For our colleague and friend
Rabbi Julie Ringold Spitzer
(1958–1999)
May her memory be a blessing

Lesbian Rabbis

Lesbian Rabbis

The First Generation

Edited by

REBECCA T. ALPERT

SUE LEVI ELWELL

SHIRLEY IDELSON

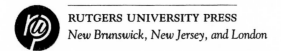

RUTGERS UNIVERSITY PRESS
New Brunswick, New Jersey, and London

Library of Congress Cataloging-in-Publication Data

Lesbian rabbis : the first generation / edited by Rebecca T. Alpert, Sue Levi Elwell,
Shirley Idelson.
p. cm.
Includes bibliographical references and index.
ISBN 0-8135-2915-8 (alk. paper)—ISBN 0-8135-2916-6 (pbk. : alk. paper)
1. Lesbian rabbis—Biography. 2. Jews—Biography. I. Alpert, Rebecca T.
(Rebecca Trachtenberg), 1950– II. Elwell, Ellen Sue Levi. III. Idelson, Shirley.

BM753 .L47 2001
296.6'1'086643—dc21

00-045751

British Cataloging-in-Publication data for this book is available from the
British Library

Manufactured in the United States of America

Contents

Acknowledgments   *ix*

Introduction   *1*
SUE LEVI ELWELL WITH REBECCA T. ALPERT

Part I   Serving a Denominational Movement

Chapter 1   Struggle, Change, and Celebration:
My Life as a Lesbian Rabbi   *39*
LINDA HOLTZMAN

Chapter 2   A Practical Theology of Presence   *50*
NANCY WIENER

Chapter 3   Working from the Inside, Out   *57*
JULIE R. SPITZER

Chapter 4   Wholeness and Holiness: A Life's Journey   *66*
SUE LEVI ELWELL

Chapter 5   Being a Lesbian Rabbi   *75*
ELIZABETH TIKVAH SARAH

Part II   Serving Congregations

Chapter 6   Ten Years on the Journey toward Wholeness   *93*
LEILA GAL BERNER

Chapter 7   Carrying On: A Lesbian Rabbi, Jewish Seekers,
and All the Voices of Our Lives   *106*
ELLEN LIPPMANN

Chapter 8   *Shlichut:* Claiming My Mission   *116*
KAREN BENDER

Chapter 9   *Ger V'toshav:* Member and Outsider   *131*
               SYDNEY MINTZ

Part III   Serving Gay and Lesbian Congregations

Chapter 10   Gay and Lesbian Synagogue as Spiritual Community   *141*
               SHARON KLEINBAUM

Chapter 11   Why I Choose to be a Rabbi of a GLBT Synagogue   *152*
               LISA A. EDWARDS

Chapter 12   Ten Years and Counting . . .   *161*
               DENISE L. EGER

Part IV   Working with Jews
              "at the Margins" and on Campus

Chapter 13   On Being a Rabbi at the Margins   *173*
               REBECCA T. ALPERT

Chapter 14   My Piece of Truth   *181*
               JULIE GREENBERG

Chapter 15   My Language Is My Country   *190*
               SHIRLEY IDELSON

Part V   Lesbian Rabbis and Conservative Judaism

Chapter 16   Saying No in the Name of a Higher Yes   *197*
               BENAY LAPPE

Chapter 17   Notes from the Underground   *217*
               DAWN ROBINSON ROSE

Chapter 18   In Hiding   *226*
               ANONYMOUS

              Glossary   235
              About the Contributors   243
              Index   247

Acknowledgments

THE IDEA FOR this book was born in the context of B'not Esh (literally, Daughters of Fire), the ongoing Jewish feminist spirituality group to which the three editors belonged. *B'not Esh* was the place where we began to tell ourselves that it was possible to be a lesbian and a rabbi, and where our stories were heard and understood. Without that group this book could not have been written.

When we contacted the fifty or more rabbis and rabbinical students we knew to be lesbians, the response we received was overwhelming. That all their stories are not here is a function of the limits of space, time, and opportunity, both theirs and ours. It is our hope that the eighteen stories that are told here do justice to the lives and experiences of all of us. We are also aware that we have omitted the stories of rabbis who define themselves as bisexual. We would have liked to include essays by these rabbis, but we live in a Jewish world where it is very difficult to write or speak from that personal perspective.

We acknowledge our debt to those bisexual, questioning, and heterosexual colleagues who have been our allies for all these years. Without their support, we would not have been able to survive, and we are grateful for everything they have given us.

We are also grateful to work in settings with colleagues and mentors who acknowledge the importance of this book: the Women's Studies Program and Religion Department at Temple University; the Union of

American Hebrew Congregations Pennsylvania Council; Macalaster College; and Minnesota Public Radio.

The Reconstructionist gave us permission to reprint the article by Rebecca Alpert, "On Being a Rabbi at the Margins."

Each of us wants to acknowledge the support of our networks of family and friends:

Rebecca wishes to thank her life partner, Christie Balka, and her children, Lynn and Avi Alpert.

Sue wishes to thank her partner, Nurit Levi Shein, her daughters Hana and Mira Elwell, and her parents, Claire and Charles Levi.

Shirley wishes to thank her partner, Alexis Kuhr, and her parents, Martin and Paulette Idelson.

David Myers did not intend to work on this book; it was handed to him when he arrived at Rutgers University Press. Since taking on the project, David provided help beyond measure. His vision, insight, gentle criticism, and editorial support were more than we could have hoped for, and we are deeply in his debt.

Finally, we are grateful to each other for the experience of working together. We are blessed to enjoy one another's friendship. This book is a gift we give one another.

Lesbian Rabbis

Introduction

SUE LEVI ELWELL
WITH REBECCA T. ALPERT

Why a Book on Lesbian Rabbis?

LESBIANS ARE CREATING a new rabbinate.* This book tells the stories of
eighteen individuals whose lives and work are informed by a commitment to wholeness and holiness, women dedicated to transmitting a
five-thousand-year-old tradition while living lives and making personal
choices that have never before been considered sanctified. Living lives
of integrity, creating systems of meaning and connections between
Judaism and lesbianism and religious leadership, forming and celebrating new kinds of families, lesbian rabbis are transforming tradition.

For many, the idea of a lesbian rabbi is simply an oxymoron. How
can a lesbian speak in the name of a patriarchal tradition that silenced
women? How can she represent a culture that denies her very existence?
How can an individual whose choice of a life partner challenges heterosexuality stand for a tradition that celebrates traditional notions of
marriage and family? The essays in this collection, taken together,
answer these questions. They reflect a bold insistence on living with con-
tradictions, and forging sometimes tenuous truces between seemingly
irreconcilable principles and beliefs. The writers of these essays have created complex, intentional identities that push the boundaries of convention and open the way for change. The lives reflected in these pages

---

* You will find the definitions of terms and phrases that may be unfamiliar to you in the glos-
sary at the back of this volume.

are studies in courage, innovation, and deep commitment to the values these rabbis see at the core of Judaism: honesty, family, rigorous intellectual and spiritual inquiry, and the commitment to a spiritual tradition that is rich and varied and perpetually engaging.

This book is written by women who refuse to choose between their Jewish and their lesbian identities, preferring instead to bring those identities together in new ways. The writers of these essays represent a first, full generation of lesbian rabbis. These are the stories of those who were the first to come out, women who risked the consequences of losing their rabbinic positions in order to speak publicly about the truths of their lives. These essays also include the stories of those who followed in the footsteps of these pioneers, waiting for an opening, or for a sign of hope that they could indeed pursue the career that called to them, as well as those who wrestled with an internalized homophobia that threatened to undermine both their professional and their personal lives. Also included here are the stories of those women we might call the last of the first generation: those who, as beneficiaries of societal changes, knew clearly from the start that their identities as lesbians and rabbis could be complementary, who believed that their insights and understanding of the challenges presented by each of these identities enhanced the other. The voices represented in this collection claim the right to be a part of an ancient tradition, and to reflect a continuity and connection with the Jewish people. At the same time, these lesbian rabbis proclaim their difference, and assert their right to create alternative interpretations of Jewish tradition.

Jewish and Cultural Contexts at the End of the Twentieth Century

The last quarter of the twentieth century has been a time of transformation of attitudes and behaviors of Jews in communities across the world and particularly in the United States. Responsive to the secular culture of the countries in which they live, post-Enlightenment Jewish communities have tended to reflect their host cultures and to adopt local norms of structure and organization. Distinctive approaches to Jewish belief and practice, first introduced in Europe in the nineteenth century by liberal reformers, developed into full-blown "denominational" differences in the United States and, subsequently, in Western Europe and Israel. Each of these denominations has reacted differently to the presence of lesbian rabbis.

Judaism is a tradition that began in the cultures of Israel and Judea and developed in the academies of Babylon and ancient Palestine in the first five centuries of the Common Era. However, Judaism as it is lived in the United States at the beginning of the twenty-first century can be understood only in the context of modern European history. The political and social emancipation of the Jews and the intellectual movements known collectively as the Enlightenment brought Jews into the world as citizens and as participants in the development of European culture. These eighteenth-century political and social movements acknowledged for the first time in Christian history that the Jew was a human being. It is not a coincidence that as Jews gained rights, enlightenment thinkers also acknowledged the humanity of women as persons, not simply as sisters, daughters, and wives of men.

As Jews gained rights of property ownership, enfranchisement, and entrance to the professions, they began to consider themselves and their traditions in a new light. The religious reforms that had transformed the face of European Christianity opened, for some, a line of questioning about traditions and ceremonies that had never before been questioned. Wissenschaft des Judenthums, the scientific study of Judaism, enabled both Jews and non-Jews to consider the development and practice of Judaism with the skills of contemporary scholarship. And women, too, began to emerge as actors in the unfolding of history. The convergence of these two factors provides the historical foundation for the ultimate emergence of lesbian rabbis. An examination of the denominational development of modern Judaism, and the growth of these denominations in America, will help to set the stage for this study.

REFORM JUDAISM

In the first half of the nineteenth century, a series of religious reforms were initiated in Germany to respond to the needs of Jews who wanted to bring together their commitment to tradition with their embrace of their new status as citizens in Christian society. Reflecting the hunger of many to identify as Jews while living in increasingly open cultural contexts, a generation of rabbis and scholars trained in European universities developed the philosophical and ideological foundations for the most significant modern challenge to traditional Jewish thought and practice. The changes began with the creation of new prayer books that shortened liturgy and added prayers and sermons in the vernacular. While some early reformers insisted that such changes did not challenge traditional ways of understanding Jewish law, others saw these initial reforms as an opening to question the divine origin of postbiblical writings, the source and nature of Jewish law, and the practices that reflected adherence to these beliefs. Abraham Geiger (1810–1874), the leading philosopher of the German Reform movement, redefined Judaism as a religion that is perpetually evolving.

Reform-minded immigrants to the United States discovered a political and intellectual climate based on the prophetic ideals of religious freedom and universal justice that are at the heart of Jewish tradition. In addition, the open culture supported and encouraged the ritual innovations that had set these reformers apart from more traditional Jews in Europe. By the middle of the nineteenth century, Reform synagogues had been established in Charleston, Baltimore, New York, Albany, and Cincinnati, offering individuals and families the opportunity to identify with a Jewish religious community that was grounded in a commitment to Jewish continuity and also reflected the American ideals of self reliance and self determination.[1] As an increasing number of Jews sought identification with this American version of Reform Judaism, a movement was established through the organization of the Union of American Hebrew Congregations (1873), the first American confederation of synagogues and, two years later, by the founding of Hebrew Union College to train rabbis for American pulpits.

In 1885, a small group of rabbis gathered together to articulate their vision of a distinctly American Judaism in what became known as the Pittsburgh Platform. The theological convictions reflected in this statement defined American Reform Judaism for much of the next century. Building on the work of Geiger and others, the rabbis called Judaism an evolutionary faith, proclaiming themselves bound only by Judaism's "moral laws" and rejecting dietary restrictions and the traditional practice of mitzvot, divinely commanded behaviors. The Pittsburgh Platform provided the philosophical and ideological foundation for the establishment and maintenance of a movement nurtured by those who understood their Judaism to be a faith commitment very much like the religious commitments of their American Christian neighbors. For this generation of Reform Jews, Jews were a religious group, not a people or a nation with a divine purpose or a historic mission. Defining Jews in this new way also opened the way to considering all Jews, not just males, to be full members of the Jewish people.

The twentieth century was a time of great change in American Judaism. Several million immigrants from Eastern Europe flooded America seeking safe haven from the anti-Semitic pogroms that preceded the destruction of European Jewry during the Second World War. Bringing with them Jewish traditions from Eastern Europe, these immigrants challenged what they saw as a Judaism that had abandoned its roots. The Reform movement responded by reclaiming some traditional concepts and practices it had previously rejected. Reform rabbis articulated those changes in a new set of guidelines in 1937.

The 1999 Pittsburgh Principles reiterated the Reform movement's historic commitment to individual autonomy and communal self-determination, while opening the way to reclaiming an increasing number of traditional Jewish behaviors and beliefs. At the same time, the document affirmed the movement's historic commitment to gender equality, and also acknowledged the presence of people "regardless of their sexual orientation" who make up the Reform movement. The principles also recognized that Reform Jewish congregations include those who are born Jews, those who convert to Judaism, and those who live in Jewish households although they themselves may not choose Judaism.[2]

The Reform movement, which began by demanding liturgical change, developed by century's end into a federation of nine hundred synagogues providing education and support for individuals and families, as well as a context for ongoing discussion, conversation, and debate about the nature of Jewish identity and commitment in the modern world. As the first movement to encourage female leadership, the first movement to ordain women, and the first to welcome synagogues with outreach to gay and lesbian Jews and their families, the movement has continued the dynamic vision of its founders and early proponents.

ORTHODOXY

The term "Orthodoxy" was used in nineteenth-century Germany to distinguish traditional Jewish practice and belief from the growing Reform movement. Among the rabbis and leaders in the traditional community who wrestled with their response to the Enlightenment and the changing political and social structure that enabled Jews to enter the larger world was Samson Raphael Hirsch (1808–1888). In 1836 Hirsch published *Nineteen Letters on Judaism* in response to the innovations of early reformers in his native Germany. Hirsch argued that the timeless truths of Torah and mitzvot are the only path to the redemption of humankind, and living according to their dictates is the only expression of authentic Judaism. Unimpressed by Enlightenment ideals of the equality of women, Hirsch rejected any change in women's status under Jewish law. He encouraged his readers to maintain their distance from those who advocated change and modernization, beginning a debate that continues in the Orthodox community to this day. The Orthodox (sometimes called neo-Orthodox) response to Reform found expression throughout Germany, in Hungary, and across nineteenth-century Europe.

In America, traditionalists created a network of synagogues, and in New York City in 1898 they established what became Yeshiva University, a center intended to educate both rabbis and those who wished to complement secular studies with intensive traditional Jewish learning. However, unlike the members of progressive movements, traditionalists did not create a large American movement with a single seminary or spokesperson.³ All those who call themselves Orthodox, however, agree that Torah, understood as an inherited system of divinely revealed and immutable texts, frames the life and decisions of every Jew.

The last quarter of the twentieth century witnessed an increase in the number of Jews who identify themselves as Orthodox. While there is a range of sociological expressions of modern Orthodoxy, all Orthodox Jews support and attend synagogues that separate men from women with a mechitzah, all observe strict kashrut, all follow the laws of niddah, observe regulations concerning proscribed dress, and pay careful attention to ritual observance. While some among the Orthodox follow traditional proscriptions against higher education for women, a growing body of literature celebrates the unique and specialized gifts and talents of men and women and argues in favor of women's scholarship.[4] The Orthodox have yet to accept women as rabbis, and are not prepared at this point in history to consider the possibility of openly gay men serving in leadership roles. Unlike the other movements, Orthodoxy continues to claim to be the single path to authentic Jewish practice and belief.

CONSERVATIVE JUDAISM

Like Reform and modern Orthodoxy, Conservative Judaism began in Germany, where it was known as the Historical School. This movement attempted to chart a middle path between the Reform movement and Orthodoxy by affirming emancipation while continuing to embrace biblical and rabbinic tradition. The emerging movement was called Conservative Judaism in America, and its path was charted by Isaac Leeser (1806–1868), a pioneering educator and organizer who attempted to create a unique version of Judaism for America. Leeser's vision differed from the perspective articulated by Isaac Mayer Wise (1819–1900), the architect of the American Reform movement on issues of Jewish observance and ritual.

The focal point of the Conservative movement became the Jewish Theological Seminary, as reorganized in 1902 by Solomon Schechter (1847–1915), whose scholarship distinguished him as a spokesperson for traditional Judaism. Schechter assembled a exemplary faculty, and the seminary became known for scholarship based on understanding Jewish law as the primary source for framing and living lives of Jewish integrity and continuity.

Conservative Jews are committed to studying and interpreting Jewish law, which is understood as divine revelation, in light of traditional commentary and with a consideration of contemporary understandings of ethical behavior and communal norms. The authority of law is not questioned, but the application of that law is open to the interpretation of trained scholars. The organization of Conservative rabbis, the Rabbinical Assembly, includes a Committee on Jewish Law and Standards that considers legal questions. In the past two decades, the committee has wrestled with issues such as whether and how to consider women as members of a minyan, how to respond to kol isha, the traditional prohibition against women's voices being heard in public, and the implications for women as shlichei tzibur. The committee's interpretation of these issues led to the acceptance of women as candidates for the rabbinate in 1984, but has yet to lead to the ordination of openly gay or lesbian rabbis.[5] By the end of the twentieth century, nearly eight hundred congregations were affiliated with United Synagogue, the organization of Conservative congregations. Students prepare for the Conservative rabbinate in New York, at the Jewish Theological Seminary, and in Los Angeles, at the University of Judaism.

RECONSTRUCTIONISM

Reconstructionist Judaism, the only denomination that started in the United States, was built on the philosophy of Mordecai Kaplan (1881–1983), a professor of homiletics at the Jewish Theological Seminary. Kaplan's ideas distinguished him from his colleagues at the seminary. His teachings included a belief in religious naturalism; the concept that American Jews live "in two civilizations," the Jewish and the American; a commitment to Jewish law as sacred but nonbinding; and a repudiation of the concept of Jews as the chosen people. Kaplan's philosophy became the foundation for the Reconstructionist Rabbinical College (RRC), established by his followers in 1968. From the outset, Kaplan was committed to a Judaism that not only included but celebrated women's contribution to and participation in Jewish life. In fact, Kaplan welcomed his daughter, Judith, as the first bat mitzvah in recorded history, when she led her congregation in prayer shortly after her twelfth birthday in 1922.[6]

The Reconstructionist movement has also proved to be a welcoming place for lesbian and gay rabbis. This movement has grown steadily over the last twenty years. At the end of the century, the Jewish Reconstructionist Federation numbered one hundred synagogues. The Reconstructionist Rabbinical College is located in Philadelphia, as are the headquarters of the Reconstructionist Rabbinical Association.

THE "NEW JEWS"

The patterns of identification, affiliation, and worship that were established in the late nineteenth century and solidified in the first half of the twentieth century were challenged and changed by the generation born after the Second World War, a generation who questioned their parents' and teachers' approaches to Jewish education, to the Jewish community, and to the Jewish family. The American youths who self-consciously named themselves "New Jews" responded to contemporary secular demands for civil rights, gender equality, and an increasing sensitivity to difference as a source of strength by adapting their parents' institutions and creating new organizations and communal forms. Some challenged large synagogues to respond to the needs of individuals and particular membership constituencies by creating chavurot. Others worked in the inner cities as members of social justice "mitzvah corps." Others reclaimed discarded traditions and infused them with new life through song, dance, and celebrations that challenged the reserve and intellectualism that distanced many from the heart of Judaism.[7] By the 1990s, many institutions of the Jewish community, from community centers to rabbinical seminaries, had begun to consider alternatives to long accepted norms of leadership, rigid concepts of authority, and narrow interpretations of both the Jewish community and Jewish tradition.

THE CHALLENGE OF GENDER

Of all the challenges presented by the cultural, sociological, and intellectual realities of the worlds in which Jews live, the most powerful has been the questioning of long-accepted norms of gender roles and behaviors. The feminist movements of the 1960s and 1970s forced Americans to examine assumptions about appropriate behaviors of and expectations for women. Religious communities were challenged by questions of women's equality, gender roles, privilege, and power. The work of some Christian feminists provided a catalyst for Jewish women to think about confronting problems within Jewish tradition.[8] These questions had been raised in Jewish communities at various times and in various ways at several junctures over the previous century.[9] But just as secular feminism had to reinvent itself in the 1970s, Jewish feminism had to find a new voice and a new generation of proponents in the last quarter of the twentieth century. Only in the past two decades have feminist issues come to be taken seriously within the Jewish community, thanks to the pioneering work of talented theologians, historians, writers, and artists, and to the contributions of both clergy and lay members of a wide range of Jewish organizations and denominations that have finally embraced women's issues as issues of import and primary consideration.[10]

The secular feminist movement claimed the goal of moving the concerns of women from the periphery to the center. But like that of the patriarchy they challenged, the vision of many feminists was also circumscribed. For many in the early feminist movement, "women" meant heterosexual white women. For some, it meant heterosexual white Anglo-Saxon Protestants. Jewish feminists challenged the exclusion of Jews from universal definitions of womanhood,[11] and lesbians challenged the emphasis on heterosexual issues in early second-wave feminism.

Some secular Jewish lesbian feminists who had experienced this exclusion began to think about the connections between anti-Semitism and homophobia. The first book to consider these questions and to raise issues about being lesbian and Jewish was published in 1982. Evelyn Torton Beck's *Nice Jewish Girls: A Lesbian Anthology* included a broad range of personal stories and essays on political, religious, and cultural issues. It was one of the first books to confront the mistaken assumption that all American Jews come from European backgrounds and are white. Beck's book offered a challenge to a generation of women who could barely say "lesbian" and "Jewish" in one phrase.[12] Seven years later, *Twice Blessed: A Lesbian and Gay Jewish Anthology* extended the conversation to include gay men and included groundbreaking essays that confronted the problems in the Jewish religious tradition and communities that were not raised in *Nice Jewish Girls*, but were reflected in the gay synagogue movement.[13]

GAY AND LESBIAN JEWS

As the women's liberation movement raised questions about women's roles and sexuality, the gay liberation movement provided the impetus to raise issues of gay and lesbian invisibility in the liberal Jewish community. Following in the path of their Christian counterparts, by 1973 gay and lesbian Jews had established their own congregations in New York, Los Angeles, and San Francisco.[14] Typically, Jewish congregations attract people who share a philosophy, an orientation to Judaism, or geographic proximity. Gay congregations, however, attract gay and lesbian Jews who may have very different Jewish backgrounds and few common attitudes toward rituals and traditions. For many gay and lesbian congregations, this has meant a struggle over religious practice. And often, especially in the early days of these congregations, feminist concerns were not on the agenda of traditionalist gay men who were the founders of many of these groups. Some lesbians, who felt invisible among some Jewish feminists, also felt uncomfortable in predominantly male and traditional gay and lesbian synagogues.[15]

But the gay and lesbian synagogue movement awakened awareness and provided important communal organizations for the gay and lesbian Jewish movement. Today there are gay and lesbian synagogues in most major U.S. cities, and many around the world. A large number of these congregations are affiliated with Reform Judaism, which set a strong example by providing outreach and support in the early years. Ironically, with the exception of Sha'ar Zahav (Golden Gate) in San Francisco, no gay synagogue was served by an openly gay or lesbian rabbi until the late 1980s, although many gay and lesbian rabbis attended these congregations prior to entering rabbinical school.

These synagogues formed in response to the overt and subtle discrimination against and ambivalence toward gays and lesbians in the Jewish community. Gay and lesbian Jews also received unexpected support from a number of rabbis across the country and across the denominational spectrum who, in public presentations and in print, urged the Jewish community to welcome gay and lesbian Jews. While their points of departure and their conclusions varied widely, these individuals became valued and honored allies to the gays and lesbians who were no longer willing to be silent or invisible.[16]

The last fifteen years of the twentieth century witnessed a sea change of visibility and acceptance of gays and lesbians as American citizens, as coworkers, and as family members. An important factor in that process was the AIDS epidemic, which brought gay men and their families out of the closet, and gay and lesbian activists and allies into the street. AIDS was a catalyst for conversation about the presence of gays and lesbians in the Jewish community. Jewish groups across the country began to offer a wide range of services to individuals and families battling the disease. National Jewish organizations created task forces and program materials, and for the first time in history, gay men and lesbians were sought out as experts.

As a result of these changes, the Jewish community began to confront a wide range of issues of concern to gays and lesbians: the persistent assumption of heterosexuality, joint synagogue membership for gay and lesbian couples, civil and religious marriage, access to donor insemination and adoption, medical and inheritance benefits, and the acceptance of gay men and lesbians as Jewish teachers, cantors, and rabbis.[17] By the end of the twentieth century, the patriarchal and heterosexist assumptions of Jewish tradition had been irrevocably shaken by the actual presence of heterosexual women, openly gay men, and lesbians who were powerful and insistent lay and professional leaders in Jewish communities, and by the deep and persistent questions of Jewish feminist and queer scholars and teachers in Jewish seminaries and schools across the spectrum of Jewish belief and practice.[18] The presence of lesbian rabbis in the Jewish community is a significant part of this challenge to the traditional male, heterosexist, and patriarchal world of Jewish scholarship.

This work focuses on the unique role of lesbian rabbis, who represent the simultaneous challenge to Judaism of gender and sexual orientation. While these struggles are connected, they are also separate.[19] The issues that confront women rabbis are distinct from those faced by gay rabbis. Lesbian rabbis are unique in that we experience both.[20] Along with all other women in the rabbinate, we as lesbians must face a tradition that has silenced us and circumscribed our public and ritual roles, has rendered us sexual objects and limited our power. Along with gay men in the rabbinate, lesbians must face a tradition that has directed hatred and contempt toward our sexual choices and orientation, and has sought to keep us silent, to make us disappear.

If the lesbian rabbi faces a double burden as a gay person and a woman, she also is heir to a double legacy of the feminist and gay movements. Lesbian rabbis are in a unique position to create change on both fronts. Through access to leadership, the lesbian rabbi can challenge stereotypes of women and gay people, reminding Jews by her presence that we are all human beings, created in God's image. She can make a commitment as a feminist to "hear women into speech," or as a gay rights activist to gain religious equality for the Jewish gay, lesbian, bisexual, and transgender community, defying cultural and sexual expectations. Although we are different from both gay men and heterosexual women in the rabbinate, these two other groups are an important part of the story of lesbian rabbis.

Women in the Rabbinate

There would be no lesbian rabbis without the ordination of women to the rabbinate. For many, the challenge to Jewish patriarchy is embodied by women rabbis, whose very voices shatter the long-observed prohibition against Jewish women speaking or singing in public.[21] Women rabbis, whether they preach before thousands in a High Holiday service, or teach one youngster how to chant from the sacred Torah scroll, defy years of male hegemony and control of public Jewish ritual life.

The idea of women rabbis was first presented to American Judaism when Ray (Rachel) Frank, a thirty-one-year-old charismatic lay preacher and service leader, began attending classes at Hebrew Union College in 1893. However, neither she nor Lena Aronsohn, who attended the seminary at the same time, completed the program. Ten years later, Henrietta Szold was admitted as a special student to the Jewish Theological Seminary with the clear understanding that she would not pursue a course of studies that would lead to ordination. In 1921, after two years as a student at Hebrew Union College, Martha Neumark (like Szold the daughter of a rabbi) asked permission to lead High Holiday services like her male classmates. Her request was granted, and the college president subsequently convened a faculty committee to consider the question of women's ordination. The faculty deliberations were undercut by the lay board of governors of the college, who voted in 1923 to bar women from rabbinic ordination.

In the 1930s, Regina Jonas matriculated at the prestigious Berlin Academy for the Scientific Study of Judaism. When she completed her studies, her professors disagreed about the propriety of ordaining a woman as rabbi, and Jonas was ordained privately in 1935. As the number of her male colleagues diminished because of emigration, arrests, and deportation, she was invited to serve several congregations in Berlin until her own deportation to Terezín. She died in Auschwitz in 1944.[22]

Influenced by societal changes wrought by the women's liberation movement, in 1972, on the very campus where Ray Frank, Lena Aronsohn, and Martha Neumark had studied years before, Rabbi Sally Priesand became the first woman in history to be ordained by a rabbinical seminary.[23] Priesand's ordination was followed by the graduation of Rabbi Sandy Eisenberg Sasso from the Reconstructionist Rabbinical

College in 1974, and by the ordination of Rabbi Amy Eilberg from the Jewish Theological Seminary in 1984. In 1975 the Leo Baeck College in London ordained Rabbi Jacqueline Tabick. As the twentieth century drew to a close, the total number of women graduated from or ordained by seminaries or by individuals in America, Europe, and Israel totaled more than five hundred.[24]

MORE THAN JUST "ADD WOMEN AND STIR": BRINGING WOMEN INTO JEWISH STUDY AND PRACTICE

Few of those who worked to secure women's admission to seminaries as candidates for ordination imagined the far-reaching challenges that women students and, subsequently, women rabbis would bring to the study of traditional texts, to the concept of rabbinic counseling, and to rabbinic practice. Often, students begin their study of the Mishnah, a second-century legal treatise, with the first chapter of *Pirkei Avot* (the *Sayings [or Ethics] of the Fathers*). It begins, "Moses received Torah at Sinai and handed it to Joshua who handed it over to the elders who handed it over to the prophets who handed it to the men of the Great Assembly. The latter said three things: Be deliberate in judgment, raise up many disciples, and make a fence around the Torah."

A clear line of transmission and rabbinic authority is established from Moses to those who compiled, and subsequently, all who study this sacred text. The line of succession is unbroken from Sinai to the present. The message is powerful and succinct: Keep the chain of tradition strong by intentional behavior, teaching generations to come, and securing the boundaries between the sacred and profane. Students who can read themselves into the tradition, that is, men, can feel elated by this opening section, which implies that by the act of studying this text, one becomes a link in the chain of tradition. Those who are made invisible by this progression throughout history, the women whose bodies make generations possible, are reminded once again that they are written out of history. Women, who are traditionally barred from acting as witnesses, can hardly fulfill the challenge to "be deliberate in judgment." Traditionally, women are barred from teaching, so they cannot "raise up disciples," who are often called "son" by their teachers. The fence around the Torah that the reader is charged to raise is a fence that seals men in and effectively keeps women out, out of the line of succession, far away from the rich inheritance, distanced from any possibility of entering the conversation between God and the Jewish people that is Torah.

When women first study this paragraph, some realize that this is the first chapter in a rabbinic education that demands a constant, daily struggle for visibility, to themselves, to one another, and to their teachers. For many women, the effort to become visible is an empowering process of discovery of the imperative of reading texts with new eyes, reading between the lines, asking questions that have never been asked before. One perceptive scholar has written that "the decision to ordain women as rabbis, to have them engage in public roles of religious leadership within the Jewish community, must . . . be considered revolutionary. The ordination of women as rabbis has brought into focus the dynamics of a gendered religious life that has both silenced women's voices and muted feminist values of cooperation, mutuality, and equality. It has spoken directly to the reality of how power is gendered as well as conceptualized within our community and its traditions."[25]

Although feminist teachers suggest that the values of "cooperation, mutuality, and equality" are embedded in traditional Jewish texts such as the Song of Songs, these values are accessible only when those texts are read with an inclusive, expansive vision that sees the lovers as peers and companions, equal in their desire for and power with one another. These teachers help students learn how to "depatriarchalize" traditional texts by asking questions and forming theories of inquiry that acknowledge traditional gender bias.[26]

Women rabbis can catalyze discussions about God's gender, the gendered language of prayer, and the challenge of reading Jewish texts with women's eyes. Some women rabbis introduce new life cycle ceremonies and rituals, including innovative covenant ceremonies for both girls and boys at birth, coming of age ceremonies for boys and girls at puberty, rituals for marking a range of adult transitions and life changes, and ceremonies that celebrate the contributions and lives of elders. Others have created rituals and guides for infertility and pregnancy loss. Women rabbis have pioneered what is now known as the Jewish Healing Movement, creating and sustaining centers for spiritual support and sustenance for the ill and the dying and those who care for them, and have been among the first to write about spiritual counseling in Jewish contexts. Women rabbis have brought new insights to the feasts and fasts that define the Jewish year, reclaiming the monthly celebration of Rosh Chodesh, and teaching women and men how to lead inclusive Passover seders that emphasize the exodus and liberation of the entire community of Israel. Building on their socialization as caregivers and nurturers, some women bring fresh perspectives to their work as hospital and college chaplains. Others use their understanding of the role of outsider to create synagogue infrastructures or nonsynagogue organizations that include those who have traditionally felt marginalized in Jewish institutional life, including singles, people with disabilities, and older people.[27]

Women rabbis' family choices—to remain single; to share their work and personal lives with a partner; to parent, alone, with a partner, or in a larger family situation, a family of blood or a family of friends—opened the issue that, for some, was at the heart of the question about women rabbis. Exercising these choices reflects the fact that women make sexual choices as well as vocational choices, for women, like men, are sexual beings. What does it mean to acknowledge the sexuality of a role model and guide?

Rabbis as (Hetero)Sexual Beings

Traditional Judaism celebrates sexuality, when that sexuality is expressed in the context of a heterosexual marriage.[28] However, most Jews would rather not think about their rabbis as sexual beings. In a traditional context, where rabbis are presumed to be male and heterosexual, marriage is the preferable state for rabbis, for then the rabbi's sexual needs and desires are focused on and fulfilled within the private context of his relationship with his wife. Unmarried male and female rabbis are viewed as candidates for marriage. If they appear to be disinterested, they are viewed with suspicion, and may lose their jobs. For that reason, many rabbis in the past who knew themselves to be gay hid their sexuality in heterosexual marriages. In fact, the rebbetzin fulfills an important role in the community simply by virtue of her intimate partnership with the rabbi. Many communities expect rabbis' wives to play a range of public roles, reflecting the couples' symbolic modeling of marriage as the norm for successful adult behavior.

A woman rabbi, particularly when she is introduced into a community as an assistant or associate working with a chronologically and experientially senior male, may be symbolically viewed in similar ways. The female rabbi may be seen as the assistant to the rabbi, perpetuating hierarchical social expectations of women's subservient status. A female rabbi may also play "mother" to the male rabbi's "father" figure.[29] Both of these roles may hint at a sexual subservience of the female to the male rabbi, whether or not any sexual awareness or tension exists between the two.

THE DILEMMA OF THE PREGNANT RABBI

At the end of the twentieth century, the preferred norm for rabbis, both male and female, remained heterosexual marriage. Since most rabbis serve congregations, and since most congregations are made up of people living in heterosexual nuclear families, rabbis, who are often seen as the models for their congregants, are expected not only to be married, but to raise children. But where the rabbi's pregnant wife is a positive symbol of male potency and efficacy, the pregnant rabbi presents a more complex challenge for a population still struggling with women in positions of authority and religious leadership.

During the first fifteen to twenty years of women serving in the rabbinate, a great deal of attention was focused on how congregations, Jewish institutions served by women professionals, and women rabbis themselves should respond to pregnancy and child care concerns. What are appropriate maternity benefits for rabbis? How long should a congregation have to do without their rabbi, or, asked differently, how long might a rabbi stay home with her newborn? What allowances should be made for breastfeeding? What kind of child care arrangements are appropriate or desirable for a working rabbi, male or female, with a young child? The women who pioneered in the rabbinate often had to work out their own solutions to these questions, for it took each of the movements several years to develop suggested policy guidelines to assist congregations and their rabbis as they approached this issue.

The married rabbi's pregnancy not only raised questions about supporting the rabbi during this time of transition; the pregnant rabbi's expanding girth also proclaimed her sexuality. For much of the first half of the twentieth century, it was not appropriate for pregnant women to appear in public. Pregnant women were even forbidden from entering

American public school classrooms as teachers. Beginning in the late 1970s, congregants in both synagogues and churches struggled with the same unconscious discomfort when thinking of their clergy as sexual beings. While some rabbis joked about the protection from detection afforded by the clerical robes worn in some synagogues, all women knew that they were facing a prejudice that none of their male colleagues had ever encountered.

Faced with little support and a stunning lack of creativity about designing work environments and options that would accommodate changing family needs, some women decided to drop out of the rabbinate for a number of years until their children were older. Other women, afraid to ask for any "special" considerations, returned to work after very short leaves, and struggled to juggle nursing schedules in a work environment that was hostile at worst or ambivalent at best. Some rabbis were faced with either blatant or veiled resentment from male colleagues, who protested that they had not been afforded any benefits when their children were born. Certainly, as more and more women entered the profession, and an increasing number became mothers while working, the people who staff and sustain synagogues began to adapt and, in many cases, to appreciate the particular contributions of rabbis who are mothers.

By the late 1990s, many Jews had become accustomed to the idea of a pregnant rabbi, and were able to celebrate with their rabbis and their families as those families expanded. But changing understandings of family and the availability of an increased range of fertility and adoption opportunities raise new challenges to Jewish communities. The desire to parent the next generation of Jews is shared by many whose families will never include one mother, one father, and their biological offspring. Just as many Americans are creating families through adoption and donor insemination, so are rabbis, single and partnered, expanding the idea and the reality of Jewish families.

Gay Rabbis

Along with changing understandings of family, changing perceptions about sexuality made it possible for some men in the rabbinate to begin to come out as gay, but only, of course, if they were willing to serve in gay congregations. In 1979, Rabbi Allen B. Bennett became the first rabbi to serve San Francisco's synagogue with outreach to the gay and lesbian community, Sha'ar Zahav. Bennett, who was ordained by Hebrew Union College in 1974, was the first rabbi to identify himself as a gay man.[30] In 1985, Yoel Kahn was ordained by Hebrew Union College in New York, and assumed the pulpit at Sha'ar Zahav. Kahn, who had studied with lesbians and other gay men both at the University of California at Berkeley as an undergraduate and at rabbinical school, became an important source of support for gay and lesbian colleagues who were serving mainstream synagogues or working in the Jewish community and were not yet ready to come out.[31] For three years, Kahn was the only gay rabbi of a gay synagogue, and his success in his position as the solo rabbi of a large congregation was a source of pride and hope for gay and lesbian students who aspired to service in the gay community. In addition, he served as an invaluable link between closeted students and colleagues. In his public presentations and publications Kahn served as an articulate advocate for his congregants and colleagues and as a powerful interpreter of gay Jewish experience to non-gay colleagues.[32]

The number of out gay rabbis, while growing, remains quite small.[33] Whether this is because of the explicit proscription of gay male sexual relations in Leviticus, or because gay male sexuality is still more threatening than lesbian sexuality, or because gay men are not themselves attracted to the rabbinate, remains an open question.

The cultural presumption of heterosexuality enables most people in public life to have some control about their presentation of self. In the case of gay and lesbian rabbis, a professional new to a community who depends on such a presumption can attempt to present herself as a scholar, social activist, counselor, teacher, and more. However, as soon as a community learns that a rabbi is gay or lesbian, all other descriptors become eclipsed. Just as rabbis who are women spend years establishing themselves so that the modifier "woman" is not used every time they are referenced, so do rabbis who are gay or lesbian face the challenge of proving themselves as professionals whose commitments, abilities, and talents are of equal importance to their sexual identity.

Lesbian Sexuality

Unlike gay male sexuality, which is explictly proscribed in Leviticus 18 and subsequent rabbinic texts, when lesbian sexual practices are mentioned in Jewish textual tradition, they are not taken seriously as a threat to male sexual hegemony or to the social order.[34] Lesbian sexuality is never mentioned in the Hebrew Bible, and is described in the Talmud as a minor infraction. Despite the warning of the twelfth-century philosopher Maimonides that cautions husbands to keep their wives away from rebellious women who "copy the practices of the land of Egypt" (Leviticus 18:3), a euphemistic reference to lesbian sexual practices, lesbianism was not considered a serious problem.[35]

However, as it has become increasingly possible for lesbian partnerships to be seen as positive and healthy in contemporary society, traditionalists have begun to speak out, often justifying their prejudices with reference to ancient Jewish texts. When lesbians' preference for women as intimate partners is understood only as a rejection of men, lesbians become projections of others' deep misandry or gynephobia. Fantasies of lesbian sexuality may titillate, disgust, entice, or challenge. People may assume that, without a penis involved, what lesbians do is not sex at all. Or they may form their opinions of lesbian sexuality based on pornographic representations of two women together, whose sole purpose is to provide erotic stimulation for men. Whatever their preconceived notions, when Jews discover that their rabbi is a lesbian, many face the significant challenge of reconciling their fear of sexuality in general and their misunderstanding of lesbian sexuality with their positive experience of this rabbi as a real person.

Some lesbians live without partners. Some live with one partner for much of their adult lives. Some have a series of relationships. For some, those relationships have been alternately with men and women. Some speak of lesbianism as a choice or a sexual preference. Others believe that sexual orientation is a biological characteristic not subject to change.[36] Some lesbians also identify as bisexual, although no bisexual rabbis have written about their stories for this volume.[37] Some of us marry men and become mothers before we acknowledge our lesbianism, and others choose motherhood in the context of our lesbian lives, through donor insemination or adoption. Unlike that of partnered heterosexual women, a lesbian's fertility is not at all dependent upon or linked to the fertility of her partner. This independence from traditional modes of conception can also be a source of deep discomfort to those who are conflicted about separating sexuality from reproduction.

Jewish communities and congregations must face the process of demystifying lesbian sexuality as purportedly exotic, alternative, or unnatural. Working alongside, studying with, learning from, and sharing community with lesbian, gay, bisexual, and transgender people, both lay and rabbinic, our communities are enriched by coming to know us as whole persons with rich and complex intellectual, spiritual, and social lives. Some even learn to cherish and take greater pleasure in their own intimate lives as a result of coming to know others whose lives and expressions differ from their own. Congregations and communities also gain from their exposure to the rich and varied familial and friendship networks established by lesbians, and expand their own understanding of family.[38]

Lesbian Rabbis: Beginning to See Ourselves

Despite numbers greater than 10 percent of women in the rabbinate,[39] until very recently, many lesbian rabbis kept our lesbianism secret or were silent about our personal lives. For some, it seemed enough that we, as women, could enter the rabbinate. Silence about our sexual orientation seemed a small price to pay for the opportunity to serve the Jewish people as teachers, counselors, and guides. For some lesbians, as for some women who define themselves as heterosexual, our gender and sexual identity are not primary. But however we named ourselves, as women, as feminists, as queer, or as those who refuse to be labeled, by the 1980s, lesbian students began to come out to one another, to teachers, and in some cases, to colleagues in the field.

In the early years of women in the rabbinate, coming out as a lesbian was a dangerous proposition. In February 1976, women students from the Hebrew Union College-Jewish Institute of Religion (HUC-JIR) and the Reconstructionist Rabbinical College (RRC), the first two seminaries to include women among their graduates and ordinees, gathered together in New York. They formed the Women's Rabbinical Alliance (WRA), with the purpose of identifying and addressing their common concerns as the first women to become members of this time-honored profession. Very early in the life of the organization, the presence of lesbians presented a challenge to the group. For some, including those unable or unwilling to articulate this, the presence of lesbians seemed to intensify the marginality of the entire group. Lesbians who were just beginning to reconcile their sexuality and their spirituality were also conflicted about how they would ever serve the Jewish community while maintaining their own sense of integrity as women who love other women. Within three years of the founding of the WRA, women in the Reform movement focused their energies on forming a women's organization, the Women's Rabbinic Network (WRN) within their larger rabbinical union, the Central Conference of American Rabbis (CCAR). The WRA foundered for an additional two years, and then disbanded. None of the women involved were ready to explore the role of homophobia of both heterosexuals and lesbians either in the demise of the joint organization or in the silence about lesbians and lesbianism in the new organization.

THE PIONEERS

Rabbi Laura Geller has written about the loneliness of being one of only two female students at Hebrew Union College in the mid-seventies: "Only other women understood the pain of patriarchal texts, the confusion of finding myself absent in the stories that shape our tradition, the desperate need to re-envision a Judaism that includes the experience of all Jews. Only other women understood the pressure of being a pioneer, of wanting to be considered as capable as the men without being forced to give up my own sense of balance, of wanting a life where work is a blessing within the context of other blessings—family, commitments, friends."[40]

The first lesbian rabbis also experienced loneliness, and the pressure of being pioneers. In 1985, Rabbi Linda Holtzman, a graduate of the Reconstructionist Rabbinical College who had been serving a small Conservative congregation, gave up her congregational position and returned to RRC to serve as the director of the practical rabbinics program. At that time, she came out as a lesbian. In 1987, Rabbi Stacy Offner, a graduate of Hebrew Union College, was promoted to associate rabbi by the large Midwestern Reform congregation where she served, and her promotion was celebrated at a special Shabbat service. Six months later, after she confirmed what was assumed to be "a false and malicious rumor" about her lesbianism, the congregation offered her a substantial severance package.[41] Later that same year, Julie Greenberg, then a student at the Reconstructionist Rabbinical College, became pregnant with her first child. Each of these women was breaking significant barriers by being open about her sexuality: one in her work as a rabbinical school professor, one as a congregational rabbi, and one as the first openly lesbian mother preparing for the rabbinate. Ultimately, all of them created professional options that would enable them to live openly as lesbians.

Those of us who were either in the rabbinate or in school at that time followed these stories closely, even as we traded our own stories. We remained in the closet for a variety of reasons; some of us were barely out to ourselves. Others were not yet out to our families. Some of us were married to men, and thought that we wanted to preserve those marriages. Others of us considered ourselves to be bisexual, and sensed that if lesbians were under attack for their openness, we would be foolish to broadcast an identity that, for some, reflects an even greater challenge to Jewish values.

Throughout the 1980s, lesbians were ordained and graduated by both HUC-JIR and RRC. Some of us were married, others single. Only a very few of us were open at school or, subsequently, at work about our sexual orientation. One lesbian chose not to interview for congregational positions because she did not want to answer any questions about her personal life. Another took a congregational position but was always on guard, installing two telephone lines at home so that she could have a professional line that her partner would never answer. An experienced rabbi in a Jewish institution lost her job because "we have one lesbian rabbi on staff. We're too small to have two." Gay students in the 1980s learned that they had two choices: Be out and go for a job in a gay congregation, or remain silent and perhaps pass in another area of the rabbinate. Yet even these circumscribed choices were problematic: When Denise L. Eger, out as a lesbian while she was a rabbinical student, was ordained in 1988, she was warned against applying for a position as the rabbi of a lesbian and gay congregation because it would "mark you for life." Some of us despaired of ever having a rabbinate in which we could be whole.

Institutional Responses to Gay and Lesbian Rabbis: Seminaries and Rabbinical Organizations

Initially, the administrators of the seminaries did not know how to deal with either the admissions process, the training, or the graduation of lesbian or gay students. In 1979 an openly gay man applied to the Reconstructionist Rabbinical College and was denied admission. In 1984 the RRC reversed that decision but did not publicize this change. Nevertheless, a significant number of lesbians and gay men learned about the policy and began to attend RRC, changing the climate of that institution. The Reconstructionist movement responded as well, issuing a significant statement in support of gay and lesbian rabbis and teachers, and the performance of gay marriages, and encouraging synagogues to become "welcoming congregations."[42] Linda Holtzman's essay documents these years of transition at the RRC.

Throughout the 1980s, a small number of gay and lesbian candidates were admitted to Hebrew Union College, most notably through interviews at the California campus, through an unspoken "don't ask, don't tell" policy. The essays by Julie R. Spitzer, Nancy Wiener, Ellen Lippman, and Karen Bender reflect the experiences of students who were admitted to HUC-JIR immediately prior to or during these years.

Gay and lesbian students met one another while they were in seminary. In their essays in this volume, Julie Greenberg, Linda Holtzman, and Sharon Kleinbaum document the founding and early years of Ameinu, a secret organization of gay and lesbian Jewish professionals and students. Students at the Hebrew Union College, New York, campus, created an organization that, as Ellen Lippman writes in her essay, was also a secret group for several years after it was founded. Dawn Robinson Rose writes of the founding of the Incognito Club at the Jewish Theological Seminary. Because of an increasing number of venues where lesbian/bisexual/gay/transgender students can meet and connect, none of these organizations still exist. In fact, the changing political climate is reflected by the founding, in 1997, of the Gay and Lesbian Rabbinical Network (GLRN), an affiliate of the Central Conference of American Rabbis. Patterned on the successful Women's Rabbinic Network, this organization, which now boasts more than fifty members, serves as a support and advocacy group for Reform rabbis. Meetings of gay and lesbian

Jewish professionals also take place in the context of the annual meeting of the World Congress of Gay, Lesbian, Bisexual and Transgendered Jews, the umbrella group for gay synagogues around the world.

In 1989, after several years of discussion, the CCAR's Committee on Human Sexuality presented a recommendation to the national convention for a nondiscrimination policy for admission to the college and for rabbinic placement. Julie R. Spitzer documents the passage of this problematic recommendation in her essay in this volume. Twelve years later, a CCAR resolution supporting rabbinic officiation for gay and lesbian ceremonies was debated and deferred for years until the Women's Rabbinic Network sponsored the resolution and brought it to the floor of the annual convention in 2000.

Both the Conservative Jewish Theological Seminary and the Rabbinical Assembly, the professional organization of Conservative rabbis, continue to wrestle with the issue of how to speak and write about the gay and lesbian individuals who aspire to become rabbis and those who have somehow completed the course of training for the Conservative rabbinate. In spite of the meticulous research and compelling arguments advanced by some of the movement's most talented scholars, lesbian and gay rabbis are not yet welcome in the Conservative movement.[43] Three essays, by Benay Lappe, Dawn Robinson Rose, and a rabbi who cannot use her own name, chronicle the experience of lesbian students at the Jewish Theological Seminary.

The First Generation

Some of us choose the rabbinate and the study of Judaism because we hope to come home to a world of moral discourse and ongoing conversation of the ingredients of a just, inclusive society that we believe is our inheritance as Jews. When we enter the world of Jewish studies, however, we often find ourselves in a hierarchical, heterosexist, deeply patriarchal universe. We marvel at the ability of our teachers, many of whom we respect and admire, not only to make peace with, but to become advocates for a tradition that can seem elitist, particularistic, and narrow. We find ourselves multiply marginal, as women, as queers, and as lesbians whose primary intimate constellation is other women. Others of us come to the rabbinate out of a conviction that the experience of the outsider, or the outlaw, is essential to understanding the human condition, and that those who ask questions from a particularly lesbian perspective will help Judaism to survive. This book attempts to explore, for the first time, how lesbian rabbis approach Judaism, how we read and interpret the tradition, how we teach that tradition to others, and how we transform that tradition with our lives and our work.

The eighteen essays included in this book present a rich spectrum of experience, personal and professional, spiritual and intellectual. This collection includes the voices of rabbis who are beginning their professional careers, and those who have worked as Jewish teachers for nearly a quarter of a century. It includes the voices of rabbis whose professional experiences are rich and varied, including congregational life, organizational work, pastoral counseling, and work with students in Jewish schools, on college campuses, and as community educators. There are also essays by rabbis who have chosen to work outside the Jewish community, and essays of graduates of all four major liberal American and European seminaries, representing each of the world's liberal Jewish movements.

The collection includes the voices of women who knew they were lesbians as young women, as well as those whose lesbianism became apparent only in later life, after they had followed more traditional paths of heterosexual marriage and bearing or raising children. This process of self-definition is further complicated by the fact that these women experience and interpret their lesbian identity in a wide range of ways. For some, lesbianism is primarily a sexual identity of women who choose women as our most intimate partners. For others, lesbian sensibility extends well beyond the most immediate circle of intimacy to friends we may consider as family. Some of us see our political work on behalf of women and girls, and our advocacy of gay and lesbian civil and religious rights and rites, as an imperative reflection of our personal commitments. Others of us define ourselves as lesbians because we are gender nonconformists. The essays collected in this volume reflect a range of sensibilities about what it means to be a lesbian, personally and politically, in one's intimate world and in the wider worlds of friends and community.

Several of the contributors write of the enormous challenges of confronting and wrestling with the many-headed demon of heterosexual presumption and heterosexual privilege, and battling the overt and subtle homophobia that poisons our culture. Several also write about how this homophobia too often works on our own spirits like a powerful virus, infecting our own sense of holiness. All of these essays document the dynamic tensions between spirituality and sexuality. All reflect a passion to serve the Jewish people, and to speak truths that have never before been recorded.

Together, the essays in this volume pose and address the questions about tensions between lesbian identity and Jewish identity; about whether there are particular lesbian readings of traditional texts; about what images, symbols, and language of Jewish experience illuminate our lives and experiences as lesbians, as Jewish teachers and leaders; and about lesbian challenges to traditional notions of Jewish family.

The book is organized around the contexts and institutions in which the contributors serve as rabbis or studied as students. We have organized the book this way because most of our contributors have chosen to focus on the ways in which their lesbian identity has affected them in their professional lives and choices. The reason for this is probably best reflected by a comment made by Elizabeth Tikvah Sarah in her essay. She declares, "I am a lesbian rabbi. It's not a job I do."

The essays collected here are written primarily by those who serve denominational movements and congregations. The single essay by a campus rabbi reflects that until very recently, lesbians serving in such positions could not be open about their lesbianism. Although many lesbian rabbis also serve as hospital or community health care chaplains, their experiences are not reflected in this volume.

SERVING A DENOMINATIONAL MOVEMENT

The first part includes essays by those who serve a denominational movement as a seminary teacher or administrator, or as an organizational executive. Linda Holtzman writes about her experiences leaving the congregational rabbinate and playing a pivotal role in the Reconstructionist movement's developing openness to gay and lesbian rabbis. Nancy Wiener and Julie R. Spitzer write about their journeys from being outsiders to working inside the Reform movement. Searching for a rabbinate in which she could be fully present, Wiener found herself teaching rabbinic students and modeling the possibility of a lesbian rabbinate to a new generation of rabbis. Spitzer, who spent the first seven years of her rabbinate living what she calls a "compartmentalized" life, became the highest-ranking lesbian in the hierarchy of the Reform movement before her tragic death in 1999. After years of hiding, she boldly used her new position to place gay and lesbian issues in the forefront of the movement's concerns. Sue Levi Elwell writes of her struggle to speak honestly about her life to her children, her parents, and those Reform Jews with whom she works. Elizabeth Tikvah Sarah writes of her attempts to create a rabbinate of integrity within the Reform and the Liberal movements of her native Britain.

SERVING CONGREGATIONS

The second part of the book includes essays written by rabbis serving congregations that include both gay and nongay congregants. Leila Berner had served her small, suburban congregation for several years when an unexpected hospitalization forced her to realize that she could no longer keep her lesbianism, and her partner, in the shadows. In search of a community where she could study, pray, and celebrate, Ellen Lippman became one of the founders of a synagogue that intentionally welcomes and serves sexually diverse individuals and families. Her essay documents the early years of a synagogue that has only a small number of analogues across the country.[44] Karen Bender was hired by a large synagogue whose leaders were not only aware of, but supportive of her lesbianism. But when Karen and her partner returned from their honeymoon, the virulence of the homophobic backlash Bender experienced nearly drove her from her pulpit. Singular in this book is the experience of Sydney Mintz, who both interviewed for rabbinical school and was ordained as an out lesbian. Her success as an assistant rabbi in a large urban synagogue is a powerful testament to the attitudinal and policy changes that have transformed some Jewish institutions in the last decade.

SERVING GAY AND LESBIAN CONGREGATIONS

The third part of this volume provides reflections of rabbis who work is in congregations with primary outreach to the gay, lesbian, bisexual, and transgender community. It also deals with the differences between serving a "mainstream" congregation and working exclusively in this community. The strong voices of Sharon Kleinbaum, Lisa A. Edwards, and Denise L. Eger reflect three perspectives on how their synagogues have provided a unique crucible for Jewish queer activism and creativity, even as they have served as safe havens for gay, lesbian, bisexual, and transgender Jews who felt unsafe elsewhere in the Jewish community. Kleinbaum shares her circuitous journey from a yeshiva into the rabbinate and writes about her continuing commitment to the gay and lesbian Jews of New York through her leadership of Congregation Beth Simchat Torah in Manhattan. Edwards, the rabbi of Beth Chayim Chadashim in Los Angeles, challenges us to reconsider the essential radicalism of Judaism as she makes a case for how gay and lesbian synagogues continue that tradition. Denise L. Eger, founding rabbi of Congregation Kol Ami in West Hollywood, describes her extensive outreach work to gay Jews who, with her help, have learned to name their social justice work as Jewish. All of these rabbis are repeatedly called upon to represent Judaism and the Jewish community in a wide range of gay and lesbian contexts, just as they represent the GLBT community's concerns to the large organized Jewish communities in their respective cities and across the country. These three essays reflect the unique historical experience, shared only by a very small number of rabbinic leaders anywhere in the world, of serving congregations whose members have been considered pariahs not only by the larger community, but also by Jews. These essays also reflect the growth and vibrancy of GLBT congregations across the country that have welcomed many who are now Jewish leaders, both lay and professional. Nearly every contributor to this volume found encouragement and support when, at some point on her journey, she visited a synagogue where being lesbian or gay and Jewish was the norm, and where she could be fully herself.

WORKING WITH JEWS "AT THE MARGINS": BEYOND THE BOUNDS OF THE JEWISH COMMUNITY

Only one half of American Jews affiliate with a synagogue. Who serves the other 50 percent? Two of the contributors chronicle serving Jews whose life experiences keep them away from synagogue life and the organized Jewish community. Julie Greenberg and Rebecca T. Alpert both write about working with Jews "at the margins." Greenberg begins her story of creating a Jewish family that defies conventional assumptions and goes on to describe how the Jewish Renewal Life Center that she founded and directs provides an alternative to synagogue-based communities and conventional study opportunities. Alpert reflects on how her work with those who are not involved in traditional denominational Judaism is enhanced by her own status as lesbian rabbi. Shirley Idelson's work as a college chaplain (not a Hillel director) also allows her some freedoms not enjoyed by many who answer to Jewish organizational expectations. Idelson chronicles her own path to the rabbinate, and reflects on the wide range of choices available to the young people she serves.

LESBIAN RABBIS AND CONSERVATIVE JUDAISM

The final section of this book points up the deep philosophical differences among the liberal Jewish movements that may seem to the outsider indistinguishable from one another in ritual, liturgy, and practice. A commitment to a particular interpretation of halachah has kept most scholars and leaders of the Conservative movement from affirming the holiness of gay and lesbian relationships and from endorsing the ordination of gay and lesbian rabbis. Benay Lappe writes about her experiences as a closeted rabbinical student, her ordination, and coming out to her colleagues and her movement. Dawn Robinson Rose catalogues her painful years as a seminary student, years that left deep wounds in spite of her successful completion of her doctorate from the same institution that refused to allow her to continue in the rabbinic program. Anonymous tells the story of how she survived her years at the seminary and her continuing sense that she must remain closeted to live as a Conservative rabbi. In 1989, when she contributed her essay to *Twice Blessed*, Leila Berner also felt the need to be closeted in order to speak.[45] The past decade has made an enormous difference for Reform and Reconstructionist rabbis; it is our hope that the next decade will allow Conservative rabbis the same freedom from fear and reprisal.

From these stories, we learn that making our voices heard does indeed make a difference. When we listen to the voices of lesbian rabbis, our understanding of Jewish experience and Jewish life is enriched. The voices that speak in this volume are the first to challenge previous assumptions of heterosexual Jewish leadership, and expand our visions of powerful Jewish teachers. The voices that teach in this volume spark new understandings of Jewish texts, of Jewish ritual, and of Jewish living. The voices that sing through this volume challenge us to hear harmonies and dissonance that could not be heard before. These voices shatter silence. The Jewish community is challenged by the commitment of those who have had to overcome great obstacles to make room for their leadership. The Jewish people is enriched by these strong, articulate testimonies of faith and faithfulness from the first generation of lesbian rabbis.

Notes

1. Michael A. Meyer, *Response to Modernity: A History of the Reform Movement in Judaism* (New York: Oxford University Press, 1988), 226–235.
2. *Reform Judaism* 28, 1 (fall 1999):10–11.
3. Jacob B. Agus, "The Orthodox Stream," in *Understanding American Judaism: Toward the Description of a Modern Religion*, vol. 2, ed. Jacob Neusner, (New York: Ktav Publishing House, Inc./Anti-Defamation League of B'nai Brith, 1975), 107. For a comprehensive discussion of the European roots of contemporary Judaism, see Robert M. Seltzer, *Jewish People, Jewish Thought: The Jewish Experience in History* (New York: Macmillan, 1980), 580 ff.
4. See, for example, Blu Greenberg, *On Women and Judaism* (Philadelphia: Jewish Publication Society, 1981); Tamar Frankiel, *The Voice of Sarah: Feminine Spirituality and Traditional Judaism* (San Francisco: HarperCollins, 1990); Debra Kaufman, *Rachel's Daughters: Newly Orthodox Jewish Women* (New Brunswick, N.J.: Rutgers University Press, 1991); several of the essays in Susan Grossman and Rivka Haut, ed., *Daughters of the King: Women and the Synagogue* (Philadelphia: Jewish Publication Society, 1992).
5. For a comprehensive discussion of the process of these decisions, see Sydelle Ruth Schulman, "Faithful Daughters and Ultimate Rebels: The First Class of Conservative Women Rabbis," in *Religious Institutions and Women's Leadership: New Roles Inside the Mainstream*, ed. Catherine Wessinger (Columbia: University of South Carolina Press, 1996), 311–317.
6. See Rebecca T. Alpert and Goldie Milgram, "Women in the Reconstructionist Rabbinate," in Wessinger, 291–295.
7. *The New Jews*, compiled by James A. Sleeper and Alan L. Mintz (New York: Vintage Books, 1971) was the first work to "name" the new generation of Jews who were claiming and transforming the Jewish world as they applied their values to the traditions and attitudes inherited from their parents and teachers. *Response* magazine, which was first published in New York City in 1967 and moved to Boston in 1970, was an important journal for many young voices. Also in 1970, a group of like-minded individuals connected to the Hillel Foundation at the University of California at Los Angeles began publishing *Davka: A Journal of Jewish Concerns*. Both magazines took risks by speaking about issues of feminism, sexuality, and the legitimacy of a range of posthalachic approaches to Judaism that had not been discussed in other cross-denominational Jewish publications. *The Jewish Catalogue*, edited by Richard Siegel, Michael Strassfeld, and Sharon Strassfeld (Philadelphia: Jewish Publication Society, 1973), styled after the *Whole Earth Catalogue*, became the movement's bible and banner. It

extended the reach of the Boston community across the country, and surprised even its editors when it sold more copies than any previous publication of the then century-old Jewish Publication Society.

8. Jewish feminists were indebted to the writings of Rosemary Radford Ruether, *Sexism and God-Talk* (Boston: Beacon, 1993) *New Woman, New Earth: Sexist Ideologies and Human Liberation* (Boston: Beacon, 1995), and *Womanguides: Readings Towards a Feminist Theology*, 2nd ed. (Boston: Beacon, 1996); Phyllis Trible, *God and the Rhetoric of Sexuality* (Philadelphia: Fortress Press, 1978); Nelle Morton, *The Journey Is Home* (Boston: Beacon, 1985); Mary Daly, *Beyond God the Father* (Boston: Beacon, 1973) and *Gyn/Ecology: The Metaethics of Radical Feminism* (Boston: Beacon, 1987); and Elisabeth Schussler Fiorenza, *In Memory of Her* (Philadelphia: Crossroad Press, 1984) and *Bread Not Stone: The Challenge of Feminist Biblical Interpretation* (Boston: Beacon, 1996). These works and others helped some Jewish feminists to frame their own questions.

9. The changes in Jewish worship made by the Reform movement (e.g., ending separate seating and altering the marriage ceremony and divorce proceedings) were certainly influenced by early efforts at women's equality in Europe and the United States. And Mordecai Kaplan's institution of the bat mitzvah and other innovations were the direct result of the suffrage movement. Some outstanding individual women were also early feminists. Bertha Pappenheim's visionary Jewish feminism is still largely undervalued. See Daniel Boyarin, *Unheroic Conduct: The Rise of Heterosexuality and the Invention of the Jewish Man* (Berkeley: University of California Press, 1997), 313–359; and Marion Kaplan, "Anna O. and Bertha Pappenheim: An Historical Perspective," in *Anna O: Fourteen Contemporary Reinterpretations*, ed. Max Rosenbaum and Melvin Muroff (New York: Free Press, 1984), 101–117.

10. The vibrancy of Jewish feminism's rebirth depends on the invaluable contributions of, among others, theologians Judith Plaskow, *Standing Again at Sinai* (New York: Harper and Row, 1990) and Rachel Adler, *Engendering Judaism* (Philadelphia: Jewish Publication Society, 1998); historians Paula E. Hyman, *Gender and Assimilation in Modern Jewish History* (Seattle: University of Washington Press, 1995), with Deborah Dash Moore, *Jewish Women in America: An Historical Encyclopedia* (New York: Routledge, 1997), and with Charlotte Baum and Sonya Michel, *The Jewish Woman in America* (New York: Dial Press, 1976); Judith R. Baskin, who edited *Jewish Women: In Historical Perspective* (Detroit: Wayne State University Press, 1991) and *Women of the Word: Jewish Women and Jewish Writing* (Detroit: Wayne State University Press, 1994); Ellen Umansky, who with Dianne Ashton, edited *Four Centuries of Jewish Women's Spirituality* (Boston: Beacon, 1992); and writers Esther Broner, *Weave of Women* (Bloomington: Indiana University Press, 1978), and Letty Cottin Pogrebin, *Deborah, Golda and Me: Being Female and Jewish in America* (New York: Crown, 1991). In addition, several Jewish women's organizations, including the National Council of Jewish Women (NCJW), Hadassah, and the Women of Reform Judaism (WRJ, formerly the National Federation of Temple Sisterhoods), remind their members that their organizations have always advocated for women, providing services for women and their families and supporting the empowerment of women in Jewish religious life, in the workplace, and in society in general.

11. See, for example, Letty Cottin Pogrebin's "Anti-Semitism in the Women's Movement," *Ms. Magazine* X:12 (June 1982):45–49, 62–74.

12. *Nice Jewish Girls: A Lesbian Anthology* (Boston: Beacon, 1989). Other secular lesbian feminists whose work has been essential to the development of a Jewish les-

bian identity are poets Adrienne Rich, whose corpus includes many poems and essays in a range of collections; Irena Klepfisz, *A Few Words in the Mother Tongue: Poems Selected and New (1971–1990)* and *Dreams of an Insomniac: Jewish Feminist Essays, Speeches and Diatribes* (Portland, Oreg.: The Eighth Mountain Press, 1990); and essayist and social critic Melanie Kaye Kantrowitz, *The Issue is Power: Essays on Women, Jews, Violence and Resistance* (San Francisco: aunt lute books, 1992).

13. *Twice Blessed: On Being Lesbian or Gay and Jewish*, ed. Christie Balka and Andy (Avi) Rose (Beacon: Boston, 1979).

14. For a description of the beginnings of the gay and lesbian synagogue movement, see Aaron Cooper, "No Longer Invisible: Gay and Lesbian Jews Build a Movement," *Journal of Homosexuality* 18 (1989–90):83–94.

15. See Aliza Maggid, "Joining Together: Building a Worldwide Movement," in *Twice Blessed*, 165.

16. The earliest rabbinic allies included Herschel Jonah Matt, "Sin, Crime, Sickness or Alternative Life Style? A Jewish Approach to Homosexuality," *Judaism* 27:1 (winter 1978):13–24, and "Homosexual Rabbis?" *Conservative Judaism* 39:3 (spring 1987):29–33. Reprinted in *Walking Humbly with God: The Life and Writings of Rabbi Hershel Jonah Matt* by Daniel Matt (Hoboken, N.J.: Ktav Publishing House, 1993); Janet Marder, "Getting to Know the Gay and Lesbian Shul," *Reconstructionist* (October–November 1985):20–25; and "Jewish and Gay," *Keeping Posted* 32, 2 (November 1986), reprinted in *Jewish Marital Status*, ed. Carol Diamant (Northvale, N.J.: Jason Aronson, 1989); and Erwin Herman, "A Synagogue for Jewish Homosexuals?" *CCAR Journal* (summer 1973):33–47.

17. The Reconstructionist movement published *Homosexuality and Judaism: The Reconstructionist Position*, ed. Robert Gluck (Wyncote, Pa.: Federation of Reconstructionist Congregations and Havurot and The Reconstructionist Rabbinical Association, 1992). The Reform movement's recommendations were published as *Kulanu (All of Us): A Program for Congregations Implementing Gay and Lesbian Inclusion*, ed. Julie R.Spitzer (New York: Union of American Hebrew Congregations, 1998).

18. The term "queer" serves both to reference the field of study of those who defy normative gender definitions and, at times, to designate the lesbian/bisexual/gay and transgender movement.

19. Cheshire Calhoun reminds us that "challenging heterosexual society and challenging patriarchy are not the same thing" and that "heterosexuality and patriarchy are analytically distinct social systems." "Separating Lesbian Theory from Feminist Theory," *Ethics* 104 (April 1994):572.

20. See Rebecca T. Alpert, *Like Bread on the Seder Plate: Jewish Lesbians and the Transformation of Tradition* (New York: Columbia University Press, 1997), ch. 1, for a further discussion of the unique situation of lesbians vis-à-vis gay men and heterosexual women.

21. The phrase *kol isha*, literally, "a woman's voice," is traditionally associated with the rabbinic dictum "Kol isha erva," meaning that a woman's voice is provocative and should therefore not be heard in public.

22. Gary Zola, "Twenty Years of Women in the Rabbinate," in Zola, ed. *Women Rabbis: Exploration and Celebration: Papers Delivered at an Academic Conference Honoring Twenty Years of Women in the Rabbinate, 1972–1992* (Cincinnati, Ohio: HUC-JIR Rabbinic Alumni Association Press, 1996), 4–5; and Ellen Umansky, "Women's Journey toward Rabbinic Ordination," in Zola, 31. Articles on Regina Jonas: Katarina von Kellenbach, " 'God Does Not Oppress Any Human Being,'

The Life and Thought of Rabbi Regina Jonas," *Leo Baeck Institute Year Book* 39 (1994):213–225; and Alexander Guttman, "The Woman Rabbi: An Historical Perspective," *Journal of Reform Judaism* (summer 1982):21–25.

23. Other women had attended HUC-JIR and also the Conservative movement's Jewish Theological Seminary over the years, but none were admitted to rabbinic candidacy. See the essays by Zola and Umansky, and "Women Who Would be Rabbis," by Pamela S. Nadell, in *Gender and Judaism: The Transformation of Tradition*, ed. Tamar M. Rudavsky (New York: New York University Press, 1995), 123–134. See also Nadell's *Women Who Would be Rabbis* (Boston: Beacon, 1998); and Guttman, "The Woman Rabbi: An Historical Perspective," *Journal of Reform Judaism* (summer 1982):21–25.

24. Including the classes of 2000, the following seminaries reported these numbers: Hebrew Union College-Jewish Institute of Religion 344, Jewish Theological Seminary and University of Judaism 118, Reconstructionist Rabbinical College 93, Leo Baeck College (London) 27. This does not include women ordained privately or at nondenominational seminaries.

25. David Ellenson, "Transformation of the Rabbinate: Future Directions and Prospects," in Zola, 96.

26. This concept was first suggested by the Christian feminist Phyllis Trible, in *God and the Rhetoric of Sexuality* (Philadelphia: Fortress Press, 1978). See also the work of Rachel Adler; Alicia Ostriker, *The Nakedness of the Fathers: Biblical Visions and Revisions* (New Brunswick, N.J.: Rutgers University Press, 1994); and others.

27. See *Wisdom You Are My Sister: Twenty-five Years of Women in the Rabbinate*, special issue of the *CCAR Journal* (summer 1997). For feminist textual analysis, see Elyse Goldstein, *ReVisions: Seeing Torah Through a Feminist Lens* (Woodstock, Vt.: Jewish Lights Publishing, 1999). For new rituals, see Debra Ornstein, ed. *Lifecycles: Jewish Women on Life Passages and Personal Milestones*, vol. 1 (Woodstock, Vt.: Jewish Lights Publishing, 1996), and Ellen Umansky and Dianne Ashton eds., *Four Centuries of Jewish Women's Spirituality* (Boston: Beacon, 1992). On infertility, see Nina Beth Cardin, *Tears of Sorrow, Seeds of Hope: A Jewish Spiritual Companion for Infertility and Pregnancy Loss* (Woodstock, Vt.: Jewish Lights Publishing, 1999). Rabbis Rachel Cowan, Amy Eilberg, Nancy Flam, and Dayle Friedman are among those most closely associated with the Jewish healing movement. On spiritual counseling see Naomi Levy, *To Begin Again: The Journey Toward Comfort, Strength, and Faith in Difficult Times* (New York: Alfred Knopf, 1998), and Karyn Kedar, *God Whispers: Stories of the Soul, Lessons of the Heart* (Woodstock, Vt.: Jewish Lights Publishing, 1999). Among the many haggadot compiled by rabbis are Sue Levi Elwell et al., ed. *The Journey Continues: Ma'yan Passover Haggadah* (New York: Ma'yan: The Jewish Women's Project, 1999).

28. David Biale, *Eros and the Jews: From Biblical Israel to Contemporary America* (New York: Basic Books, 1992).

29. This was suggested by Rabbi Elizabeth Weiss Stern in a talk delivered at the 1995 Biennial Convention of the Women's Rabbinic Network in Oakland, California.

30. Author's conversation with Rabbi Allen Bennett, 27 September 1999. Two other synagogues with outreach to the gay and lesbian community had been established in Los Angeles (Beth Chayim Chadashim, 1972) and in New York City (Congregation Beth Simchat Torah, 1973), but neither used the services of a gay rabbi.

31. On one occasion, Kahn was able to make a connection between two lesbian colleagues, both of whom were in the process of ending heterosexual marriages. They were able to provide one another considerable support as each of them confronted the challenges of coming out to their husbands, their children, and their parents, and restructuring their professional lives.

32. See, for example, Yoel H. Kahn, "Judaism and Homosexuality: The Traditionalist Progressive Debate," *Journal of Homosexuality* 18(3/4):47–82, and "The Liturgy of Gay and Lesbian Jews," in Balka and Rose.

33. To the best of our knowledge fifteen rabbis are out gay men.

34. See Rebecca T. Alpert, "Challenging Male/Female Complementarity: Jewish Lesbians and the Jewish Tradition," in *People of the Body: Jews and Judaism from an Embodied Perspective*, ed. Howard Eilberg-Schwartz (Albany: State University of New York Press, 1992), 364–366.

35. Alpert, *Like Bread on the Seder Plate*, 29–35.

36. See Judith Plaskow, "Lesbian and Gay Rights: Asking the Right Questions," *Tikkun* 9 (March–April 1994):31–32.

37. Women rabbis who identify as bisexual were invited to contribute to this volume. Several considered writing, but ultimately chose not to. Bisexuality is still highly stigmatized in the Jewish community. It is often misunderstood as a challenge to monogamy, although most bisexuals, like their gay and heterosexual counterparts, are serial monogamists. It is perceived as threatening because it involves the idea that people may not divide so neatly into categories of gay and straight, and opens up the possibility that many individuals may be capable, at different times in their lives, of different sexual choices.

38. See Alpert, *Like Bread on the Seder Plate*, 71–96, for a discussion of Jewish lesbian reconstructions of the family.

39. An informal census of ordained rabbis and rabbinical students indicate that between 11 and 13 percent of the approximately 580 women rabbis self-identify as lesbians. Rebecca T.Alpert corroborates the figure of greater than 10 percent, and goes on to explain, "Note that self reporting is the definition being used. There are also women in the rabbinate who define themselves as bisexual or queer, or choose not to label themselves with any sexual identity, and these numbers may increase in the future as language and custom change. However, most of the non-heterosexual women rabbis are comfortable with the label lesbian and so identify." "Lesbian Rabbis and the Politics of Visibility," paper presented at the American Academy of Religion, November 1997.

40. "From Equality to Transformation: The Challenge of Women's Rabbinic Leadership," in Zola, 69–70. An earlier version of this essay appears in Rudavsky.

41. Author's conversation with Rabbi Stacy Offner, 26 September 1999.

42. *Homosexuality and Judaism: The Reconstructionist Position: Report of the Reconstructionist Commission on Homosexuality*, rev. ed. (Wyncote, Pa.: Federation of Reconstructionist Congregations and Havurot, 1993).

43. Bradley S. Artson, "Gay and Lesbian Jews: An Innovative Legal Position," *Jewish Spectator* (winter 1990–1991):6–14; "Enfranchising the Monogamous Homosexual: A Legal Possibility, a Moral Imperative," *S'vara: A Journal of Philosophy, Law and Judaism* 3, 1 (1993):15–26; Elliot N. Dorff, *Matters of Life and Death: A Jewish Approach to Modern Medical Ethics* (Philadelphia: Jewish Publication Society, 1998), 139–150; Gordon Tucker, "Homosexuality and Halachic Judaism: A Conservative View," *Moment* 18, 3 (June 1992):40–43; Howard Handler, "In the Image of God," Rabbinical Assembly Committee on Jewish Law and Standards;

and Harold Schulweis, "Morality, Legality and Homosexuality," *Jewish Spectator* 57, 3 (winter 1992):23–27.
44. Shir Tikvah: The New Reform Congregation of the Twin Cities (Minneapolis and St. Paul, Minnesota), founded by Rabbi Stacy Offner, is one such synagogue community. Reconstructionist Congregation Mishkan Shalom in Philadelphia is another, and Central Reform Congregation in St. Louis is a third.
45. La Escondida, "Journey Toward Wholeness: Reflections of a Lesbian Rabbi," in Balka and Rose, 218–227.

Serving a Denominational Movement

Part I

Chapter 1	Struggle, Change, and Celebration

LINDA HOLTZMAN   *My Life as a Lesbian Rabbi*

I GRADUATED FROM THE Reconstructionist Rabbinical College in 1979, accepted a position as the sole rabbi of a Conservative congregation, and began my fifteen minutes of fame. Newspapers from around the world ran stories about me, the first woman rabbi serving in such a position. Calls from radio programs, magazines, television programs poured in. Everyone wanted to interview a woman rabbi. While I was overwhelmed by the attention, I also enjoyed it. I had worked hard to reach that point in my life, and it felt good to be celebrated. Sort of . . .

During my fourth year of rabbinical school, while I was in Israel, I had a relationship with a woman and began to explore my identity as a lesbian. This was new and exciting to me. I wanted to share my experience with everyone I knew. Wouldn't everyone who cared about me be as excited as I was, learning that I was exploring a profound aspect of my identity? Needless to say, in 1978 there was little excitement from anyone, except perhaps other lesbians. The Reconstructionist Rabbinical College had been a haven for me in many ways. Within its walls, I was able to question commonly accepted ideas about God and Jewish tradition and know that my questioning would be acceptable. I was able to challenge instructors, and was celebrated for my willingness to honestly express my opinions. I was able to argue with my colleagues about political and social issues, and it was always comfortable. Yet would I be able to return from Israel and be open? I realized early on in my coming-out process that this issue was different.

Having spent a year of rabbinical training in Israel, I returned to the United States in the fall of 1978, ready to begin my final year at RRC. I had barely settled in to the year's routine when a major issue was raised. A graduate student at the Jewish Theological Seminary had spoken to the dean explaining that he was interested in transferring and becoming a Reconstructionist rabbi. He was highly skilled, a brilliant academician, a deeply knowledgeable Jew, and seemed to be the perfect candidate for admission but for one factor. The candidate was gay, and he was interested in applying to RRC only if he could be open with the college community about his life. He wanted to know whether RRC would be comfortable considering an openly gay man for admission. The dean was dumbfounded; the issue had never been raised at RRC so directly before. He brought the question before both the faculty and student bodies before he would respond to the potential applicant.

I was immensely grateful. Here was an opportunity to see the reactions of my colleagues on the question of gay and lesbian rabbis without being open myself. I was still so unsure of my own identity and so uncertain about the direction of my own career that anything that required that I be more self-revelatory would have felt much too unsafe. This event provided the opportunity to safely discuss issues that I needed to explore. I also felt certain that my colleagues would all be accepting and open. How could they not be?

The students began the discussion of this issue with an exploration of traditional Jewish texts on homosexuality. In 1978 there were no contemporary writers doing a serious critique of the traditional texts, and only a few of us cared enough to uncover the layers of homophobia that formed the texts. I watched while a group of well-meaning yet largely uncomfortable students grappled with texts that made assumptions about my life that were unfounded and absurd. Yet I too was a novice at delving into the heart of the texts and unmasking the assumptions at their core. I found the process frustrating and disheartening. The texts themselves were clearly homophobic, but more disturbing to me was the homophobia that some of my colleagues brought to their study of the texts. Any sense I had of trust that my colleagues would be automatically supportive of me evaporated as I watched their ambivalence about admitting an openly gay student.

At the end of our conversations, we communicated our thoughts to the dean. It seemed unlikely we could ever reach a consensus on any one view, so a few of us took the situation into our own hands. We wrote a strong letter saying that after examining the traditional texts and exploring the issues concerning gay and lesbian rabbis, we could not think of any valid reason why someone should be deemed inappropriate for the rabbinate because of his or her sexual orientation. We then shared our letter with the whole student body. Approximately half of the students were prepared to sign the letter. For a variety of reasons, the other half of the student body refused to sign, sending no message of their own to the dean. Needless to say, a letter from merely half of the students was not sufficient, and after a negative faculty vote, the potential student was called and advised not to apply.

I was devastated. If at the Reconstructionist Rabbinical College, the most progressive rabbinical school on so many important social issues, the student body could not be open to the possibility of ordaining a gay or lesbian rabbi, what hope was there? My dream in life had been to serve as a congregational rabbi. I had long seen myself as leading a congregation, and I was now uncertain that I would ever be able to do so. It meant giving up a dream that I had been working toward for years: the dream of helping shape a community according to the values that were central to my life. It meant giving up the possibility of working with children, with older people, with a whole Jewish community in deep and significant ways. It meant that I had to choose: between the career that I had long imagined and prepared for and the whole person that I was beginning to see myself to be. I felt alone and torn.

The one person from whom I received support for my conflict was the then dean of students at the Reconstructionist Rabbinical College, Rabbi Rebecca Alpert. She had had a similar conflict in her life, and was in the process of determining the direction of her life and of her career. She listened to me for hours and really heard the pain in my conflict. Yet even she was not open about her sexual orientation. In 1978 it did not seem as if there was anywhere in the Jewish community where a gay or lesbian rabbi would be tolerated, let alone embraced.

When I graduated from rabbinical school in 1979, I had several major decisions to make. Should I interview for pulpit positions and remain in the closet? Should I try to find a different kind of job, one that would allow me to be out? Were my years of studying for the rabbinate going to come to naught because there were no Jewish institutions that would consider hiring a lesbian rabbi? It was not a difficult decision. When I first entered the Reconstructionist Rabbinical College, I did so because of a deep desire to serve the Jewish community as a rabbi. I loved the pulpit: leading services, speaking publicly, teaching, officiating at life cycle events. I desperately wanted to work with people of all ages, to be with them at their most powerful moments, to celebrate their joys and support them through their sorrows. Now that I had the opportunity to reach for my dream, I was not going to give it up.

I had a strong belief in my potential as a rabbi. I knew that I could be successful. Deep down I felt that if I was good enough, I could be a congregational rabbi and be out as a lesbian and make it all work well. Maybe others wouldn't be able to do it, but I could. (I have heard this expressed by many other women through the years. I have come to real-ize that one's ability is certainly crucial, but that it takes a lot more than ability to enable someone to succeed in a community as an open lesbian rabbi.) I felt as if I was embarking on an extended test. I would certainly not be open at the start of my work in a congregation, but in time, I would be able to be open—even in a small town's conservative/Conser-vative congregation where being a woman rabbi was considered quite radical; even in a community where the process for hiring a rabbi was extended by months while the congregation debated whether or not they could tolerate a woman rabbi; even in a community where the words "gay" and "lesbian" were never publicly spoken. It might take a little while, I reasoned, but I could do it.

When I moved to Coatesville, Pennsylvania, to be the rabbi of a small congregation located forty miles west of Philadelphia, I began liv-ing two very lovely—and very separate—lives. Work was rich and sat-isfying, and took up most of my days and many of my evenings. No one in my congregation knew anything about my personal life, and while people were often curious, they allowed me to maintain a high level of privacy. Whenever I had any free time, I left Coatesville and headed to Philadelphia, where my social life existed, where I could be open about my lesbianism, where I could feel whole.

I have often been asked about those years: Were they very sad? Was I often depressed? How did I cope with the separateness of my personal and professional lives? The truth is that I was not unhappy. I loved the rabbinate, adored my work, enjoyed the congregation I was serving. I also loved my friends in Philadelphia, developed important relationships, and had a satisfying personal life. While I began the six years by living in Coatesville, I took the forty-mile drive to Philadelphia every few days to see friends, to date, and to have a social life. The underlying fear of being caught and the stress that it added to my life were not pleasant, but they were not all-consuming. I enjoyed my life, and accepted its limitations as inevitable; in 1979 they certainly seemed to be.

In 1981 I met Betsy Conston, the woman who was to become my life partner, and in 1982 I moved into her house in Philadelphia. For the next three years I drove to and from Coatesville six times every week. It was very important to me to be available to my congregation, while also building a partnership with the woman I loved. I was determined to have the career I had dreamed of as well as the relationship I treasured, even if it meant that the parts of my life would be totally separate.

While I was not open in my congregation, during the six years that I served them, while in Philadelphia, I made inroads into the gay and lesbian Jewish community. I spoke at an International Conference of Gay and Lesbian Jews, and while I never publicly discussed my own sexual orientation, simply presenting myself as an accepting rabbi brought me many referrals. There were so few rabbis who were open to gay and lesbian people that, even in that, I made a contribution. People began to call me to perform commitment ceremonies and baby namings, to counsel their parents who were having difficulty with their children's coming out, to discuss with them their possible inclusion in the Jewish community as fully open gay or lesbian members. By this time, there were other gay and lesbian rabbinical students who were searching for role models. While I was not out to my congregation, I made certain that I was open and available to anyone who wanted to talk. Sadly, the advice I gave students then was not very hopeful; it was hard to believe that at any time soon the Jewish community would change its negative attitude about homosexuality.

The mid-eighties were a time of major change for the gay and lesbian Jewish community in general and for gay and lesbian rabbis in particular. In 1984 my life partner and I decided to celebrate our commitment in a ceremony, officiated at by two good friends and attended by lots of our friends and the few family members who were

ready at that time to accept us. I was clearly walking a tightrope; I had a
large open ceremony in Philadelphia, but did not let anyone in my congregation know that it was happening. I was too excited about the ceremony and about my life with Betsy to see how dangerous this was. We
were planning our life together, dreaming of the children we would raise
together, imagining the home we would build. My contract in Coatesville
was due to be renegotiated during the spring of 1985. I knew that remaining in Coatesville depended on the congregation's ability to be more
accepting of me and of who I was. If Betsy and I were going to have children together, I could lead only one life. If I was going to be a mother, it
was not going to be acceptable for me to lie about my status or to pretend
that my child did not exist. And I could certainly not expect a child to
keep our relationship a secret. I had been teaching children long enough
to know that children are the most open people imaginable. I wanted our
children to be open and proud of their home life. The world would do
enough to make them ashamed; I would not add to it.

During a meeting of the synagogue board of directors, I gave the
congregation my terms for contract renewal. I informed them that my
"housemate" was planning to have a child. I was going to be helping her
raise the child, and I wanted two weeks' coparenting leave written into
my contract. Next month, I expected to hear from board members as
they discussed my demand. And hear from them I did. One by one
board members came into my office and sadly explained, "Rabbi, it's not
me. I would be perfectly happy to have this clause written into your contract. The rest of the board, however, would never be able to live with
it. They're just not ready." The message was clear. At the next month's
meeting, I informed the board sadly that I would be leaving the congregation at the end of the year.

It was now 1985, and change was in the air. I began to work part-
time for Beth Ahavah, the gay and lesbian synagogue of Philadelphia,
and part-time at the Reconstructionist Rabbinical College. Now, several
years later, it was acceptable for me to be open as a lesbian and to teach
at RRC. Now there were gay and lesbian students at RRC who were
beginning to talk more openly about who they were and who were
mostly supported by their colleagues and by the faculty. Yet there was still
a lot of fear in the air. Could an openly gay or lesbian rabbi ever serve a
mainstream congregation? No one was certain. Could the Reconstruc-

tionist movement, as small and insecure as it was, be supportive on this controversial issue and continue to grow and thrive? Was RRC willing to be the first rabbinical school to take a stand on the question of gay and lesbian rabbis?

This time, RRC accepted the challenge that this issue presented. Under the leadership of RRC's then president, Ira Silverman *z'l*, a small committee was formed to write a policy statement for the college on admitting openly gay and lesbian students. The committee consisted of Rabbi Hershel Matt *z'l* and me. After briefly meeting, we wrote the simple statement that formed RRC's policy: "RRC does not discriminate on the basis of sexual orientation." The faculty overwhelmingly passed this policy, proud that we had achieved something significant, but quite naive about the ramifications of our vote.

RRC's new policy meant that gay and lesbian students at RRC could be open and unafraid while at school. It meant that there would be a more relaxed atmosphere at the college. It meant that an open conversation about having gay and lesbian rabbis in the field could begin. And it meant that openly gay and lesbian rabbis would soon be graduating.

The Federation of Reconstructionist Congregations and Havurot and the Reconstructionist Rabbinical Association were furious. How could the RRC not consult them about an issue that would affect them too? Congregations might not be ready for gay and lesbian rabbis. How dare the college put them in a position where they would be forced to accept them?! It was clear to us at RRC that we had voted in something with far-reaching ramifications that, to us, had simply felt like the right thing to do.

In retrospect, I strongly believe we did the right thing. Had we waited, it might never have happened—not because the rabbinic and lay leadership of the Reconstructionist movement would not have supported it, but because the discussion process about the issue might have continued endlessly. RRC's open admission policy has been inspirational to other movements as well. This policy gave impetus to Hebrew Union College, the Reform rabbinical seminary, to begin to consider its own policy on gay and lesbian issues, thus fostering greater openness in the Reform movement as well.

At RRC, while there was much jubilation, the work of implementing this policy had just begun, and there was concern among students, faculty, and administration. Would students who were out at RRC be able to find jobs? Would heterosexual students be comfortable studying together with people they knew were gay or lesbian? Could we as a community celebrate the life cycle events of our gay and lesbian members as easily and comfortably as we celebrated those of our heterosexual members? How could we help our gay and lesbian students as they made life decisions concerning being out, making commitments, having children? There was so much for us to consider, more than any of us had realized.

Sharon Kleinbaum, then a student at RRC, encouraged the faculty to listen to the students, to hear their concerns, to meet their needs. We formed an unofficial committee, the "What Now?" Committee, to tackle the issues raised. We held workshops in which homophobia was explored and expressed and sometimes overcome. We listened to speakers present the many ways this decision would have an impact on the lives of all Reconstructionist rabbis, regardless of their sexual orientation. We met for hours to think through the seemingly endless issues raised by this one simple decision.

I was honored to be a part of this process. My own life was exciting and fulfilling. In 1986 my partner, Betsy, gave birth to our son Jordan, and in 1988 I gave birth to our second son, Zachary. Now I was in a community that would celebrate the birth and growth of our children. Now I was in a community that fully understood the meaning of coparenting leave. Now I was open in every area of my life. I was home.

Yet, as comfortable as my life was becoming, there was still much work to do. I spoke before congregations every chance I could about gay, lesbian, and Jewish issues. I spent countless hours counseling gay and lesbian Jews who were excited by RRC's openness, but who weren't sure the rest of the Jewish community would accept them as rabbis. I performed more and more commitment ceremonies and baby namings for gay and lesbian people. As the AIDS epidemic grew, I worked within the Jewish community to try to lessen the terror that accompanied it and to dispel the homophobia that grew up around it. At RRC, I was often the faculty person who was the confidante of queer students of all sorts: gay, lesbian, bisexual, or transgender. I helped guide people through the RRC program at a time when that world was warm and accepting, but the world outside was often fraught with danger.

The danger was brought home to me most boldly by a short-lived but very helpful organization that I joined. Called Ameinu, this organization for gay and lesbian Jewish professionals hosted a conference every year for three years. Each conference took place in a different part of the country. The preconference material that we all received told us what airport to fly to and when to arrive, but we were never told exactly where the conference would be held. Everything was secret. If people found out about the conference's location and its nature and figured out that their rabbi or cantor or education director was there, the rabbi or cantor or education director could lose his/her job. Even in the days when I was most closeted in my life, I had never felt the level of fear that some of the other Jewish professionals lived with on a daily basis. Couples who shared apartments but not telephone numbers, couples who never drove to or from any events together, couples who were in the same congregations but would never talk to each other in public: all came to these conferences wanting support and desperately needing a place to relax. These were people who loved serving the Jewish community, but who lived in fear in order to do it. I became even more committed to working to create a safe, accepting environment within the Jewish community for queer Jews.

The Reconstructionist Jewish community proved to be a wonderful place for some of this work to be done. After the initial negative reaction of the Reconstructionist movement to RRC's open admission policy, a transformation occurred. Throughout the movement, education and discussion about gay and lesbian rabbis began to occur. This soon expanded to discussions of gay and lesbian community members as well. As a member of the Reconstructionist Commission on Homosexuality, I took part in developing a position paper and educational program for the movement that welcomed gay and lesbian Jews and that celebrated the inclusion of gay and lesbian rabbis in our community.[1] This position paper represented not only RRC, but also the Reconstructionist Rabbinical Association and the Jewish Reconstructionist Federation (the new name for the congregational body of the Reconstructionist movement). While the document did not do enough (no mention was made of bisexual or transgender Jews, for example), it was a very important step. This was the first time a major Jewish movement expressed unequivocal support for gay and lesbian Jews and rabbis. It was the first time we were celebrated, not just tolerated, by the Jewish community. It was a document built on compromise and on the integrity of its membership. The process of drafting the document was exciting and uplifting. While it is not perfect, it is a work that I am proud of.

As the director of the practical rabbinics department at the Reconstructionist Rabbinical College today, I look back over the past twenty years in amazement. It is a different world. Gay and lesbian students are often placed in congregations without difficulty. Of course, there are still some Reconstructionist synagogues that are not comfortable with the idea of a gay or lesbian rabbi. A few years ago, there were stories of new graduates being asked subtle questions in job interviews in an obvious attempt to determine their sexual orientation (Will your wife/husband be looking for a job as well? . . .). This still happens, but less frequently. With the ongoing support of the Reconstructionist Rabbinical Association, most students decide to be open. There seem to be enough progressive Reconstructionist congregations that welcome all qualified candidates.

But our work is not finished. In most of the Jewish world, gay and lesbian Jews are still invisible. In most synagogues, there are no commitment ceremonies for gay and lesbian Jews, no baby namings for their children. In most religious school curriculums there are still no families celebrated that don't include mommy, daddy, and children. To combat this problem, RRC students are required to take a two-day intensive course on "Inclusive Community." Focusing primarily on gay and lesbian issues, this course helps students explore homophobia in their lives and the effect of homophobia on their congregations. It teaches students how, as rabbis, they can help build communities like the community at RRC, one in which sexual orientation is seen as one of an exciting number of differences among community members to be understood, respected, and celebrated. The more we teach our leaders to be sensitive, the more the Jewish community will become an open, welcoming place.

We have come a long way. I am blessed by being able to live in a Jewish community that accepts me, is supportive of my family, and enables me to teach other rabbis to build such communities in their lives. The depth of change that has occurred in so few years constantly surprises and thrills me. When I graduated from rabbinical school in 1979, it never occurred to me that twenty years later gay and lesbian rabbis would be ordained and working openly in many communities; that the curricula of many religious schools would celebrate the diversity of the families of their students; that excellent educational material exploring gay and lesbian Jewish life would be available. I have been blessed by being able to be part of this process, and I anticipate the next phase of our journey with joy and excitement.

Note

1. Robert Gluck, ed. *Homosexuality and Judaism: The Reconstructionist Position* (Wyncote, Pa: Federation of Reconstructionist Congregations and Havurot and the Reconstructionist Rabbinical Association, 1992).

A Practical Theology of Presence

Chapter 2

NANCY WIENER

W<small>HILE DRAWING A PICTURE</small> to represent the pieces of my life (I was at a presemester, schoolwide retreat) in the fall of 1999, I was overwhelmed by the sea change that had taken place in my world and by the sense of profound gratitude and joy that the awareness of this engenders in me. Not only are the pieces of my life marvelously interconnected, but my relationship with my spouse figures at the center—and I can and do share this reality with my colleagues and my students, my congregants, my family and friends and neighbors, as well! Nine years earlier, I had wept with my friends and my therapist because, as my ordination approached, I feared that I would never be able to integrate my personal and professional lives. I had become quite accustomed to leaving at home all traces of my private life—even carefully choosing my words and editing the stories I told in order to avoid revealing my status as a member of a committed lesbian relationship—when I went to work. My rabbinic life was 100 percent "professional." On a personal level, my congregants hardly knew me; all they saw was a relatively shy, unattached young woman, rather than the social, outgoing partner in a relationship that my friends and family knew. As ordination approached, I was torn between my ever-growing excitement about becoming a rabbi and my profound dread of the years that lay ahead during which, according to well-meaning, more experienced rabbis and Jewish professionals, I would have to continue to perpetuate this charade.

Shortly before ordination, I wrote a letter to a close friend who had encouraged me to go into the rabbinate:

April 16, 1990

Dear Laura:

In five weeks a rabbi. Me. I can't wait . . . this is what I love doing. I just hope that I will have the opportunity over the years to experience all the different parts of the rabbinate that I find appealing. . . . I just hope there is a congregation that is ready to hire me, where Judy can be visible, and, where ideally our relationship can be open and a non-issue. . . . The reality is that few such places exist; most likely, we will live in one of the major metropolitan areas, I'll be at an in-lying suburban congregation that won't mind my living in the city and commuting; and my personal and professional lives will have to remain separate. It seems so unnecessary and so unfair!

That my sexual orientation can be viewed as a determining factor in my ability to serve as a rabbi is mind-boggling. Fortunately, the Reform movement has been actively doing outreach to gays and lesbians to encourage membership in synagogues. They've also done extensive education about homophobia and AIDS. . . . Unfortunately, there still exists a clear delineation in many people's minds between what's O.K. for everyone else and what's O.K. for the rabbi. Hopefully, that too will change over time. I'm a great congregational rabbi and Judy has a lot to offer any congregation, as she has the synagogue we attend here in the city.

At the beginning of my rabbinate, I struggled with the question, "As a rabbi, how can I have meaningful relationships with others if I can't bring all of myself into the relationship?" Knowing that I experience God through my human relationships, I wondered how I could have transformative relationships as a rabbi, if I entered the relationship with only parts of my self present. I dreamed of finding a way to get beyond the external pressures and realities of an unaccepting straight world, one that had forced so many to stay closeted. I wanted to find a means of practicing what I believed.

Initially, I sought professional venues that I believed were less likely to demand intense, personal relationships from me: a chaplaincy training program and a very part-time pulpit. I thought I could find refuge in the safety I perceived in the world of chaplaincy. I hoped that by having short-term, hospital-based relationships with patients and their families I would not have to reveal those aspects of my private life that I feared would be unacceptable. I thought it would be possible to relate fully, even though I was not bringing all of myself into the relationship. Little did I know that as my supervisor taught me and reminded me daily, "The only thing you bring into a patient's room is yourself. If you shut down part of yourself, other parts are automatically shut down as well. Either all of your being is present and accessible, or none of you really is." Prayers, rituals, and religious garb are all adjuncts to the personal, caring presence that a chaplain offers.

In addition to the chaplaincy, I'd arranged to work with a chavurah in suburban New York. It too seemed ideal: a small, committed community that wanted a part-time rabbi and had no expectation that the rabbi would live locally. And yet, every other weekend, as I drove to the chavurah, a deep sadness entered my soul as I consciously forced myself to shut down or hide away parts of myself. On so many levels, my first year in the rabbinate was unsatisfying; ultimately, my professional choices did not provide me with an escape. My full self was begging to come out in the open and function as a whole.

After that first year, I promised myself to work consciously at letting my supervisor's teaching about being fully present guide me in all aspects of my life, especially the professional. In fact, even today, I work to make my rabbinate one that allows me to be fully present, and encourages others to be fully present as well.

When I first discussed the possibility of becoming fieldwork coordinator at the Hebrew Union College-Jewish Institute of Religion, the seminary of the Reform movement, I told the dean that I could not imagine working at the school if I could not be out to students and colleagues. It was a risky statement to make, but, at the time, it seemed like a much greater risk to my personal and mental health to start the job in the closet. Much to my amazement and delight, the dean responded by saying that he felt it was important for students, both gay and straight, to know that I was there—available to support them and answer any questions or concerns that they might have. He got it! If I were to be interacting with students, I would have to be myself. And particularly if

I were going to be advising students as they developed their professional identities, I would need to be able to be fully present and a real role model for them.

In the early winter of 1991, during my first academic year working at the College-Institute, Judy and I sanctified our relationship at our kiddush ahavah. I told select colleagues and some students, but chose not to make a loud public statement. I did not yet believe, in my heart of hearts, that the institution had changed enough to celebrate with us. I still retained too many painful memories of being in semihiding during my tenure there as a student. And then, again to our utter amazement and delight, Judy and I came home after our ceremony to find a lovely basket of flowers with a card wishing us "Mazal tov" from the school administration.

Although I began to wear my wedding ring to my weekend work with the chavurah, I still did not come out. Having learned that I was not forthcoming about my personal life, few members said anything about the ring. To those few who did, I tossed off blithe, diversionary responses. Finally, nine months after our ceremony, I could no longer continue with the charade. I had grown very fond of the members and enjoyed the work I'd done with them. I wanted them to get to know a fuller me, and to know Judy. I was tired of hiding. Thus, although I was nervous that coming out would mean saying good-bye to the members of this chavurah, comprised primarily of upper-middle-class, suburban empty-nesters, I called the president to arrange a meeting, at which I planned to tell her. Again I learned that my fears, which had prevented me from coming out sooner, were far more paralyzing than responses I received from my chavurah. The president had no problem; she had gay relatives and friends herself. Moreover, she felt that most members of the group would respond the same way she did. Together, we reviewed the list of members, speculating about their reactions to my coming out and to my expressing the desire to involve my spouse in the activities of the group. There was only one family that we both felt was likely to be deeply upset by the news, perhaps upset enough to leave the group. The president seemed unfazed by this possibility. When the group gathered for its monthly meeting, and the chavurah as a whole had its first opportunity to discuss this news, it was the member whose response the president and I were most concerned about who stood up to say, "I seek a rabbi with integrity. Our rabbi has integrity! Why should we have any problem?"

Of course, as I became a multidimensional person, with a rich life of relationships, my congregants felt more comfortable sharing with me the many dimensions of their lives as well. My friendly yet withholding stance had warned them to act similarly by not talking with me about some of their more profound concerns. I had not realized how superficial my relationships had been until chavurah members began turning to me with greater ease and frequency to discuss deeply personal matters. They came now, believing that I could not only respond professionally but also empathically and personally, to their pains, confusions, and struggles.

Immediately following the meeting, Judy began coming with me to the chavurah. The members of the chavurah universally recognize her as a valued and beloved rebbetzin and integral presence in their lives. Whatever theoretical objections they may have held regarding a "gay rabbi" have disappeared as they have gotten to know us as a committed, loving, Jewishly active family. And only one year later, thanks to the chavurah, Judy and I experienced something that far surpassed any of our wildest fantasies. At the chavurah's midsummer barbecue and havdalah service, a major community outreach program for prospective members to meet the group, all those present came to help us hang the mezuzah on the doorpost of the cottage that the chavurah has made available to us. It was a joyous, warm celebration for us as a family and for the community as a whole.

My move to the college did not represent a move away from counseling and chaplaincy, but rather the opportunity for me to continue in a new venue. It has been a way to bring a new dimension to the college's supervision program and professional development courses. I introduced students and faculty to the notion that fieldwork supervision can be so much more than checking in for a progress report or cleaning up unanticipated messes. By being available to students to discuss their goals, expectations, and dreams, by offering them support and encouragement as they struggle to develop a sense of themselves as clergy, and by teaching them some theoretical frameworks and practical skills in counseling, I have been able to help students grow to understand supervision and pastoral counseling courses as a welcome and necessary part of their overall education. Through my words and my example during class and in supervision sessions, I try to model for my students the use of oneself in a counseling rabbinate.

With the support of the college, I earned a Doctor of Ministry in Pastoral Counseling degree, so that I could deepen and expand my own knowledge and practical skills. For my doctoral demonstration project, I chose to develop a counseling model for rabbis to use in work with gay and lesbian couples who wish to celebrate their unions with specifically Jewish rituals. When I submitted my proposal, I was asked whether the topic was "broad enough," whether I could be "objective enough," whether it was "doable." In spite of these concerns, I successfully completed the project, with no dearth of couples interested in participating and numbers of rabbis eagerly awaiting its completion for ideas and assistance in improving their own counseling techniques in this vital new area of clergy counseling. As a result of my research, I have been asked to lead numerous workshops on the topic for my colleagues, and to write a book for all Jewish couples, regardless of sexual orientation, to help them plan and prepare for their weddings.

At the time of this writing, most of my time at HUC-JIR is split between supervising students in their field placements and teaching courses on chaplaincy and pastoral counseling. In both arenas, I find myself teaching my students what my teacher taught me: "The only thing you bring to others is your self. The title 'rabbi' or 'cantor' may be the reason people turn to you, but what they get from you depends on who you are and what you are willing and able to bring to the relationship you create with them. You are a religious being, an intellectual being, a social being, a sexual being. And so are the people with whom you interact. How do you acknowledge this? How do you nurture it?"

To ask these questions of my students with any integrity, I must hear them daily as questions and challenges for myself as well. They serve as my barometer for measuring how I am doing in all aspects of my life. When students struggle to find time for school and work and family, and wonder how to manage it all, I share parts of my own ongoing struggles, as well as patterns and priorities that friends of mine and I have articulated over time. I draw on personal stories to highlight the tough choices that all clergy face. The ease and comfort with which students come to me to discuss personal and professional issues affirms for me the power of an open, caring presence.

The simple acts of asserting my desire for wholeness, and directly, unequivocally, but nonconfrontationally making my presence as a lesbian rabbi known, has been transformative in ways unimaginable and unfathomable to me just a decade ago. From dreading an existence that demanded a split life, I have come to enjoy my life, living openly and lovingly with my spouse, in all spheres of my personal and professional life. I thank God that this is true, and recognize my partnership with God in making this so. Slowly and often subtly, I have seen miraculous and unpredictable changes in the people whose lives I touch. My colleagues and students have matured in their sensitivity toward gay men and lesbians, and are eager to learn more about issues affecting our lives. Members of the chavurah, couples with whom I work prior to their marriages, people I meet when I lead workshops and give lectures, family members and friends, find that their presuppositions about our differences and their lingering fears dissolve when we encounter each other as multidimensional human beings. We share as much as we allow ourselves to see and experience. Individually and collectively, my gay and lesbian colleagues and I have contributed to tikkun olam, merely by being present. May others come to know this same richness and joy. Ken yehi ratzon (may it be so)!

Working from the Inside, Out

Chapter 3

JULIE R. SPITZER

THERE WAS SO MUCH riding on my success that first year of the rabbinical program. I was going to be the first woman from my hometown to become a rabbi. I was a role model to all my friends in high school and college. I was the only one from my family to travel this particular life path. And the first-year program in Israel meant I could return to the country in which I had spent a wonderful six months as an exchange student during my junior year in high school. Academically, that first year was superlative. Emotionally, the first year of my rabbinical training was impossibly difficult.[1]

For some lesbian colleagues, applying to the Hebrew Union College-Jewish Institute of Religion in the late 1970s meant having to worry about being "discovered" during the battery of psychological testing. It was a standard part of the admissions procedure then, as it is now. For most lesbian applicants, the admissions procedure mandated telling only part of the truth, committing the sin of omission. But for me, the admissions process was smooth, and I was untroubled. I had nothing to hide because I simply did not identify myself as a lesbian.

However, once I arrived in Israel for my first year of rabbinical school, my assumptions about my place in the world began to be challenged. I tried to do what was expected, dating an Israeli man for part of the year. I also developed a very close friendship with a female classmate. After I broke up with my boyfriend, I realized that I was quite hostile toward my best friend's boyfriend. I only realized later that I wanted to be with her, and was jealous of him.

Once I returned to the States in the fall of 1980 to continue my studies in Cincinnati, I threw myself into my academic work. Intense friendships with women, so much a part of my new life as a rabbinic student, grew more and more compelling. When one of those friendships blossomed into full-blown mutual attraction, I acted on it. The next day, all I could think about was that somehow, "it" would show. My first intimate experience with another woman, I feared, would appear as a scarlet "L" across my forehead for everyone to see. I would certainly be banished from the rabbinic program. I would return in shame to my hometown faster than you could say "bad role model." Fortunately, my fears were more powerful than my reality. I learned to be discreet. I learned to live in the closet, to compartmentalize my life: one corner for rabbi, one corner for lesbian. It was a complex existence that left me more enriched than scarred, like the patina on a gold ring.

Ten years later, I had been working for three years as an associate rabbi at a very large synagogue. In June 1990, I traveled to Seattle to attend the annual convention of my professional organization, the Central Conference of American Rabbis. I knew that this meeting had the power to change my rabbinate, for my colleagues and I would be voting to accept the recommendations of a report prepared by the Ad Hoc Committee on Homosexuality and the Rabbinate. During the debate on the floor, the minutes seemed to stand still; indeed, my memories have a dreamlike quality to them. Would the more than five hundred rabbis from the United States, Canada, Europe, and Israel vote to affirm me as a lesbian rabbi?

The report seemed to give us hope by validating our existence, noting that "all rabbis, regardless of sexual orientation, be accorded the opportunity to fulfill the sacred vocation which they have chosen." But the report also stated, "Publicly acknowledging one's homosexuality is a personal decision which can have grave professional consequences. Therefore, in the light of the limited ability of the Placement commission of the Central Conference of American Rabbis to guarantee the tenure of the gay or lesbian rabbis who 'come out of the closet,' the committee does not want to encourage colleagues to put their careers at risk." And then it continued, "to the extent that sexual orientation is a matter of choice, the majority of the committee affirms that heterosexuality is the only appropriate Jewish choice for fulfilling one's covenantal obligations."[2] The report was far from perfect, but for me, and for many colleagues, the fact that the conference was addressing the reality of our being rabbis was powerful and affirming. After the final vote was taken, and the report was accepted, those of us who had stood anxiously together during the voting went out to celebrate. We were unsure of how and whether this report would make a difference in our lives or our careers, but were grateful to have been members of the body that had affirmed this first, if flawed, affirmation. Would this report mean that someday we would be able to be out as lesbians and gay men in the rabbinate?

At the conclusion of the conference, my partner of four years, Abbe, flew to meet me so that we could travel in the Pacific Northwest. We checked in to a grand old hotel in Victoria, British Columbia. We were walking very close to one another, engaged in intimate conversation on our way to high tea, when we quite literally ran into my senior colleague from Baltimore Hebrew Congregation and his wife. They were staying at the same hotel. We mumbled surprised greetings and introductions, and accepted an awkward invitation to meet for breakfast the next morning. All evening, Abbe and I debated: Did this man, with whom I worked every day, know that I am a lesbian? Should we say something?

Shortly after I had arrived at the congregation, my colleague told me that someone had shared with him a rumor about my personal life that he had chosen not to believe. Our breakfast made it clear to me that any discussion of my sexual orientation should continue to be kept off the table. Abbe and I made it through an uncomfortable meal, and swore we would never vacation after a CCAR conference again. Clearly, I had to remain in the closet as long as I kept that job.

Like my time in rabbinical school, the seven years I spent as a congregational rabbi were characterized by extreme discretion, bordering on paranoia at times, and by a total compartmentalization of my life. I became very good at maintaining professional boundaries: work on this side of my life, personal activities on the other side. Certainly, there were individuals who "knew," congregants who became friends and figured out that I did not live alone, and was, in fact, very happily partnered. With these people, it became a kind of "Hamevin yavin," and I hoped, accepted my lesbianism. Abbe grew to appreciate her role as a rebbetzin, albeit an invisible one. In retrospect, I realize that my next career move would have been very different had being a lesbian been truly acceptable in the congregational rabbinate.

After leaving Baltimore Hebrew Congregation in 1992, I went to work for the Union of American Hebrew Congregations, the organization of Reform synagogues in the United States and Canada. It is essentially a volunteer organization, and the work of UAHC is overseen by lay leaders from across the country. The professional staff work for the lay leaders through fourteen regional offices. I was offered the position of regional director for the Mid-Atlantic region, a prestigious and exciting administrative assignment. Several of the people on the search committee for the director's position had known me while I was at Baltimore Hebrew Congregation. While I did not use the world "lesbian" during the interview, I felt certain that my sexual orientation was no surprise to anyone, and was of no interest to anyone. This, after all, was the UAHC, the same organization that, under the leadership of Rabbi Alexander Schindler, boldly proclaimed full equality for gay and lesbian Jews in 1987, unlike the compromise resolution passed by my rabbinic body three years later. And yet, when I met with Rabbi Schindler in applying for the Washington position, I realized that I just couldn't let my guard down completely until I knew that the job was mine. Despite everything that I had heard about his leadership on the issue of equality and inclusion for lesbian and gay Jews, I had internalized so much fear that I did not fully answer his questions about my family. When he asked, I spoke only of my parents and my sister, and not of my partner of seven years. Perhaps I feared that it was one thing to support a principle of equal treatment, but quite another to hire a regional director who was gay. Thankfully, I was wrong.

By going to work for the UAHC, I had finally escaped the fishbowl of congregational life. My partner and I were finally both living in Washington, the city where we both worked; she had commuted from Baltimore to Washington for almost five years. And best of all, I was working for an organization that did not consider my sexual orientation to be a disability. I was growing increasingly visible as an advocate for lesbian and gay issues in the Reform movement. In many ways, I was coming out every time I used the word "we" in reference to lesbian and gay Jews. Initially, I felt a bit of trepidation. Eventually, it became quite comfortable, but never without some thought about who was in earshot. Old habits die hard.

Five years after the Seattle CCAR conference, my life was in transition. I had just announced that I was going to be leaving Washington, D.C., and my job as director of the Mid-Atlantic regional office of UAHC. My partner had been offered a wonderful position in New York City, and it was my turn to move for her career. It was hard to realize that my life had changed so dramatically compared to my first two positions as a congregational rabbi. Not only was I out of the closet, but I was relocating because of my partner's new job!

When I made the decision to leave the Washington regional office, I felt that I needed to send a letter to the congregational leaders and the rabbinic colleagues with whom I worked. I did not want to hide behind the curtain of "leaving for personal reasons." I wanted to be honest about leaving for my partner's career opportunities. I thought it would be a "teachable moment." I waited for the response with some nervousness. One person misunderstood what I meant by "partner." "I didn't know you were in business. . . . " Another understood, and appreciated my candor. A third told me that her daughter was a lesbian and was in the process of applying to HUC-JIR. Then she asked if I would be willing to speak with her daughter about what she might expect as a gay rabbinic student. For that reason alone, I was happy I had chosen to express my reasons for leaving my position. This particular member of my board of trustees had never before shared this information with me. In fact, there were probably very few people she had told. It gave me great pleasure to get to know her daughter. I look forward to counting her among my colleagues.[3] No one, to my knowledge, called to complain.

In my transition from Washington to New York, I took one major responsibility with me. I was the UAHC staff liaison to a new Task Force on Lesbian and Gay Inclusion. This group had grown like a pearl in the UAHC structure. A few irritants who persistently requested greater visibility in the UAHC committee and commission structure were finally successful in establishing an independent task force. To the initial small group, we added representatives from the CCAR and from the rabbinical college, the Hebrew Union College-Jewish Institute of Religion. Women of Reform Judaism, our powerful national women's organization, and a few other affiliates and UAHC departments sent representatives to at least one of our meetings. Under the direction of committed volunteer chairs and cochairs, the group produced *Kulanu: A Program for Congregations Implementing Gay and Lesbian Inclusion*. I was honored to serve as one of the primary editors for the volume.

Kulanu was the product of many contributors. Some wrote chapters; others sent us material from their own congregations, ranging from sermons to fliers for programs. The volume was published by the UAHC Press, and thanks to the generosity of a number of benefactors, was distributed free of charge to the more than 860 UAHC congregations in the United States and Canada. The handbook included chapters on Jewish texts, programs for inclusion, educating the leadership of a congregation, life cycles, and employment issues. One of the most important sections was a compendium of the resolutions passed by all the arms of the Reform movement calling for civil and legal rights of gay and lesbians, access to equal employment and leadership opportunities, elimination of antigay discrimination in the U.S. military, support for domestic partnership legislation and civil marriage for gays and lesbians, and clear and unequivocal support for welcoming gay and lesbian individuals and families into Reform synagogues. The resolutions represented decisions ratified by the UAHC, NFTY (National Federation of Temple Youth, the Reform youth movement), the WRJ (Women of Reform Judaism), the NFTB (National Federation of Temple Brotherhoods), and the CCAR through June 1996. Our primary motive was to provide tools for the congregations of a movement that, in principle, stood for full inclusion of gay and lesbian Jews, including Jewish professionals. A resolution is relatively easy to pass, but far more difficult to implement. *Kulanu* provided clear guidelines for realizing the commitment for inclusion that had been endorsed by the members and affiliates of the Reform movement, giving congregational leaders and congregants the tools to challenge and change institutional structures and policies that stood in the way of full inclusion for lesbian and gay synagogue members.

While a growing number of congregations throughout the Reform movement are working toward inclusion, one area, in particular, has become an increasing concern: employment issues for lesbian and gay synagogue professionals. When the report of the Ad Hoc Committee on

Homosexuality in the Rabbinate was accepted by the CCAR membership in 1990, it had little apparent connection to the professional placement process. Increasing numbers of openly gay rabbis, cantors, educators, and synagogue administrators are completing their training, and today they face lay leaders who are largely unprepared to hire them. Several of us have been working with the director of placement for the CCAR, and the joint commission that assists him, in an effort to correct this problem. There are a few models for educating search committees and synagogue boards of trustees. In the early years of women in the rabbinate, placement assistance teams were prepared to visit with prospective congregants and prepare the way for female candidates to be considered fully and equally. Some have suggested a similar approach for lesbian and gay professionals. In fact, there are individuals who are available to meet with search committees to help them examine their own feelings and understanding about what it might mean for them to hire a gay or lesbian candidate, but their numbers need to increase. Copies of *Kulanu* have been donated to the Placement Commission to be given to leaders of search committees, but like any initiative, there needs to be consistent and reliable follow-up to insure implementation.

Placement of lesbian and gay rabbinic students into initial positions is improving every year. There are an increasing number of senior colleagues, for example, who are willing to guide and instruct their congregations that being a lesbian or gay rabbi is no impediment to serving a congregation as an effective assistant or associate rabbi. However, for colleagues in the field seeking a second or third position, applying openly as a lesbian or gay rabbi is far more challenging. Here, the issue of being the only rabbi, the role model, the representative of the congregation to the community is of paramount consideration to the search committee. Few can honestly say a rabbi's sexual orientation is of no concern.

From my vantage point as a regional director in the Reform movement, and as a lesbian, I see that progress is slow and sometimes painful. And yet, looking back a decade, or even just five years, I can see that lesbian and gay colleagues have made quantum leaps. Today, there are a number of openly gay colleagues who serve congregations with an outreach into the queer community. There are also a handful of colleagues around the country who openly serve the general community. Some come out as they begin the interview process. Others wait until well into the interview process, when it seems that there is some mutual interest, and then reveal their sexual orientation to the head of the search committee, or to the entire group. Still others wait until an offer is extended before sharing their truth. Some even wait until they have completed one year with the congregation, or until it is time to renew a contract. And some choose to remain closeted indefinitely. No single way works for everyone. Much depends on the comfort level of the candidate and the prospective congregation. Search committees or congregational leaders may instruct a potential rabbi not to "make an issue of this." Can we imagine asking a heterosexual candidate not to bring a spouse to a "get to know the candidate" evening? Can we imagine asking a straight, married rabbi to pretend to be single or not to share information about their personal life with the congregation? Of course these questions are absurd, but lesbian and gay colleagues face them on a regular basis.

Certainly, not receiving an offer from a congregation can be based on many factors, not exclusively sexual orientation. As more lesbian and gay rabbis, with diverse skills and personalities, seek placement openly, I hope this will become more apparent. I look forward to the day when being lesbian or gay will no more influence a decision to hire a given candidate than whether or not she/he writes or speaks well. As our numbers grow, and hiring of gay and lesbian professionals becomes normalized, we hope that we will be judged on our character and our knowledge, on our ability to relate to others and to teach Judaism. What should set us apart from other candidates should be the characteristics, talents, and abilities that make each of us unique as individuals, and the particular passions that bring each of us to the rabbinate. We know that many people want to "do the right thing," yet, in the vast majority of our congregations, full employment equity continues to be an issue.

For those of us who came of age during the period of "don't ask, don't tell" in the rabbinate, coming out of the closet took some time. In fact, even to this day, there are still times when I consider answers about my family and my personal life very carefully. I am currently in my seventh year of work with the Union of American Hebrew congregations, and I write this in my fourth year as director of the New York Region. A funny story from my interview for this position demonstrates just how far I, and we, have come: In this case, it was clear that I was available for the job because of my partner's relocation. I suppose there was a little too much comfort with who I was. One member of the committee asked me if I could commit to a real future in the position because Abbe might again be relocated by her company. I didn't know whether to be insulted or to jump up and hug the questioner! On the one hand, this seemed typical of the demeaning attitude faced by many of our heterosexual female or male congregants whose qualifications for a give position are judged on the basis of their spouse's employment. On the other hand, our relationship was so normalized that the questioner could seriously worry about the duration of my stay in the New York area.

Looking back on my thirteen years in the rabbinate, I am pleased with the journey I have taken thus far. If I had known I was a lesbian when I applied to Hebrew Union College in 1979, I probably would not be where I am today. I envy younger lesbian and gay colleagues who don't have to face so many of the difficult personal decisions I had to face. No doubt, they must make new choices: how far to come out and when, whether or not to start a family. I still think of myself as a role model, albeit cautiously. From the "inside" of the Reform movement, I hope to be able to clear away a few landmines for my colleagues in the trenches. I take great pride in knowing that, institutionally, the UAHC provides insurance coverage for domestic partners, and that the same welcome extended to all families is extended to mine. Bringing that same level of inclusion into all congregations of the Reform movement, despite our good intentions, will take some time.

If not now, when?

Notes

1. Rabbi Julie Spitzer died at age forty-one in September 1999. This essay was written just before she was diagnosed with ovarian cancer, and she was not able to edit it before her death. With heavy hearts and deep respect, the editors have attempted to preserve Julie's distinctive voice in their preparation of this essay for this volume. They acknowledge the assistance and editorial support of Julie's partner, Abbe Tiger.
2. "Report of the Ad Hoc Committee on Homosexuality and the Rabbinate of the Central Conference of American Rabbis Annual Convention, 1990" in *Kulanu (All of Us): A Program for Congregations Implementing Gay and Lesbian Inclusion*, ed. Julie R. Spitzer (New York: UAHC Press, 1996).
3. Elyssa Kohen was ordained in 1999, and serves Congregation Beth Israel in West Hartford, Connecticut.

Chapter 4	Wholeness and Holiness

SUE LEVI ELWELL   *A Life's Journey*

W<small>HEN</small> I <small>APPLIED TO</small> rabbinical school in 1980, I could not have imagined how my journey into and through the rabbinate would alter my life
forever. I knew I was dedicating myself to study and to learning to pass
on a rich and ancient tradition. I knew I was opening myself to texts that
would challenge my intellect and my spirit. I knew I was committing
myself to a venerable and complex people with a rich and often painful
history, a living people whose care is demanding and uplifting. I did not
know that the truths I would confront, both in the texts and in the lives
of the Jews I served, would force me to examine the deepest commitments of my own life.[1]

Twenty years ago, when I began my rabbinic journey, I could not
have imagined that my rabbinate would provide the context and the catalyst for me to claim my commitment to women as an essential and
defining passion in my life, even as my rabbinate would be the vehicle
through which I would express my commitment to Judaism and the
Jewish people.

I entered rabbinical school after completing a doctoral dissertation
in women's history. My research took me to the excellent American Jewish Archives, located on the campus of the Hebrew Union College-
Jewish Institute of Religion in Cincinnati. While I was there, I began
thinking about further studies in Judaica. I had been fortunate to have
been able to pursue graduate study at Brandeis in the department of con-

temporary Jewish studies, and while subsequently completing my doctorate at Indiana University, I had continued my study of Jewish texts. But I was hungry for more. I had been warned by Professor Jacob Rader Marcus ʒ'l, director of the Archives, that the only way to complete my dissertation was to "avoid the tributaries," to chart and keep to a firm course on the seas of research and avoid the distractions that often seduce both novice and experienced scholars. But my investigation into the evolution of American Jewish thought and belief and the changing mores and practices of American Jews tantalized me, and I wanted to better understand how and where women's lives fit into Judaism and the American Jewish experience. I wanted to learn more about the history and context of these issues, and to follow their development beyond the purview of my historical research and into the present.

In the course of my dissertation research, I had also discovered what historian Carroll Smith-Rosenberg called "The Female World of Love and Ritual," as she described relationships between women in nineteenth-century America.[2] The subjects of my dissertation and many of their contemporaries were women whose lives were characterized by rich friendships and deep devotion between women, connections and intimate relationships that often sustained women throughout their lives. I wondered whether and how Jewish women created, sustained, and nurtured such connections in the patriarchal culture of Jewish tradition.

In September 1981, I matriculated at the Hebrew Union College. I was thirty-three years old, in a decade-long stable, heterosexual marriage, and pregnant with our second child. My seminary years were intellectually intense and spiritually rich. From the beginning, I integrated my family life into my studies, hosting study groups at our family's expansive dining room table, clearing away piles of books to offer steaming bowls of homemade soup or freshly baked coffee cakes during our study breaks. After the birth of my second daughter, working in the college's cooperative day care center became an integral part of our lives. My older daughter spent many hours when she was too sick to attend school but not sick enough to stay home sitting in the back of my rabbinical school classrooms, coloring, reading, or sitting on my lap cuddling while I tried to take notes. Many of my classmates considered her our class mascot. My life was busy and full. Most of the time, I felt whole and fully visible as a student, a parent, and a colleague to a diverse group of classmates. Sometimes, I'd be filled by a sense of longing for a world for which I had no model, no analogue. I would dismiss my daydreams and return to my rich present of studies and children and challenging student internships.

When I was offered what seemed to be a perfect position in Los Angeles after ordination, we moved across the country. I immersed myself in the life of the large, affluent, politically active congregation, and my husband and I worked hard to juggle the competing claims of our two young children and two careers. But our move across the country was more than a change of geography. In some ways, my world split open with that move.

Because we could not move into our new home for six weeks after we arrived in Los Angeles, we stayed in the home of friends who were conveniently working and traveling during that time. For a month and a half we lived in a gracious, expansive, beautifully decorated house that was home to two women who loved one another. Both of them worked as professionals in the Jewish community. As I spent my days registering my children for day camp and for school, opening bank accounts, and learning my new job, I was living in a house that represented a reality that I had only imagined—women living together openly, joyfully, celebrating their lives and their Judaism as family.

I remember sitting on the floor of that bright living room, looking out the windows at the San Fernando valley, which stretched all the way to the horizon. I could not see my own future, but feared that this move might be taking me away from, rather than toward, my life's work. I had hoped that by moving to California I would simplify my life: I'd become a rabbi and fulfill our parents' expectations, and my own, for myself and my family. But my heart would not be silent, and I worried about how I could serve my people when I was at war with myself.

My congregational work was both emotionally and spiritually demanding. As the months passed, I was increasingly brought into the intimate places in congregants' lives: sharing a parent's desperation with his ten-year-old's overtly aggressive behavior; holding the hand of a recently widowed writer, who wept as he told me that I should not mind that my voice reminded him of his beloved wife, and therefore made him cry; watching a forty-year-old psychologist waste away from AIDS, as his seventy-year-old widowed mother asked me why this was happening to her only child. I began to learn how to serve as a safe and compassionate vessel for the outpourings of others' hearts. But too often, the pain of others threatened to pull me under, for I, too, was mourning a deep and terrible loss. Adrienne Rich writes that "in fact we were always like this / rootless, dismembered: knowing it makes the difference. / Birth stripped our birthright from us, tore us from a woman, from women, from ourselves . . ."[3] I felt that loss keenly.

I worked hard to design and teach classes and to write sermons that would touch both hearts and minds. I sat through meetings planning programs to promote social justice, and helped to organize workdays and interracial and interfaith dialogue groups to confront prejudice and build bridges between people of faith and goodwill. I felt proud to be serving a community that confronted hard truths, that worked diligently to find language to address difficult topics, a congregation of individuals who attempted to use a Jewish vocabulary to speak about issues of poverty and injustice and the rampant disease of materialism we named "affluenza." But in a community that emphasized integrity of word and deed, I began to feel like a fraud, for I knew that my marriage was coming apart. And the issue that was turning my life upside down was barely on the congregational agenda. It was only later that I could name the homophobia that was so subtle and insidious that I did not know how powerfully it had infected my own sense of integrity. I feared that if I followed my heart, I would lose my children, my parents, and my career. But I knew that if I closed my heart, I could never parent, or be a daughter, or serve as a rabbi. So I began to learn a new language in which to speak to myself, to my children, and to those I loved. I hoped that this new language of honesty could also become a vehicle for speaking the Jewish truths inscribed on my soul.

I left the congregation after three years, and soon afterward, my husband and I separated. We had worked very hard, over a period of years, first to save and then to reimagine a partnership that could provide a context in which we and our beloved children could thrive. We concluded, with deep and searing sadness, that we could not repair our marriage. We both agreed to try to construct new lives. I worried that I would not find firm ground on which to stand. Again, in the words of poet Adrienne Rich, "no one who survives to speak / new language, has avoided this: / the cutting-away of an old force that held her/rooted to an old ground. . . ."[4]

The opportunity to create a Jewish women's center enabled me to integrate my commitments to feminism and Judaism. In 1990 Rabbi Laura Geller offered me the opportunity to join her in the creation of what became Los Angeles Jewish Feminist Center as a project of the American Jewish Congress. Through classes, rabbinic counseling, consultation, and rituals and ceremonies, we offered a proud and unapologetically feminist interpretation of Jewish history, Jewish texts, and Jewish culture. During my tenure as director, we initiated lecture series, programs, and a feminist seder that were adopted by synagogues, community centers, and institutions of higher Jewish learning across the county. I was deeply gratified to work with many people who had not felt welcome in traditional contexts of Jewish study and celebration because of their gender, their sexual orientation, their family status, or their sense of being different from a Jewish community that was perceived as affluent, materialistic, androcentric, coupled, and monolithic. By presenting programs in a range of contexts and venues, and utilizing the talents of teachers from across a wide spectrum of the rich and diverse Los Angeles Jewish community, the Feminist Center touched many who had either intentionally or unintentionally remained beyond the reach of mainstream synagogues, community centers, and institutionally sponsored adult education programs.[5]

As I began to become more visible to myself, I was able to work with a community that had not been visible. As I began to heal my own sense of brokenness and sense of disconnection, I attempted to begin the work of healing the Jewish community by making it more inclusive. I was finally able to name my hunger as a hunger for wholeness, a wholeness I hoped would lead to holiness.[6] I was finally able to claim that my passion for women was not only a hunger to learn about women's experience and to integrate women's stories into the tradition. My energy for the creation of women's rites and rituals was fueled not only by my sense of justice to tell the complete story of the Jewish people.

My truth was a deep truth of my body and soul, for as Judaism is my home, my body is my home. And Judaism teaches that this physical vessel that we call the body is most whole when it is united with another. My body, created in God's image, finds deepest comfort in the embrace

of another woman. Claiming this essential truth was a source of celebration for me, and I was profoundly thankful to finally unlock the gates
of confusion and self-doubt that had imprisoned and threatened to cripple my spirit.

I had begun to acquire a new language. Now the time had come to
speak. I worked hard to find the words and the contexts to speak to my
daughters, one a teenager and the other a preteen, about what my lesbianism meant to me and what it might mean for them. I was blessed
that others shared their stories with me, so even as I groped for my own
words, I knew that others had traveled this difficult path before me.[7] I
knew that in some ways, I would be the same mother after the revelation
as I was before I "told." But I knew, too, that I would never be the same,
for I would no longer feel compelled to avert my eyes from the gaze of
another, or to invent elaborate strategies to pretend to conform to an
expected heterosexual norm.

Once I had spoken to my children, I faced the dilemma of speaking
to my parents. My siblings, ever my most dependable source of support,
advised me to write a letter. I wrote, "In one of the services we used on
Shabbat at the synagogue at which I worked were these words: 'The freedom we strive for means more than broken chains. It means freedom
from the enslavements that warp the spirit and blight the mind, that
destroy the soul and cripple the body. . . . When people are forced to give
up their way of life, to abandon their culture, to deny who they are to
obtain work and to live safely without bigotry—they are slaves.'[8] I used
to think about how much I was hiding—out of desire, out of necessity,
out of shame. I knew that I was, in a fundamental way, denying a part of
who I am in order to maintain my work and my family life. I knew that
my desire for a life of my own was enslaving me." I continued, writing
about why it had taken me so long to come out to myself, and then to
those I love. "I feared that if I came out, I would jeopardize my professional life. I am so clear about my rabbinate; I am blessed to have found
a calling that so well suits my gifts and abilities. And I did not want to
lose it."

I concluded, "It has taken me years to write this letter. I understand
if it takes you time to respond. I hope that someday, you will accept me
as I am, who I am. I hope that someday you'll see that my marriage ended
because of love and respect, not anger and resentment. And that my

coming forth now is an act of growth and hope and love for the future that all of us share."

Years later, my oldest daughter, my mother, and I prepared and presented a panel, "Straight Mothers, Lesbian Daughters; Lesbian Mothers, Straight Daughters," at a regional conference of Hadassah, the largest women's organization in the world. I joked that I created the panel to deal with my then twenty-year-old daughter's sexuality.[9] The panel was in fact a celebration of our deep mutual love and respect, and a reflection of our collective and individual journeys toward claiming and expressing those commitments. In 1998 my partner Nurit and I were married in the backyard of the home we share. The chuppah was held by my two daughters and two of our nieces. My parents and Nurit's father blessed us with their presence and words of the traditional sheva brachot. Among our guests were over twenty-five rabbis, who, along with our mesaderet kiddushin, offered this prayer to seal our union: "You have set one another apart from all others in the eyes of the people of Israel. As you have come under the chuppah and signed this lover's covenant, may you continue to study and teach Torah and to fulfill the mitzvah of working towards the repair of the world." The colleagues present, who included rabbis ordained by the seminaries of the three liberal movements, sealed a covenant that both continues and challenges Jewish tradition. The ceremony concluded with a single shofar blast, celebrating a season of jubilee and proclaiming our hopes for a future when all can celebrate love.[10]

My rabbinic journey continues. After my older daughter graduated from high school, Nurit and I decided to move across the country to Philadelphia so that my younger daughter could continue her middle school and high school years in the city in which both her parents lived. I was fortunate to be invited to create and produce Jewish feminist programs, this time with the innovative project Ma'yan, conceived and overseen by the visionary Barbara Dobkin. Together, we pioneered a range of programs to promote women's creativity and visibility that could not have been attempted in most heterodox contexts.[11] When I had an opportunity to return to the Reform movement as a regional administrator, I hoped that I would be able to continue to bring women's issues out of the closet, and to challenge the lay and professional leaders and the million and a half members of the nearly nine hundred syn-agogues of the movement.

"The task is great and the workers are sluggish," teaches the classic Mishnah text, *Pirke Avot* (2:15). The Reform movement, despite a proud history of commitment to gender equality, is still a male-dominated organization, in which men have a clear advantage in securing and maintaining top leadership positions. We are still struggling with issues of gender bias in the Jewish classroom and continue to face the formi-dable task of creating curricular resources that integrate women's history and stories into Jewish studies at all levels. And acceptance of gay and lesbian clergy depends more upon geography and accepted norms of gender presentation and behavior than on ability, talent, or professional experience.

But the text also teaches, "It is not up to you to complete the task, but neither are you free to desist from it" (2:16). I am blessed to work in the Reform community, which is made up of people philosophically committed to the full inclusion and justice for women, gay men and les-bians, and other sexual minorities as part of a broader commitment to social justice for all who are disenfranchised and marginalized. I am also blessed by extraordinary colleagues and companions with whom I share the responsibility of making the lives and the truths of women, and of lesbians and gay men, visible, just as we strain to listen to the voices of all who continue to live in worlds of darkness and pain, and to sing with them songs of liberation and peace. I pray that my own sense of integrity, my sense of full presence, enables me to serve with a deeper compassion and empathy than I could previously, celebrating the holiness of each individual who is a part of my beloved Jewish community.

My personal journey continues, with my beloved family at my side. Together, we wrestle with a tradition that, perpetually renewed by our devotion and attention, has the power to heal this deeply troubled world. With God's help, we will continue this work—making a place for wholeness, finding language for holiness, for many years to come.

Notes

1. I am indebted to many beloveds and friends whose choices cleared paths so that I could begin to find my way. My thanks to each one who walked with me, shar-

ing silence and speech. I am especially in awe of my daughters, whose journeys we share with joy. May such words and examples mark the way for future travelers.

2. See Nancy F. Cott and Elizabeth H. Pleck, *A Heritage of Her Own* (New York: Simon and Schuster, 1979).

3. "Transcendental Etude," in *The Dream of a Common Language: Poems 1974–1977* (New York: W. W. Norton, 1978), 75.

4. *Ibid.*

5. The center received both funding and guidance from the Nathan Cummings Foundation and its Jewish Programs officer, Rabbi Rachel Cowan. Among the teachers in the first classes of the Jewish Feminist Institute were Professors Rachel Adler, Tamara Eskenazi, and Shoshana Gershenzon; Rabbis Jacqueline Koch Ellenson, Emily Feigenson, Laura Geller and Jane Litman; Anne Brener, Olivia Schwartz and Dr. Savina Teubal. I was humbled to join their ranks.

6. I used this phrase in my chapter, "The Lesbian and Gay Movement: Jewish Community Responses," in *Twice Blessed: On Being Lesbian or Gay and Jewish*, ed. Christie Balka and Andy Rose (Boston: Beacon, 1989), years before I came out as a lesbian.

7. I am particularly indebted to my B'not Esh sisters, who have been such an amazing source of friendship and support to me since our founding in 1981.

8. This was adapted from Mordecai Kaplan's *The New American Haggadah* (1941), which has recently been reissued, ed. Gila Gevirtz (New York: Behrman House, 1999).

9. The panel was first presented at the Fourteenth International Conference of Gay and Lesbian Jews in July 1995 in New York City, and subsequently at the New York Regional Conference of Hadassah, Sarah Lawrence College, April 1996.

10. Our wedding took place during the year that both Nurit and I marked our fiftieth birthdays, celebrations we shared with the State of Israel. We followed the biblical custom of marking the fiftieth year with a blast of the ram's horn (Leviticus 25:9 ff), and were honored that my godson, twelve-year-old Noah Myron Cohen, sounded the blast.

11. I am grateful to have worked with talented and dedicated individuals in the gay and lesbian-friendly context of the Jewish Community Center of New York's Upper West Side and to create bold programs that have been replicated and imitated across America and Canada.

Chapter 5   Being a Lesbian Rabbi

ELIZABETH TIKVAH SARAH

Context

THE FIRST GENERATION of lesbian rabbis. A factual statement. The implications are clear: We are the pioneers. But the full implications depend on the context. In the United States there are forty openly lesbian rabbis; in Britain there are three. I am one of them: one of the first two to receive smichah in 1989; the third was ordained in 1996.

We three are the first generation of lesbian rabbis in England (there aren't any in Wales or Scotland). The Jewish community in Britain as a whole currently stands at around three hundred thousand. So, comparing this figure with the Jewish population in the United States, the proportion of lesbian rabbis is probably about right. But the reality is, there are only three of us, and we are all in London.

When my colleague, Sheila Shulman, and I began to study for the rabbinate at the Leo Baeck College in 1984, we were the first "out" lesbians in the mainstream community—indeed, we were the first "out" homosexuals" altogether. The combined progressive movements that fund the college were in a state of shock.[1] In addition to being lesbians, we were also radical feminists. The movements had only one radical feminist, Barbara Borts, originally from the United States, who sponsored my application. A dynamic individual, who was ordained in 1981, Barbara had already played a major role in putting feminism on the Jewish agenda in Britain. Now there were three radical feminists, and two of us were lesbians.

So what did the so-called progressive establishment do with us? We were put on probation for the full five years of our training. We were told that we could be thrown out at any time. We had to be exemplary in every respect. No one could tell us what actions on our part might constitute grounds for expulsion.

We were exemplary. The reports from our congregational placements were excellent. And despite both coming to the college without any prior Jewish study experience, and having learned to read Hebrew only the year before, we did very well academically: We were each awarded a distinction for our rabbinic theses. One of the Liberal congregations I served in my fourth year and the Reform one I worked with in my fifth year—both of which had relied on student rabbis for years—offered me a job. I decided to take the Reform post because it was full-time. Sheila succeeded in launching a new alternative synagogue. We had made it.

And that was the problem. No one thought we would overcome the obstacles. So what now? We might have graduated from Leo Baeck College with flying colors; we might have found work, but were other rabbis prepared to accept us as colleagues? The Reform Assembly set aside a whole day to discuss whether or not to allow us to be members. In the end, the majority ruled in our favor.

That's the bare bones of act 1 of the drama. It is impossible to express the pressure of those years—the stress, the fear—and, yes, the moments of exhilaration and joy. We felt under siege; we were scrutinized constantly; we were cold-shouldered and bad-mouthed by our detractors; we also received a great deal of support from both rabbis and laypeople who wanted us to play a part in the Jewish community.

Radical Feminist Lesbian—Rabbi?

In order to understand how I got through those first five years of immersion in the mainstream—how I managed not to drown in the bitter waters of hostility and prejudice—I have to go back to the time before the beginning. I came out as a lesbian in 1978 in the context of the women's liberation movement. I was married in 1975, a couple of months prior to my twentieth birthday. I had tried to repress my lesbian feelings and my sense of being different for several years. My engagement with feminism, my increasing awareness that lesbians not only existed but celebrated their lives, helped me to come out. As an active radical feminist, like other women whose otherness was not limited to our sexuality, I began to explore my Jewishness together with other Jewish women, both lesbian and heterosexual.

I had always had a strong Jewish identity, although my Jewish knowledge was patchy. I had always lived through the cycle of the Jewish year and enjoyed the celebratory ritual but did not have any sense of what it meant for me to live as a Jew. Rejecting the prescriptions of Orthodoxy, the perceived "Englishness" of Progressive Judaism, the inward-looking parochialism of the Jewish community as a whole, my Yiddish-speaking mother and my Viennese-Jewish father belonged to a synagogue—which they never attended—only until my brother became bar mitzvah (when I was eight years old). The Jews I knew as a child were family members and friends—at school, in my street, among my parents' varied social circle. As I grew up, I continued to encounter individual Jews, but the Jewish community was somewhere else. I knew where it was, I knew who belonged to it. I knew it had nothing to do with me. Because my family was "different," because I was "different" again.

I had no experience of the mainstream Jewish community at all before I decided to embark on a career in the rabbinate. I was part of a Jewish lesbian group that included women with very varied Jewish backgrounds. We met each week to share food, our stories, our questions, our rage, our joy in one another, our vague and painful Jewish yearnings. And then Israel marched into Lebanon in 1982. *Spare Rib*, the feminist journal, following in the well-trodden footsteps of left-wing anti-Zionism, condemned the "nazi" invaders. None of us identified as Zionists, but we were Jews and we knew who the Nazis were. We wrote a letter. *Spare Rib* refused to publish it. We wrote another letter. Fierce arguments blazed through the pages of the internal Women's Liberation Movement Newsletter. Suddenly, we were all screaming our conflicting allegiances. From that time onward, *Spare Rib* ceased to be the mouthpiece of the movement as whole. Lebanon touched the raw nerve of all our particular identities, and feminists were never the same again.

I was never the same again. Up to that point, my young adult life had been dominated by successive passions: antiracism, socialism, feminism, lesbianism (I accumulated them in turn, but also privileged each new revelation). It was only when I began to explore my Jewishness that I recognized my vocation in life: to be me; to be all of who I am simultaneously and so be able contribute to life. And somehow, becoming a rabbi represented that quest. Becoming a rabbi—are you serious? Yes, because I am a very serious person (who has only discovered her sense of humor quite recently)—becoming a rabbi became the key to my personal integration, an integration that has freed me to be in the world.

What did I know about rabbis? Before the autumn of 1983, when I met Barbara Borts, Rodney Mariner, who taught me and thirty-odd others the alef/bet, and Lionel Blue, who became my tutor through Leo Baeck College and ordained me, the only rabbi I had knowingly encountered was a young man in a stylish double-breasted suit who had officiated at my wedding at a West London synagogue in 1975. My husband-to-be and I met him only twice: once in his office, and once under the chuppah. I knew nothing whatsoever about rabbis and was even less interested in finding out. From the time I first discovered the black civil rights movement in the United States, I loved Martin Luther King and found his preaching speeches—two of which I read again and again—absolutely compelling. I even wrote a dissertation while doing a sociology degree at the London School of Economics on "The Role of Religion in American Slave Resistance" in which I discussed the key contribution made by slave preachers. But while part of my agenda at the time involved challenging Marxism's materialist determinism, I made no connection with my Jewish identity. I didn't know about prophetic Judaism; I didn't even know that progressive rabbis marched in the freedom marches, too.

And when I became a feminist, it didn't help. Judaism is a patriarchal religion; rabbis are its key practitioners. But that crude dismissal didn't last long. In my heart I knew it was more complicated—and then I met Barbara Borts: a radical feminist and a rabbi, too. She didn't explain what rabbis were about, or even why she had become one; she simply demonstrated to me for the first time in my experience the unity of theory and practice. Up to that point most of the socialists I had encountered were so preoccupied with right-thought that they had little time for engaging in social change, most of the antiracist activists I had campaigned with were just that—activists, and most of the feminists I had worked with on various collectives felt that intellectual activity was male. Barbara was the first person I met who embodied both theory and practice. And she was—is—a rabbi. As I watched her in action—teaching, singing, studying, challenging injustice, arguing, holding someone's hand—I recognized myself; I was coming home.

An engaged lesbian feminist Jew, all right—but why a rabbi? There are two aspects to this question: the religious dimension and the leadership dimension. When I first began to talk about becoming a rabbi, people were obsessed with the religious bit: my mother, aleha hashalom, worried that I might start imposing the halachic strictures she had rebelled against on the rest of the family; feminists of all persuasions thought I had sold out to a gray-bearded grandfather in the sky. However, I wasn't overtly interested in religious issues at all at the time. The big question for me revolved around leadership. Unlike socialism, feminism not only challenged who was in power; it challenged power structures altogether. And what was a rabbi if not an authority figure, a representative of Jewish male power?

But does that still hold true when the rabbi is a woman? Watching Barbara, I discovered the difference between being a powerful person who empowered others and using one's position to exert power over others. That doesn't mean that women necessarily express power differently from men. It doesn't necessarily mean that men can't express power differently. I began to realize that power and domination are not the same thing.

I also began to acknowledge that power is a potential within all of us; I began to acknowledge my own potential. But did that mean I should be a communal leader? In theory, feminism scorns leadership as a characteristic of hierarchy; in practice, although there are no leadership structures, there are many feminist leaders—indeed, there are as many leaders as there are women who acknowledge their own ability to make a contribution to the community and whose contribution is valued by other women.

But did becoming a rabbinic leader fit the bill? When I talked about training for the rabbinate, it became clear that most of my feminist sisters did not see it as a way of making a valued contribution—on the contrary: I was abandoning the marginal women's community for the mainstream. I saw it—and to a certain extent still see it—differently: I was tired of the feminist and lesbian agenda being confined to the margins, and

I was entering the mainstream in order to assist in the struggle to bring it center stage. For that to happen, more Jewish women, more lesbian Jews, had to achieve leadership positions within the Jewish community.

Having struggled so hard with myself, with others, around the complex issues associated with becoming a rabbi, once I applied for rabbinic training and was accepted on the program—albeit on five-year probation—I was totally resolute, and determined not to allow any external obstacles to stand in my way; if I changed my own mind, that would be a completely different matter.

And so I survived those five years—I even flourished. What I didn't realize until I began to work as a rabbi was that the reasons for my survival had a lot to do with the religious dimension that I spent much less time exploring prior to embarking on my journey. From the outset, becoming a rabbi represented a way of being all of myself; when I became a rabbi, I discovered that being me also included embracing my spirituality, which, until I began to recognize it directly, wore various political masks. Thinking back to my first stirrings of political awareness, what was it about Martin Luther King, about what he said and did, that had such an immense impact on me? I realize it now: not just the powerful plea for justice, not just the assertion of human dignity, not just the vision of a better world—it was also the way his soul seemed to fill his body, strong and still, and radiating from every pore. Martin Luther King had charisma, of course, but it was the source of his charisma that made him shine with spiritual integrity.

So I received smichah from my tutor, Lionel Blue, one of the best-known voices of spiritual concern in Britain today, and also a gay man who eventually came out officially when he retired from his post as convener of the beit din of the British Reform movement. Years ago, Lionel Blue wrote "Godly and Gay," which was published as a pamphlet by the lesbian and gay Christian movement in Britain. It was only when I began to practice as a rabbi within a congregation that I began to recognize the link between my sexuality and my spirituality.

Practicing What I Preach

I survived rabbinic training in one piece with my vision intact. But now I was an employee of a small congregation with their own expectations about what they wanted from their first full-time rabbi. I began to real-ize the extent that practicing effectively involved a host of skills that I had in unequal measure: diplomacy, tact, tolerance, patience, generos-ity of spirit, the ability to listen and to negotiate. Patience was my biggest challenge. It still is. Tolerance comes a close second. I don't like the word. But it's the only one that really encapsulates what it takes to work with those whose views and values are radically different from my own. It's not just accepting that not everyone is a feminist, it's recog-nizing that many members of Reform synagogues are not Reform Jews and dealing with the consequences. Diplomacy and tact? I can manage both if I'm not feeling too stressed. I am thankful that being prepared to listen and to negotiate and feeling essentially generous toward others has usually helped me through.

When I began my rabbinate my agenda included: facilitating the participation of all members in synagogue activities; enabling all adult members to engage in prayer and ritual; enlivening and enriching prayer and ritual and making it genuinely inclusive; fostering an atmosphere in which youngsters enjoyed learning about and living their Jewishness and continued to actively participate in congregational life after they became b'nai mitzvah; generating continual Jewish learning opportuni-ties for all ages; creating an environment in which members with diverse identities, experiences, and life-situations might find a home; expanding the range of ways members expressed their Judaism to include social action and dialogue with other groups. A very ambitious program! Of course, working together with real live Jews involved modifying it in response to their needs, grappling with limited resources, confronting pockets of entrenched conservatism, of apathy and disenchantment, dealing with interpersonal rivalries and conflicts.

When it came to measuring my achievements, I soon learned to appreciate that "small is beautiful." In small ways, working with the members of my congregation, I realized aspects of my dream; the com-munity wasn't transformed, but individuals within it changed and began to develop and realize their aspirations.

In small ways I was able to practice what I preach, but interestingly, preaching what I practiced proved more problematic. I gave very few explicitly feminist sermons—although the handful of feminists appreci-ated them, it seemed that talking about what we were doing within the congregation, and what was happening within the Jewish community as a whole, in the context of a wider framework of feminist meaning, seemed to be unhelpful for some and irrelevant for others. The all-encompassing theory of feminism was threatening; the particular examples of feminist practice members engaged in—like the equal participation of females and males in prayer services—were not. And when it came to speaking about sexuality, the response was similar: My partner and I were treated as a couple, membership of the synagogue was on a household basis, all adults irrespective of personal status paid the same fee, but there was little space to talk about lesbian and gay issues, beyond the odd reference in the context of discussions of equality and inclusivity.

And yet, although directly naming and defining feminist and lesbian and gay concerns was not welcome, I became aware that my spirituality was emerging out of the totality of my being as a woman and a lesbian working as a rabbi within the congregation: the sense of wholeness I felt, particularly during communal prayer and study and life cycle ceremonies; the way I was able to be present with people in times of pain, loss, and grief. Engaging in the heart of my rabbinic work I felt full and alive in ways that I had never before experienced. And I knew that because I was being myself I was able to forge connections with those around me and enable others to be themselves and make connections. In small ways, the ordinary mainstream congregation I worked with knew moments of real community in which its members recognized their own value and cherished one another.

But there is much more to the synagogue than its beating heart. The body politic looms large and can become a prison, the structure of the synagogue a punctilious regime run by officers dedicated to the task of keeping it running as smoothly as possible, who derive their sense of achievement and well-being more from fulfilling their functions than from engaging in the life of the community. And then there are the personalities. In my experience, the lay leadership can have a huge impact on what one does and can do as rabbi. And matters are compounded if the principal players change continually. In the period of five years I spent with the congregation, I worked with five very different chairpeople. Charting my rabbinate, the impact of these five individuals proved critical: I began on an up that continued for a good while, had a singular low point—which included the chair and a small band of supporters trying to get rid of the lesbian feminist rabbi in their midst—and then things improved markedly when a feminist took the chair!

I left on an up, because an opportunity arose that I couldn't miss. Because, even with a feminist chairperson, the full-time rabbinate left little space for me and my life. I went into the rabbinate because it represented bringing all the different parts of me together. When it came to engaging in my rabbinic work—despite all the practical and political issues involved—that's in fact what happened: I brought all of who I was as to whatever I did, whether it was reinterpreting Torah or being with a dying person. But in practice that meant that although I felt spiritually fulfilled, the private me got squeezed out—almost completely. Ironically, perhaps if I had worked in a more formal established institution with a professional staff that expected the rabbi to play a discreet, predetermined role and left me less room for creative maneuver, I might have preserved more of myself for myself and my partner.

The Pitfalls of Leadership

The not-to-be-missed opportunity came in the form of a new leadership position within the Reform movement, as director of a new division, which involved putting the values of Reform Judaism into practice in eighteen program areas including spirituality, social action, music, and Jews in the FSU/Eastern Europe and Israel; and responsibility for the religious, cultural, and interfaith programming of the Sternberg Center in North London, the largest Jewish center in Europe.

While the content of the work was very close to my heart, the context was extremely daunting: I had never worked in an office environment, and now I was responsible for managing a budget and eleven variously part-time members of staff. Within five weeks of starting I had to produce my first budgeted plan of work for the year ahead.

But in the end, none of these things proved problematic. Planning was second nature, I learned to read figures, and I loved the team of people I worked with. The expectations attendant on being a movement employee and leader proved much more difficult to deal with. In a way, the limitations on me were similar to those imposed within the synagogue setting, but with a critical difference: As a congregational rabbi I engaged directly with the life of the community; as a movement worker

I was involved in distance-living, expected to deliver packages of potential life for distribution to the synagogues.

The movement wanted my creativity and my commitment, but not my politics. Part of the attraction of the job was the presence of boundaries: having an office to go to and return home from, resting on Shabbat. But I discovered that while the physical boundaries were there, wherever I went I was a movement representative. When I delivered a Kol Nidre sermon on the theme of "Covenant" in the autumn of 1996, I was catapulted into a realization of what it meant to be public property.

Three months earlier the Reform Assembly of Rabbis had established a working party on "Same-Sex Commitment Ceremonies" on which Sheila Shulman and I both sat as members, with colleagues who spanned the whole spectrum of opinions on the issue. From the time in 1981 when the Reform movement published the pamphlet "Jewish and Homosexual" by a well-respected movement member, Dr. Wendy Greengross, there had been several references to same-sex relationships in various publications, including in the widely publicized book *Faith and Practice: Reform Judaism Today* (1995) by Jonathan Romain, a leading Reform rabbi. The line to date was that rabbinic involvement was appropriate so long as it was confined to private home rituals—like the fixing of a mezuzah—in the context of the rabbi's pastoral responsibilities. But the climate was changing: Lesbian and gay Jews were becoming more visible on the margins of the Jewish community. Indeed, once a month I convened a Shabbat morning service of lesbian and gay Jews at the Sternberg Center.

Almost a year before the working party was set up, a couple who had begun to participate in that chavurah said they wanted a commitment ceremony and asked me to conduct it. The issue was, where to hold it? They wanted a Jewish setting. Perhaps the Sternberg Center? After months of deliberation, the Reform lay leadership decided that location of the ceremony at the Sternberg Center might be construed as Reform endorsement. The couple went in search of a neutral venue, which, fortunately, they found.

The need for a working party on the issue was becoming pressing. On a personal level matters were complicated because, a year after I had separated from my partner of seven years, I met another woman, and we changed each other's lives. Simply put, we felt we were mates, and we wanted to establish our brit ahavah in the presence of our family and friends. Knowing that our relationship needed to be tested by time, we set a date for June 1997. I made an announcement at the Assembly of Rabbis in July 1996, and a few colleagues wished me mazal tov, including the chief executive of the Reform movement. The announcement was recorded in the minutes.

I was on a high: Although I had been angered by the lay leaderships refusal to allow a commitment ceremony to be held at the Sternberg Center, I felt that at long last the movement I had been contributing to for thirteen years was tackling the issue of the expressed need of lesbian and gay people for recognition of our relationships in public; I felt acknowledged as a lesbian, as a Jewish woman in a loving partnership with another Jewish woman.

And so when I was asked to guest preach on Kol Nidre at the synagogue where I had begun my rabbinic journey, working there as a cheder teacher and junior warden (youth group leader) for three years, I decided to explore the theme of brit, in the context of both the increasing demand of parents to have brit, ceremonies for their baby sons b'li milah, and the growing desire of lesbian and gay couples to celebrate their brit ahavah. What did these living Jewish needs tell us about the living meaning of the key Jewish concept of brit?

I knew it was challenging stuff, but I felt I was sharing my reflections with friends who, on the most challenging night of the Jewish year, were open to reflect with me. I was both right and wrong. Many of the six hundred people present were friends, and they accepted the challenge. When I began to talk about conducting a brit ahavah ceremony for two women, one man screamed, "It's an abomination!" and he and four others walked out in protest. How this "event" got to be the lead story on the front-page of the *Jewish Chronicle* the following Friday comes down to the one dimension that I hadn't considered at all: that even when I wasn't officially working in my Reform movement post, I was seen as a movement spokesperson. Perhaps it should have been obvious to me, but it wasn't until that moment.

Even before the story came out in the *Jewish Chronicle*, within two days every Reform synagogue had received a statement signed by the chairman of the movement, the chief executive, and the chairman of the Assembly of Rabbis condemning what I'd said, confirming that it was not movement policy, and stating that I would not now be conducting the ceremony. I was ordered to apologize at public meetings of the board of the Reform movement (the executive arm), the Council (which included delegates from each synagogue), the Assembly of Rabbis, and its executive arm, of which I was a member. I didn't know what had hit me. It was the beginning of the end of my relationship with the Reform movement. Both my supporters and my detractors wrote letters to me and to the movement leadership.

Over the next few weeks, while I considered my position and continued to do my work with the support both of my staff and of most of my fellow senior colleagues, it became clear that many synagogue leaders were not content with my public humiliation, they wanted nothing to do with me. As the northern conference of the movement drew near at which I was due to lead the Torah service on Shabbat morning, the northern coordinator informed the chief executive that people were refusing aliyot, and one synagogue chairman threatened to stage a walk-out in protest. The chief executive insisted that "the show must go on." My supporters among the northern congregations were identified, and they accepted the spurned aliyot. As I conducted the Torah service, the individual who had made the threat sat in front of me in the first row. The service passed without incident. I don't know how I got through it. Afterward I went to my room and wept for half an hour. At the evaluation session on Sunday, my participation was loudly applauded by a surprisingly large number of those present. I say surprisingly, because no more than a dozen people had indicated their support to me directly during the weekend.

What began as a reaction against my sermon became a massive reaction against the progress made by lesbian and gay Jews, and against me personally—not just as the embodiment of a feared phenomenon, but because, as a lesbian, I had climbed too far up the movement ladder. For many people, lesbian rabbis per se were an anathema, let alone the idea of a lesbian rabbi in a senior position in the Reform movement.

It took me a long time to decide to resign—partly because the working party was still in progress and I still hoped for a just outcome, and partly because I knew that people were rooting for me. But the strain became too much. Toward the end of March 1997, I wrote my letter of resignation, giving the full six months' notice that my contract of employment decreed. As a gesture toward me, I was allowed to leave at the end of July on full pay to the end of the six-month period.

I learned a great deal about myself during that waking nightmare, both about leadership and about the way I saw my role as a lesbian rabbi. Interestingly, it was only after I left my leadership post, without another job to go to, that I began to understand what it meant for me to be a leader. The context for that understanding was really the Jewish lesbian and gay community, which had been badly shaken by the whole debacle.[2] During the sermon crisis I learned that I was not considered a legitimate Reform leader by the majority of the movement's activists, although many people respected me and believed in equal rights and responsibilities for all Jews. At the same time I discovered that in addition to being involved member of the lesbian and gay community, I was also regarded as one of the community's leaders. That didn't mean that everyone agreed with me, simply that people saw me as an advocate for the cause of lesbian and gay Jews within the Jewish community. Even without a job, I was one of *their* rabbis. Interestingly, during the whole period, lesbians became increasingly visible and vocal in Jewish lesbian and gay activities, and after being dormant for many years, a strong and confident lesbian group has emerged. When my partner and I finally celebrated our brit ahavah in June 1998—not 1997 as originally planned—outside the mainstream community, because after almost two years of deliberation the Reform movement managed to officially confirm the status quo with regard to rabbis' pastoral involvement only in private ceremonies, it was wonderful to see so many of our lesbian sisters participating and schepping naches.

Being a Lesbian Rabbi

I am a lesbian rabbi. It's not a job I do. Since I left the Reform movement—both my employment and the Reform Assembly of Rabbis—I've discovered that in addition to the lesbian and gay community, there are also other contexts, both ad hoc and ongoing, in which I am able to work rabbinically and give a lead. The ad hoc ones are interesting: Several Reform synagogues who don't have rabbis have asked me to lead Shabbat and festival services since I left my post. The cynic inside me says, "They want to have the benefit of my skills, without having to 'own' me"; the optimist responds, "But they are asking for *me*, and they have all asked me *back*." In addition to leading prayer, I have also been invited to lead study programs. In these ad hoc contexts, I've learned that it's possible to provide leadership, in flashes, that meets people's needs at the time and kindles sparks that may burn after I have left. Some synagogues with rabbis choose to import me for my skills, again, on an ad hoc basis—whether it's running a spirituality program, a leyning course for women, or a creative midrash class. And of course, there are the women's study programs I initiate myself under the auspices of the Half-Empty Bookcase—Progressive Jewish Women's Studies Network. In all these contexts, I express my values and priorities as a lesbian rabbi and provide rabbinic leadership.

And then there are the ongoing fora. I am chairperson of Leo Baeck College's rabbinic in-service training program. When I left my Reform post, the Leo Baeck College approached me to facilitate the spirituality course with Hebrew Union College–trained Marcia Plumb and to teach the course on progressive Jewish thought with John Rayner, the Liberal movement's leading rabbi. In addition, one of the classical-Hebrew teaching posts had become vacant. I applied and was accepted. Since 1994 I had acted as supervisor for one of the rabbinic students, a young woman from St. Petersburg who was ordained in 1999. I now found myself working with students in a variety of different ways. It continues to be an enriching experience for me, which also provides an opportunity for me to contribute to the next generation of rabbis.

There have been other nourishing opportunities. As I faced the first new year after the Kol Nidre crisis, I felt overwhelmed with loss and very isolated. A lifeline came in the form of a request to lead the first Kol Nidre service at Beit HaChidush in Amsterdam. The service was held at the newly renovated Uilenburger synagogue, which had not been alive to the sound of Jewish prayer for over sixty years. Prior to the service, we fixed a mezuzah to the door of the building. Just before sunset, my partner lit the candles inaugurating both Shabbat and Yom Kippur. As the voices of the congregation filled the sanctuary, the walls seemed to echo with those of the prewar generation. In that moment, the present greeted the past, and heralded in the future. It was immensely moving to be part of such a beautiful act of renewal. I also felt the first stirrings of renewal in my own heart. Somehow, although I had no idea where I was going,

I knew on that night that the future, my future as a lesbian rabbi, was a real possibility.

And so it was. When I left the Reform movement I didn't expect that I would work for a mainstream Jewish organization again on an ongoing basis. But, fortunately, as the old cliché puts it, life is full of surprises. In June 1998, I was appointed as part-time leader of the Liberal congregation that I worked with as a student rabbi in my fourth year.[3] Ten years had passed, and the community now had a building that they had finished paying for and wanted to expand the rabbinic input they received. So when they asked me again, I accepted: When I began my rabbinic journey, I wanted nothing less than a full-time post; now I'm delighted to include working part-time with a congregation within the range of my rabbinic "portfolio." What is so surprising about this latest turn of events is not only that this congregation asked me again after ten years, but that they decided they wanted me to work for them in the full knowledge of everything that had happened. A clear indication of their acceptance of me—and my partner—came a week before the annual general meeting of the congregation, which formally endorsed my appointment, in the form of a card congratulating us on our brit ahavah signed individually by every member of the council.

Just over three years ago I thought I was drowning in a tidal wave of fear and animosity. The wave did much damage, but I am thankful that—thanks to my loving partner, some real friends both inside and outside the Jewish mainstream, my own stubborn determination, the wondrous ways of Life—I have survived. More than that, I feel that I have constructed, from the wreckage, a way of working rabbinically and being a lesbian rabbi that is right for me now. I am self-employed. While I am delighted to be teaching at the Leo Baeck College, and working with a mainstream congregation again, I have no desire to be the employee of any organization, large or small, at the moment. I open my rabbinic portfolio and see a variety of skills and special interests. But while I carry a range of goods with me to different places, they are all held together by me, by my way of being and expressing my rabbinate. Whether or not a group or an individual ask explicitly for the contribution of a lesbian rabbi, a lesbian rabbi is what they get—is what I give. That's how I pray, sing, study, teach, engage with people wherever I encounter them; that's my head and my heart and my eyes, ears, and hands—literally, not metaphorically, since I have been fortunate enough so far in my life to have all my faculties. My way of being a rabbi, my sensibility as a lesbian rabbi, has been forged by all the differing experiences and insights and areas of knowledge I have accumulated over the years—everything I have learned in the process of becoming myself.

Notes

1. Two movements constitute the progressive movement in Britain: the Reform Synagogues of Great Britain—referred to throughout as Reform; and the Union of Liberal and Progressive Synagogues (ULPS)—referred to as Liberal.
2. To date, there are no lesbian and gay synagogues in Britain. The Jewish Gay and Lesbian Group, based in London, holds monthly Erev Shabbat services that are co-led by gay liberal rabbi Mark Solomon and myself. Sheila Shulman's congregation, Beit Klal Yisrael, which is affiliated with the Reform movement, includes a large proportion of lesbian and gay people as members.
3. The congregation actually calls itself "progressive." I'm using the label "Liberal" to indicate that it belongs to the ULPS.

Part II   Serving
Congregations

Ten Years on the Journey toward Wholeness

Chapter 6

LEILA GAL BERNER

A DECADE AGO, I wrote an article entitled "Journey toward Wholeness: Reflections of a Lesbian Rabbi." At the time, I had not come out professionally (though I was on the edge of doing so), and the article was published under a pseudonym, La Escondida (the hidden one).[1] In the article, I compared myself to the hidden Jews of medieval Spain and the contemporary American Southwest, Jews who felt compelled to hide their Jewish identity for fear of victimization and rejection. Judeophobia and homophobia were profoundly linked in my heart and mind in 1988.

In the past decade, I have come out in a mainstream congregation, kept my job, left that congregation two years later, and served a predominantly lesbian and gay congregation for three years before moving more into academic life. Today, I am completely out personally and professionally, and yet I have learned that the coming-out process never ends. Even today, I find myself in professional situations in which yet again I must reveal that I am a lesbian, yet again I must prove myself worthy of functioning professionally in the straight world. I still encounter moments of awkwardness, some hostility, and some sense of exclusion as I negotiate the pathways of my professional life. I also encounter welcome and much more acceptance and understanding than I did ten years ago. There are even places in the Jewish world where my being an out lesbian is celebrated.

As I write now, I am in the process of looking for a new job as my life partner, our daughter, and I relocate to a new city. Once again, I realize that there will be doors closed to me as I seek rabbinic work because I am a lesbian. I do not know how I will be received in some sectors of my new Jewish community, but I do know that despite some closed doors, there will also be open ones. Some will welcome what I have to teach as a feminist and a lesbian, and many will welcome me in the wholeness of who I am.

Today I am much clearer about who I am, and less afraid of rejection and homophobia than I was ten years ago. I am stronger, much more certain of my own intrinsic worth, as a woman, as a feminist, as a lesbian, and as a rabbi. The experiences of the past decade have taught me some truths: that no journey is as a straightforward as we hope it will be, that people and communities that appear to be enlightened and free of homophobia aren't always what they appear to be, that keeping a job is not the ultimate measure of success, that transformation is an internal process, beginning within myself and then flowing outside, that speaking my truth publicly can be healing, for me and for others.

My generation of lesbian rabbinic colleagues has made history, and we continue to be forces of change within our communities. Some of us are the first generation of rabbis who have entered mainstream communities openly as lesbians; some of us have come out on the job and kept our jobs; some of us have lost our jobs; some of us measure success as survival within the rabbinate, and some of us use a different criterion—the degree to which we experience ourselves as whole human beings, employed or not. Some of us have succeeded in effecting important change within our communities, some of us are still hidden, and yet the substance of our work is always influenced by the fact that we are lesbians.

Because we have made history, it is appropriate, I think, to share our stories and histories. What follow are fragments of my own coming-out story in one congregation, and what I have learned from that experience. Much more has happened to me over the past decade as I have worked in several contexts as a rabbi, but some of those experiences are still too fresh and complex for me write about yet. They will await a later recording, when I have greater clarity. My story is a piece of a much larger story that I share with my lesbian colleague-sisters, bits of the tapestry that is a lesbian-Jewish-rabbinic legacy to the future.

Coming out in a Mainstream Congregation

In January 1992, after months of careful strategizing and planning with members of my rabbinical organization and leaders in the Reconstructionist movement, I came out to my congregation in suburban Philadelphia. For two and a half years, I had worked very successfully at the synagogue, never officially revealing that I was a lesbian, but also never really hiding my life.

From the beginning of my tenure at the synagogue, my life partner, Renee, accompanied me to all services and became an active member of the community. Everyone knew that we lived as housemates, that we were very close friends, and that we seemed inseparable. We said nothing, and the community said nothing. We all lived in amiable silence.

In September 1990, I discovered how insidious amiable silences can be when I became extremely ill. After a day in critical condition, I remained in the hospital for several days. During this time, my congregants sent flowers, visited, and sent cards. All were wonderfully supportive of me, but Renee, who was terrified by my illness, was completely ignored. She was treated as my friend—nothing more and nothing less.

My congregants' disregard for Renee did not occur because they were unkind or insensitive, but because we had all colluded in an amiable silence. After I came out to my congregants, they told me, "We didn't know what to do, how to treat Renee. You had never told us of your relationship, so she had no status as your 'spouse.' We were afraid to invade your privacy by acting toward her as if the two of you were partnered." In the end, my hiddenness had contributed to a situation in which the person I loved most was bereft of communal support at a crucial time. I vowed that never again would Renee be put in that position. It became very clear to me that my bifurcated, hidden life was causing much more pain than we as a couple could bear. Shortly after my recovery, we began my coming-out process.

The synagogue I served was made up of one hundred fifty mostly upper-middle-class or wealthy families. Many members were academics, highly successful professionals and businesspeople. In addition to their closeted rabbi, there were two deeply hidden single gay men in the congregation, and one lesbian. Eighteen months before my arrival there, the congregation had experienced a time of turmoil and conflict, resulting in the departure of the previous rabbi and about half the congregation with him. It was partially for this reason that I had decided to delay my coming out until the community had a time of healing. But in truth, my decision to stay closeted was based on what I believe was a correct instinct that I would never have been hired as the synagogue's rabbi had they known that I was a lesbian during the application process. When I applied for the position, it was clear that the shul, having recently experienced turmoil, wanted to avoid controversy at all costs—and as a lesbian, I would be the source of controversy. This was not a group of social activists whose priorities were to fight social injustice.

But now, I decided, it was time to come out.

First I met with the executive committee, then with the synagogue's board of directors. I prepared for the first meeting by reading the story of Reb Zusya, who said before he died, "In the world to come, they will not ask me, 'Why were you not Moses?' They will ask me, 'Why were you not Zusya?' " I reminded myself: From now on, I want to be truly Leila, myself—without hiding, without shame, without apology.

I will never forget coming out at the synagogue board meeting. As I first sat at the table, before the president officially called the meeting to order, I hid in the act of making notes on my notepad. Writing in Hebrew, I wrote everything that came to mind that could strengthen me, comfort me, remind me of why I sat in this room and why I had chosen to take my own plunge into the sea. The yellow lined sheet of paper carried on it a large "b'h." I had never meant it so sincerely as on this night. The God that I believe in was a power flowing through me, giving me courage and resolve.

The president began the meeting with the instruction that we all needed to listen with both our heads and our hearts, in an atmosphere of mutual respect and dialogue rather than confrontation. I then spoke, saying that after two and a half years with the congregation, I had too much respect for the community to continue to be dishonest by omission. I needed to be open and honest about who I am. I said that I expected that this was not a surprise to some of the people in the room, and that it might be new information for some, but that I needed to share with them the fact that I am a lesbian. I asked them to read a letter I had written to them (see appendix). I distributed the letter, and a deep silence descended on the room as everyone settled in to read.

I sat quietly, again filled with the warring emotions of serenity and terror. But a comforting calm had wrapped itself around me—like a soft tallit, sheltering me from harm, its fringes reminding me that I was free and engaged in the act of liberating myself. In biblical times, only free people were permitted to wear fringes on their clothing. Thus it was a great gift to my people when, after their exodus from Egypt, God instructed them to place fringes on the corners of their garments. "Be free people!" the Holy One was telling my ancestors—and now I was creating my own new fringed garment.

That evening I saw the best in people, the most noble impulses, the ability to be dignified, sensitive, and respectful. I saw people transcend pettiness and prejudice and look deep down into their own souls. I saw them emerge clean—in the best sense of that word. I felt deeply affirmed, honored, and even celebrated—for the person that I am, for the rabbi that I am.

Once everyone had finished reading, the congregation's president spoke first. In her leadership, I saw a timid woman become brave. I saw, in Marge Piercy's words, "a strong woman who is powerfully afraid." I watched as she looked her own fears in the face and transcended them.

Sarah spoke movingly about how the imagery of crossing the sea was so powerful to her.[2] After expressing thoughtful concerns and a commitment to working through challenges, she expressed her strong support for me, and concluded that "our rabbi has been in Mitzrayim—and it is time for her to come out from Egypt."

As more people spoke, I could feel the pall of tension palpably lift. Smiling at me, Jennifer told everyone how I had worked with her and her non-Jewish fiancé in his Jewish learning, in preparation for their wedding. "Leila is a wonderful rabbi," she said, "and has opened up new doors to Judaism for both of us." How grateful I was for so many smiles of support. But why did I feel so damned grateful? Is this the way things really are—that the victim of society's hatred and prejudice should feel grateful for a little simple human kindness? Why was I not enraged that I had to go through all of this?

Sam said, "If the purpose of religion is to push us to look deep into our hearts and souls and face our own prejudices and examine our own ethics and principles, then this situation has been a very successful use of religion." He thanked me for giving him the opportunity to search his soul. and that he was grateful to discover that his ethics and principles won out over his prejudices.

Janet offered me personal support, but expressed her concern that she didn't want Bet Ruach to become a "gay synagogue."[4] How strange it is that when it comes to the topic of homosexuality, people suddenly become irrational and fear catastrophe. The fear of a complete gay and lesbian conquest takes over otherwise rational people's thinking. It is as if on some deep-set level, gay and lesbian people are conceived of as the body snatchers, who will stealthily come and convert everyone into gay and lesbian clones! Janet's comment is so typical. Suddenly a suburban, mainstream congregation filled with 99 percent heterosexual people is in danger of becoming a "gay synagogue." When I am in a good mood, I can laugh at the absurdity of such a fear. But what's so wrong with a better balance? Does the presence of more openly gay and lesbian people imply that there is something intrinsically wrong with the shul?

Jim spoke about his work with the Reconstructionist movement's Homosexuality Commission and about how far he had come in his own thinking in the past two years. He especially addressed the issue of "flaunting," recalling that when he first joined the commission, he held the typical liberal position: "I don't care what gay and lesbian people do privately, as long as they don't flaunt it. What does 'flaunting' mean?" Jim asked. "When Sarah and I walk down the street and hold hands, no one looks twice. But if a gay or lesbian couple walk down the street holding hands, people think they are flaunting. We must help gay and lesbian people have the same rights we have—to be who they are out in the open. We must support Leila."

Elizabeth spoke simply: "Thank you for liberating yourself," she said to me, "because in the process you are liberating us."

Liberation! Recently I had been reading Letty Cottin Pogrebin's new book, *Deborah, Golda and Me,* in which she mentioned a comment her older half-sister once made: "When you have a secret, you secrete it." It is almost as if the secret oozes from the pores—and because it is a secret, it takes on a stale, almost rancid smell—and in the air, subtly but pervasively, is the odor of fear and hiddenness. What a relief it is to let in the fresh air.

Rhoda was afraid that her relationship with me as her rabbi would somehow be altered by my revelation, and she didn't want to lose me.

She needed to test me, to have me prove to her that I was still available to her as a rabbi. I was saddened by her fear and its implications—had I become someone different to Rhoda, and therefore suspect?

I felt a deep undercurrent of tension and discomfort from Jackie, who asked how I would handle the issue with the children of the congregation. I answered that I would continue to approach this issue in the same way I had over the past two and a half years—as an issue of justice. I would continue to assert the inappropriateness of offensive epithets (faggot, dyke, etc.) in the same way I would object to racial slurs or other kinds of invective. I spoke about the Talmudic dictum that "a person who publicly shames his neighbor is like someone who has shed blood."[3] I added that I would emphasize the Jewish belief that all humans beings were created in God's image and that every human being, regardless of sexual orientation, race, religion, physical shape, and so on, is entitled to be treated with respect and dignity.

Before my coming out, no one ever asked me any questions about my wisdom or judgment in handling issues of sexuality with the kids. They simply assumed that I would exercise good judgment. Why the concern now?

Looking Back

I came out to the congregation in 1992. Since then, I have come to realize that I was not being entirely truthful with myself. In my attempts to reassure the congregation of my continuing "safety" as their rabbi, I did not speak boldly enough about what, in my heart of hearts, I hoped would occur after my coming out. I am less timid now.

In my letter to the congregation, I stated that I did not want to be a single-issue rabbi; that I had no hidden agenda; and that I had no political motive or plan. Today I realize that this statement is not true. Deep within me, I did indeed have an agenda. I had hoped that there would be a communal transformation in this congregation that could be a model for other communities in their own transformative work. I wanted my congregants to explore diversity more deeply than they had, and to open their hearts and minds to create a community in which lesbian and gay Jews and their partners were not only welcomed with friendliness, but celebrated in all aspects of their identities. I have come to understand that the road between acceptance and celebration is long and arduous and that my hope for deep communal change was somewhat naive. I dreamed of an immediate shift in people's thinking, a disappearance of deep-seated (and often unconscious) homophobia in people into whom homophobia had been ingrained by society's moral messages about sexuality and sexual orientation.

My letter of application to rabbinical school had stated that I wanted to work with "just Jews"—not a special group of Jews. I wouldn't write that statement today. I have come to understand that I want to work with Jews that are committed to a vision of true celebration of diversity. I want to work Jews who want to learn with me to become deeply committed to tikkun olam. Celebration of diversity cannot be sporadic and token. It must be systemic. I want to work with Jews who understand this and who have the courage to challenge the communal systems and assumptions under which they live.

What I discovered was that the initial supportiveness of my congregation did not necessarily lead to systemic celebration. While I respect and honor that initial support, over time I have realized that it was unintentional, complacent tokenism. No one thought they were being tokenist. The members of Bet Ruach genuinely thought that by supporting me and Renee they were supporting other gays and lesbians. Nonetheless, they resisted my attempts to bring about metalevel change.

Two examples will illustrate my point. First, when I met with the committee to rewrite the synagogue publicity brochure, we agreed to keep phrases that communicated that we were a warm and welcoming egalitarian congregation, especially sensitive to the needs of intermarried families, and embracing of single people. I wanted to add a phrase to our brochure that also indicated our welcoming of lesbian and gay Jews and their partners. Several members of the brochure committee, including the current synagogue president, objected strongly that I was "banging your drum too loudly" and that there was no need for specifying a welcome to gay people. I tried to explain that for many lesbian and gay people, unless that welcome is explicitly stated by a so-called mainstream group such as Bet Ruach, the assumption is that the welcoming does not include them. This explanation fell on deaf and even hostile ears.

Second, during Pesach of that year, I presented a sermon that described my vision of true liberation: The majority culture should be ready and willing to go through the hard work of expanding its world and embracing elements of the minority culture within it. In this sermon I specifically mentioned lesbian and gay minority culture. Later, several members of the congregation objected once again that I was banging my drum too loudly, pointing out that I had mentioned lesbian and gay people more times than I had mentioned any other oppressed group; they had actually counted the number of times I had mentioned the "g" and "l" words! My congregants told me that they were becoming afraid that I was becoming what I had promised not to be—a single-issue rabbi.

The memory of this stirs up anger in me. My congregants' responses suggest that my advocacy of metalevel social change was self-serving and narrow. Instead of my helping the whole community to grow Jewishly, it was implied, my vision of Jewish life was becoming too parochial and limited in my interest in furthering gay and lesbian Jewish life. I, on the other hand, experienced myself as only attempting to broaden the already expansive commitment I had to all aspects of Jewish life and culture. My own sense was that I was offering yet another opportunity for deep ethical Jewish exploration to my congregants.

I had said in my letter to the congregation that I did not want to become a single-issue rabbi. Now, I believe my need to declare "I'm not a one-issue rabbi" was a way of acquiescing to the fears of my congregants. That acquiescence was a form of self-oppression. My reassuring my congregants in this way gave credence to their fears that because I was a lesbian, gay and lesbian issues would become my only interest. Rather than posing the challenge of transformation to my community, I sought to comfort them and assure them that I really wasn't a radical.

It has become increasingly clear to me that, while I thought the letter I wrote to the members of Bet Ruach was profoundly pastoral, I had actually written it in an attempt to reassure them and to appear safe to them. I have come to understand that I was not truly addressing my own dream and my own vision. Now I know that the communities I work with in the future must be dedicated to real embracing, to real change, to deep struggle with the demons of prejudice and bigotry. Now I know that I can more proudly be myself as a subversive in the best sense of that word—a lovingly dangerous agent of systemic social and spiritual change.

Appendix

This was my letter to the members of congregation Bet Ruach, January 14, 1992–9 Shevat 5752.

"I sit down to write this letter to you a few days before Shabbat Shirah—the Sabbath of Song—when the people of Israel crossed the Reed Sea to freedom after fleeing slavery in Egypt. After their safe crossing, Miriam and Moses sang a song of thanksgiving in celebration of their liberation. It is in this "song" that the words of "Mi chamocha" are sung—the same words that we sing each Shabbat during our services. As many of you know, the "Mi chamocha" is one of my favorite parts of our liturgy. I often speak about "taking the plunge into the unknown," each of us standing at our own personal "sea," knowing that we have to make a hard decision, knowing that we have to take risks if we are to move forward, knowing that we have to "plunge in." I stand at such a "sea" as I write this letter to you.

I believe that the time has come for me to take a risk with you now. I need to tell you that I am a lesbian. I tell you this now, not because I have any desire to share the intimate details of my personal life. That would be inappropriate under any circumstances. Rather, I share this information with you now because in the past two and half years I have gained a respect for this community that demands of me the utmost in honesty. I tell you this now because I want to be fully who I am in a community I respect and because I want to serve this community with complete honesty and integrity. I am committed to, and care deeply for this congregation and for the people in it. I believe that I have the best interests of both the congregation and myself at heart in sharing this information with you now. I believe I can be a better rabbi for you and with you if I live my life openly and honestly.

I also want to tell you that I am in a happy and fulfilled relationship with my life-partner, Renee Primack, whom you all know. We have been together for several years, and have recently consecrated our relationship in a brit ahavah ceremony, which was attended by our family and friends. We hope, God willing, to spend the rest of our lives together in a loving, healthy and mutually supportive relationship.

Though certainly not the only reason, my committed relationship with Renee is one of the reasons I feel that the time is right for me to be open with all of you. I actually reached this conclusion some time ago after a very painful experience that really got me thinking about the consequences of secrecy.

As many of you know, in 1990, just about ten days before Rosh Hashanah, I became seriously ill. During those terrible first few hours, no one really knew what would happen—and Renee, who was by my side throughout the ordeal, was terribly frightened (as was I). . . . Members of Bet Ruach . . . were very kind and solicitous and caring to me, but did not realize that my partner, Renee, also needed support. That is not anyone's fault. After all, no one knew how much she means to me—or how much I mean to her—and certainly, no one considered her my life-partner or spouse, deserving of care and support during this crisis time. As I recovered, I realized that I never wanted to be a in a situation like that again—where I had to hide my partner. Can any of you imagine hiding your wife or husband or lover at a time of danger and crisis? Can you imagine what that must have felt like for both of us? I can no longer contemplate living that way. It is simply too painful.

I want to say clearly and unequivocally . . . that I want to continue to serve as your rabbi in the same way that I have done so until now . . . that I am the same rabbi today, now that you know that I am a lesbian, as I was yesterday and that I plan to be tomorrow. I stand on my record of the past two and a half years. I have no hidden "agenda," no political motive or plan behind my revelation to you. I simply want to continue to do my job to the best of my ability—in an atmosphere of honesty and mutual trust.

I want to share a few lines that I wrote several years ago, when I was applying to rabbinical school, because my vision of rabbinical work remains the same today as it did then. It states what I want to accomplish as a rabbi:

"What I really want to do is help people reach the more profound spiritual dimension connected with their Judaism. I want to be able to work with other Jews to create meaningful rituals, to find their way toward their own religious/spiritual evolution. . . . I want to teach within a Jewish context (not exclusively in a secular university) where I am not constrained by the obligation to be objective and coldly intellectual. I want to help provide that food for the soul as well as for the mind. . . . When I dream of my work as a rabbi, I envision working with Jews, not exclusively young Jews, not exclusively old Jews, not exclusively gay and lesbian Jews, not exclusively heterosexual Jews. I simply want to work with Jews."

If I were to elaborate on those comments written in 1985, I would add for today that I don't want to change the essence of Bet Ruach and that I refuse to suddenly become a "one issue rabbi." I would add that I will speak from the *bimah* about gay and lesbian issues in the same way as I speak about other issues—feeling the freedom to express my own views and welcoming and respecting the freedom of each of you to do the same. As rabbi of Bet Ruach, I want to continue to challenge and be challenged, to teach both adults and children—and learn from them as well, to share Shabbat and holiday services and celebrations, to share in the joy of Judaism and the pride I feel as a Jew, and to organize programs and events. I want to continue to counsel those in need and visit those who are hospitalized, and share in the ongoing growth and development of this Jewish community. In short, I want to do tomorrow what I have done every day for the past two and a half years.

If I have a vision for this congregation, it is a vision that I believe I share with all of you, a vision that is expressed in Bet Ruach's recent brochure and in the congregation's Statement of Principles: "We are committed to presenting Judaism in all its diversity, as befits a congregation whose members are varied in background, marital status, age and religious training. Opinions are listened to . . . diversity is respected." I believe that Bet Ruach can be a welcoming Jewish home for all Jews—with mutual respect and understanding.

In Bet Ruach's Statement of Principles, we write, "We strive to maintain a consistency between our values, our beliefs, and the ways in which we conduct our daily lives, both in and out of the synagogue." It is important to me to live in a way that is consistent with my own values and beliefs as I am sure it is to you to be true to yours.

I want to add that I am not asking for each individual member's "approval" of me or my lifestyle. I cannot, and would not, ask that. Nor am I asking for any "official" and monolithic statement of Bet Ruach's position on gay and lesbian issues. I respect the congregation's history and the communal desire not to take "official" and monolithic "political" stands. I acknowledge each individual's right to his or her personal feelings and opinions as they are felt now on receiving this information and as they might evolve in the future. I repeat what I said earlier in this letter: I simply want to continue to do my job to the best of my ability—in an atmosphere of honesty and mutual trust.

I hope in the coming months and beyond that we may engage in an ongoing communal dialogue about the issues that may arise from this letter. I welcome a process of discussion in which everyone will have an opportunity to express her/his views, concerns and thoughts in a mutually respectful and dignified atmosphere of dialogue rather than confrontation. I will be pleased to discuss these issues with any of you, and I also recognize that there may be times when some or all of you may need to discuss these issues without my being present. I look to the leadership of the congregation to guide the way in ensuring that we continue to grow together, communicate well and constructively with each other and in so doing, strengthen the Bet Ruach community. I am committed to that—as I know all of you are.

Notes

1. Christie Balka and Andy Rose, *Twice Blessed: On Being Lesbian, Gay and Jewish* (Boston: Beacon Press, 1989), 218–227.
2. To ensure individual congregants' privacy, I have changed their names.
3. Babylonian Talmud—Baba Metzia—58b–59a.
4. Members of my former congregation may have different perspectives on my coming-out process. Thus, out of respect for them and honoring their right to communal privacy, I have changed the name of my congregation and called it Bet Ruach.

Chapter 7 — Carrying On

ELLEN LIPPMANN

A Lesbian Rabbi, Jewish Seekers, and All the Voices of Our Lives

KOLOT CHAYEINU/VOICES of our lives, the community described here, is in its seventh year as I write—a Shabbat year, time to stop, reflect, renew, and prepare for the future. We have learned much in seven years, and have much to learn. This is our story, intertwined with my story as a lesbian rabbi.

Our Story/My Story

We gathered around the dining room table, eager, uncertain, nervous—none more nervous than me. Seven people came together to talk about an idea for a possible new kind of Jewish community. The idea was simple on the face of it: So many of the Shabbat services we had all attended felt lifeless, dull; people dozed, responded listlessly, expressed no emotion. Yet these same people, given a cup of coffee and a piece of cake, or a cup of wine and a piece of challah, came alive at the oneg Shabbat or kiddush. Why not flip the order, then? I asked. Let's eat first, then bring that energy and connection into the service or study session or social action.

So seven people came to talk. We began by sharing our names and what had interested each of us in joining this discussion. My heart pounded as we began. I had decided that I would not go into this new venture in the closet, would not hide the fact that I was a lesbian as well as a rabbi, though I had tried to hide that combination for some years and some of the people at this table knew me only as a rabbi. My partner of many years concurred. Thus this first meeting took place at our home, at our dining room table. And when it came her time to speak, she said her name, and then added, "I guess I'm the rebbetzin." Much laughter, no surprise or visible discomfort on anyone's part, and the meeting moved on. It took several more minutes for my heart to stop pounding, and I still look back on this moment as the beginning of something far more complicated and wonderful than the first sharing of a simple idea would indicate.

How did I get to this extraordinary moment? I think back. . . . I entered the Hebrew Union College-Jewish Institute of Religion as a "new convert." A Jew by birth and life decisions, I had decided only a few years earlier to follow my heart and soul's directions and finally come out, become a lesbian. I fell head over heels in love with an amazing woman I met at work, who remains my life's partner sixteen years later. Although she isn't a Jew, my decision to enter this relationship and to acknowledge the path I had been unconsciously pursuing had the effect of freeing me to follow another long-hoped-for path, that of becoming a rabbi. In an unexpected way, my coming out as a lesbian led to a true coming out as a Jew. I knew that it was time, after many earlier expressions of interest, to jump into the rabbinate with full intent.

My rabbinic education was not always easy, but it was always the right choice. At its end, I realized that my job opportunities were limited by several decisions, both mine and those of potential employers: I was going to be staying in New York City where my partner and our daughter and I had established a life. I was a lesbian at a time when true welcome to gay men and lesbians in the Jewish community was in short supply. And I was effectively married to someone who isn't Jewish, strong supportive ally though she is. I put my interest in the congregational rabbinate on hold, and turned to another passion, that of social justice work and in particular, of feeding the hungry. I had founded the soup kitchen at HUC-JIR in New York, and I am ever grateful that that work led me to an early rabbinate with MAZON: A Jewish Response to Hunger, whose director and other staff were truly welcoming of me and my family. After several years there, though, I began to yearn for a different kind of rabbinate and for the joy and comfort of belonging to a true Jewish community. That yearning led me to plant the seeds that became Kolot Chayeinu. This is its story, and mine.

Seven years after that first discussion, I am the rabbi of an extraordinary, progressive, lively, surprising community that eats together almost any chance we get, a community that honors me as a lesbian and a rabbi, a community that has grown into the name we gave it in our first year: Kolot Chayeinu/Voices of Our Lives.

It is hard to gauge how the development of Kolot Chayeinu is connected to my being a lesbian. Certainly the confluence of my life experiences, circumstances, and values, and those of our members leads us to common desires and responses, and our community has developed—and is still developing—accordingly. Our early emphasis on eating together, for instance, has become focused: First we considered opening a cafe that might also help to support the community's religious activities. Later we refocused on our initial recognition of how eating together can break down walls that separate us and the idea of an actual cafe faded into the background. Now it has come to the fore again in the form of regularly scheduled coffee klatches and coffee-house-type folk concerts. At the same time, we have articulated two important goals: one, that we remember that as we offer food we are offering hospitality in a Jewish form that goes back to Abraham and Sarah, and two, that we remember the necessity for nonreligious activities and discussions in our diverse Jewish community.

Similarly, the involvement of gay men and lesbians in the community has changed. While the community defined itself from the outset as inclusive, at first some self-conscious patting-on-the-back was evident. Now, we more often want to stop noticing our still-unusual integration and get on with the work of building this community. What does this progression look like in real life? At an early meeting, a heterosexual couple, who had known me only as rabbi and had come to see what we were up to, declared that there were too many lesbians here, and left. (At that time, the lesbians present were me and my partner.) Last year, a lesbian member of the community came up to me at a monthly Shabbat dinner-service, and said jokingly (and happily), "We're kind of overflowing with lesbians here, wouldn't you say?" Yesterday, I visited a lesbian couple and their new baby, born a few days before, and later announced to some heterosexual congregants that Liz and Andrea had finally had their baby. "They did?!" they exclaimed. "That's great! How is she?"

This new baby—and all the others born or adopted into our community, whether to lesbian or to gay male parents, to married or unmarried male-female couples, to single mothers or fathers—comes into a congregation that opens its arms. I am richly blessed to be a rabbi who serves a community I would want to be part of, and this, in part, is why. My own comfort and at-home-ness has, I hope, helped to create a place of comfort for others, a haven from an often hostile world, a place in which to end a self-imposed exile from Judaism.

It is not only lesbians who feel, I imagine, an extra level of comfort when they see a lesbian rabbi in the lead. In Kolot Chayeinu, it is also gay men, interfaith and interracial families, gay or straight, single parents, and the heterosexual singles and couples who recognize a new vision and want to live it and help shape it. All of these people are represented on our board but, and this is crucial, they are on the board because of the contributions that they bring as individuals, not to occupy some artificial gay seat or interracial marriage seat. We are intentionally building an inclusive, diverse Jewish community.

One gay member of the board says it this way: "For me, the synagogue has helped to challenge some of the deepest notions of homophobia and bridge some of the deepest gaps—in my family, in my lover's family, in my neighborhood, and in the broader Jewish community. . . . Even if there were a gay and lesbian congregation [in the area], I would not switch—it is the blend of straight and gay leadership that gives the congregation its power. Whether you call it 'post-gay' or simply good coalition building, it is precisely in the ways that straight and gay experiences butt up against each other in the congregation—not always without friction, but always with a commitment to working it through—that has forced change." He adds a personal note: "I've been with my lover for seven years, but it took my bar mitzvah [as one of four adult b'nai mitzvah students one year] to get our parents to be willing to meet. That day also marked the first time in my adult life that my grandmother found herself able to visit our home. Those are small, personal changes, but they are echoed again and again at Kolot Chayeinu as straight and gay people gather to organize together, to celebrate and to mourn. That we do it equally, with respect for sexual orientations instead of undue attention to their differences, is as extraordinary and important as the small but committed group that gathers each year to march in the Lesbian and Gay pride parade."

Our vision is an integrationist one, and we recognize that that is not the only way to go with regard to gay and lesbian Jews. But we are not just gay and lesbian Jews and, ultimately, it is the Jewish part that wins out, and then we all win. Our children study with gay and straight teachers without comment, and learn in class and in community that adults can live in a variety of satisfying and committed ways. Just as important, we hope they learn Hebrew, and prayers, and how to read and understand and grapple with a Torah portion, and what tzedakah means. Adults learn to erase assumptions about one another's lives as they study Torah together or engage in social action or pray or form a shiva minyan or celebrate a brit milah or a brit bat.

All of us have learned from some single members that we can help them by looking out for possible dates for them, and so we try to help. Recently, a rabbi who is a member of the congregation had a young woman in mind for a young man who had recently joined the community. She wanted to gauge the likelihood of this match, so she asked him, "Do you date women?" Later she noted with pleasure that she could not imagine another Jewish community in which she might phrase a question like that. Another single member notes that Kolot Chayeinu is one of few synagogues where she doesn't have to check her sexuality at the door. Her comment reflects our shared vision of our sense of the integration of mind and body, and our delight at how our tradition honors us as whole beings.

Single members, gay and straight, taught us early on that they were tired of having to pay higher dues for synagogue or any other membership than do members of couples. With their urging, we developed a dues plan based on one adult–one membership. This policy has had unexpected benefits. Many couples find that only one member of the couple wants to join the congregation. With our policy, they can do so easily. If both members of a couple join, they are considered as two members. This dues policy is one tangible expression of something we had hoped for: It is clear to those looking in that many who are alienated or distant from Judaism can find a way into this community whose leadership is gay and lesbian and straight. Open the doors wider, and more people can fit through. Narrow the doorway, keep people out, and the whole place feels constricted. We prefer the expansiveness of the wilderness rather than the narrowness of Mitzrayim.

Challenging assumptions, opening doors, broadening children's horizons, developing a true haven—these are some of the many strengths of a community that has been created by many hands and hearts, including mine. Kolot Chayeinu also has developed certain hallmarks that came originally from my convictions and dreams, but have expanded far beyond all expectations.

First, we are a community with a seriousness of purpose about Judaism and adult learning. We are intentionally not engaged in what Professor Lawrence Hoffman of the Hebrew Union College-Jewish Institute of Religion has termed "pediatric Judaism." We have developed educational programs for both children and adults that, we hope, create and sustain active and engaged Jews. We offer as many study and learning opportunities as we can in a still-small, part-time congregation. One observer, participating two or three years in a row in our High Holy Day services, asked if I realized what a high level of Jewish skill our members had attained. I hadn't stopped to notice, but we do have an unusual number of members who can now read Hebrew, chant Torah and haftarah, deliver brilliant divrei Torah, and lead services. And the percentage of those readers and leaders who had never before been welcomed or recognized in a Jewish community is very high.

We are deliberately egalitarian in many ways. I have always changed some of the language of prayer, especially that referring to our ancestral mothers and to God, and many Kolot Chayeinu members follow my lead. But we do not insist: If someone studying Torah in our weekly Shabbat session wants to use more traditional language, that too is included and accepted.

We do insist on the involvement of women at all levels: on the board, on the bimah, as Torah readers, and in our examination of tradition. The women who came before us—our foremothers, for example—must be represented, as well as the women who join us today. Each year on erev Rosh Hashanah, for instance, we stop the service at the point of singing "Mi kamocha" (lines from the biblical Song at the Sea that are included in the prayer service to evoke that time of liberation from slavery) to speak and sing about Miriam, and to explicate her life in new ways.

We are egalitarian with regard to money, too. Honors are not given only to those who make large contributions, nor do we put much emphasis on the newest, shiniest, or most expensive ritual objects when the ritual itself is what we believe should be emphasized. Before Kol Nidre one year, for instance, a single gay father and his three learning-disabled sons led us in lighting the holiday candles, using the simple wooden candlesticks that they use to light Shabbat candles each week. They received this honor because they are actively involved members and because they light Shabbat candles each week in their home, not because they give money to the congregation or hold office.

Another strength of our community is our understanding of and acceptance of doubt. Many who have long been distant from Judaism and Jewish community arrive with doubts about the value of such community, about Jewish traditions, and about God, and we all share in and encourage the expression of those doubts. Children and adults are encouraged to ask questions and to express their doubts, at the same time that we reiterate our identity as a Jewish religious community that collectively engages in prayer and communal activity. As Rabbi Tsvi Blanchard, now of CLAL (Center for Learning and Leadership), once said, we want everyone involved in this great conversation that is Judaism.

Finally, we draw lines and we are willing to lose people. We develop boundaries even in our expansiveness, knowing with Robert Frost that "good fences make good neighbors," knowing from Torah that havdalah, the making of distinctions, is a crucial Jewish occupation. In drawing lines, we have kept people in and let people out. For some, as noted above, we have been "too lesbian." For others, "too Jewish." For others, too "organized religion." We joke now that my best recruitment line is, "Perhaps you'd be happier somewhere else. . . . " We are not in the business of unrestrained growth. Rather, we are in the business of shaping a community. Inevitably, that shaping will leave someone out. We are at heart a Jewish community and, therefore, decided after a painful struggle that only Jews could be board members and committee chairs and that only Jews can be called to the Torah for an aliyah or hold the Torah scroll. While these decisions are painful in all synagogues that welcome interfaith families, it may be that our decisions were additionally painful to gay and lesbian Jews who sometimes see "gay and lesbian" as an ethnic group and ask how we can divide a couple as Jew and non-Jew who are linked as gay men or lesbians.

In addition, as a community in development, we insist that each member make some financial contribution. Some of our members live on the edge of poverty, while others live from weekly paycheck to paycheck. Even so, we ask that—except in one or two extreme cases—each person contribute at least a minimum amount of dues. In our case, in 1999/5759, we established a minimum membership fee of $225, or $18.75 a month. This requirement, too, is occasionally the impetus for someone to depart.

To be as welcoming as we are and still know when to say good-bye is painful, but it is also vital, and respectful. Any newcomer is not just gay, or lesbian, or a single mother, or a straight married man; she or he is an individual with hopes and dreams and old baggage and new tools. And to be part of Kolot Chayeinu, she must also be someone who wants to have a hand in our shaping.

In this "sabbatical" year, that shaping focuses on growth and the need for funds and how we can grow and get better organized and still maintain the principles enunciated here. Some longtime members already miss the intimacy of the early years and the excitement of building this community. Now that it is built, we are in the first stages of creating new visions, new projects, new modes that can encompass our old strengths and our many new members. We have walked through the parted sea, we say, and have been to Sinai. Now it is time to build a mishkan—a tabernacle in our wilderness—so that God may, we pray, continue to dwell among us.

This sounds idyllic, so it seems necessary to admit that we struggle hard and often. As I write, our struggles focus on how to raise money in a community whose members often ran from synagogues that they perceived as focusing entirely on fund-raising, and on how to create an infrastructure that can sustain the growth we are happy to have. My personal struggles have to do with the same family-time vs. community-time issues that so many rabbis confront. I smile as I write this, recognizing that once my struggle to hide as a lesbian was over, it was replaced by the issues that plague all rabbis who have spouses and families. My partner, once kept invisible by what seemed the necessity of the time or situation, is now in many ways the rebbetzin she declared herself to be at our first meeting. And so we struggle—with how much time she will spend with the congregation, with how much time I will spend, with how to find time just for us and for our daughter, soon to enter college. These struggles are often painful and difficult. But having them feels lucky.

Seven years later I do count myself lucky. I am lucky enough to have had an engaging idea, and to have gathered people who saw it as such, and who wanted in. I know that I am also lucky to have tried this in Brooklyn, New York, home to—besides nostalgia for a long-gone baseball team and a great deal of Jewish extremism—one of the largest lesbian communities in the world. The rest of the country or even of the rest of our city does not necessarily offer such fertile ground. I know similar seeds of hope are planted and harvested daily, weekly, all across the country. But I agree with the Kolot Chayeinu member who, asked to envision a more perfect world as we prepared to chant "Aleinu," said drily (and in perfect Brooklynese), "It don't get any better than Brooklyn." It was in Brooklyn that I served as a student rabbi in the closet and in Brooklyn that I opened the closet door and walked into that first scary meeting. And it is in Brooklyn that Kolot Chayeinu has grown and thrived, in small part due to the fact that I took that risk. Our members recognize this fact, more or less.

Only I know that during my first closeted years at the Hebrew Union College-Jewish Institute of Religion in New York, I thought the college had no windows. I remember walking into that building for my admission interview and seeing a woman whom I had met at New York's gay and lesbian synagogue. I went over to her to say, "Hello! I met you at CBST [Congregation Beth Simchat Torah, New York's gay and lesbian synagogue]!" and heard her take in her breath and say, "Shhhhhhh. . . . " So perhaps only I, in all of Kolot Chayeinu, realize what a chiddush, this community is—though many know what a life-saver it is, for me and for all the voices of our lives. We have become a community that can proclaim its identity to the world. My hope is that others can do the same, or their version of the same, and that Kolot Chayeinu as an institution may thus become a teacher as well as being the home of many students. We know something worth learning, and we have plenty still to learn.

We are not completing even our own small tasks, much less the large ones of ridding the world of homophobia, or of creating justice in an unjust world. But we know, as Rabbi Tarfon reminded us, that while it is not incumbent on us to finish the work, neither are we free to desist (*Pirke Avot* 2:21). So, as the songwriter Gil Turner would have us do, we carry it on.

Chapter 8

KAREN BENDER

Shlichut

Claiming My Mission

I WAS RAISED IN Los Angeles, California, in an Israeli home. Both of my parents are sabras who met in the Israeli army and were married under a "military kibbutz" chuppah: an Israeli flag suspended by two pitchforks and two rifles. They came to the United States on student visas in the late 1950s, intending to return. But he opened a business, she became a teacher, and life unfolded for them in Los Angeles instead of Tel Aviv.

We were affiliated with the Conservative synagogue Valley Beth Shalom, headed by the extraordinary Rabbi Harold Schulweis.[1] Though my parents began as secular Israelis, they became Americanized in their Jewish observance and attitudes.

After graduating from high school I attended U.C. Berkeley, where I studied political science with the plan to become an attorney. However, after several internships that failed to really inspire me, I changed my mind. After much soul searching, I decided to become a rabbi.

Rabbinical College

I entered the Hebrew Union College-Jewish Institute of Religion as a straight woman. (I was honest with them. It was to myself that I was lying.) Very straight. During the application process, I met another Berkeley student who was also pursuing the rabbinate. By the time we became students at the College-Institute, our relationship had become quite serious. We were "engaged to be engaged," as we used to say.

But just before actually getting engaged, I left him. He later told me that he knew it was because of my sexual orientation, but didn't think that it was something that I could have heard at that time. He is probably right. I knew enough to know that even such a wonderful man could not be my life partner. But I refused to admit to myself why.

Clearly, it was dangerous to come out. If I was gay, that could mean that I'd lose everything. My parents would reject me, my friends would reject me, I could never be a rabbi, I could never be married, I could never have children, I would always be an outcast. These were not hyperbolic nightmares, hysterical fears. This was the reality I saw around me. There was no lesbian chic, just dyke perverts.

I must have dated dozens of men during the next two years in search of my heterosexuality. But each new dissatisfaction pointed me closer to the truth. And then I met Rachel. It was just my luck that we got together shortly before I flew to Israel for a year off from rabbinical school. I was going to study at Pardes, a liberal yeshiva where men and women study together.

The timing was traumatic. There I was, twenty-five years old, a third-year rabbinical student, undeniably lesbian. And believe me, at that time, if I could have denied it to myself, I would have. But for the first time since that first time with a girl when I was just sixteen, I had fallen in love. I knew that I wasn't straight, and I was quite certain that I wasn't bisexual. I was a lesbian. And my Israeli parents weren't going to like it, my brothers weren't going to like it, my rabbi wasn't going to like it, HUC-JIR wasn't going to like it, and my dream congregation somewhere out there wasn't going to hire me.

So it seemed that I had a choice faced by millions of other homosexuals throughout history. I could kill myself, but I really wasn't into that. I had thought of it as a teen, and decided against it. I could go through the motions of living a fake straight life, lying to everyone except to myself, and have a secret lesbian life. This seemed like an appealing option, since I wouldn't have to devastate my parents and I wouldn't have to destroy my career and I could have children. Unfortunately, it would mean living a lie. Another option would be to actually pursue a relationship with Rachel and be totally open about it. And the final option, which I chose, was to pursue a relationship with Rachel and be totally closeted, except to my immediate family and friends.

During my junior year at HUC-JIR New York, Rachel and I were apart. She was wrapping things up in Los Angeles, where she lived, to join me the following year in New York. The great March on Washington came upon me during the spring of 1993. I had to go, even though I was "straight." I figured that no one would find out.

While there, I bumped into two straight classmates, a married couple who were there in support of gay people. I was so impressed, but couldn't tell them so because they thought that I was there for the same reason. I marched with them, and despite the insane duplicity of marching as a straight person, it was a transformative day for me. After being exposed to so much gay pride and joy, I knew that I would have to come out.

It was a very hot and sunny day, and I got quite a sunburn. Everyone asked about it when I came back, and I couldn't lie, since classmates had seen me at the march. "Wow, Karen, you are such an incredible social activist! With your busy schedule, taking a day out to go to Washington in support of gay and lesbian people—I really admire you." I heard that repeatedly and was embarrassed.

That week, Dr. (now Rabbi) Lisa Edwards, an out classmate, delivered her "senior sermon" (they are given by juniors, for some reason) at HUC-JIR. Her sermon on Jews, homosexuality, and homophobia was extraordinarily courageous in that she essentially asserted to professors and classmates that we are here, we're queer, we're Jewish, get used to it. I was indescribably moved. Lisa had already been a courageous role model to me, but this sermon was a gift. She was modeling the courage that I would later have to summon myself.

Hours later, at Lisa's sermon evaluation, a couple of professors stood up to make outrageous comments defending their own homophobia. These were men who had fought the ordination of gays and lesbians in the past. I raised my hand and stood up. I looked at Lisa. Her gaze back into my eyes was like a crutch that held me up. Her gaze gave me courage. I knew that this would be the last time that people would hear me speak thinking that I was straight, so I took advantage of the opportunity.

These were my words: "During this past week I have been commended by dozens of you for having marched on Washington for a cause that is not mine. You have treated me like a "righteous gentile" and you have admired me.

"You too can be a righteous gentile. Each one of you. Imagine if every person in this room gave one sermon defending the humanity and rights of gays and lesbians. We alone could influence thousands of people. Be a righteous gentile. I am telling you this not because I am a righteous gentile, but rather, because I am gay."

When I sat down, I felt an incredible moment of relief. Most out-of-the-closet homosexuals wish that closeted people would come out. Sometimes we even resent them for being closeted, because we know the powerful impact of every coming out. Every individual transforms the thinking of so many. But I honestly believe that no one really comes out for the cause. People do not come out in order to further gay and lesbian rights. People come out because they can't take it anymore. I couldn't take it anymore.

The Job Search

Applying for jobs was the loneliest and most depressing experience that one could imagine. Nobody could offer me advice, saying, let me explain to you how I handled it. In fact, a lot of people offered advice, but they didn't know what they were talking about.

There was a consensus among rabbis who advised me that I ought to apply for jobs closeted and then come out to the congregation about six months later, "after they already know you and feel attached." One rabbi, who I know was trying to help me, actually said, "But I don't talk about my wife with my congregation." I tried to explain to him that there is a difference between not talking about your wife and having to hide your wife altogether.

There was only one rabbi in a position of authority who encouraged me to apply openly: Rabbi Arnold Sher, the director of placement of the Central Conference of American Rabbis. His encouragement ultimately granted me a freedom that I otherwise might not have enjoyed for a long time. He said exactly what I needed to hear: "You will get a job. The next time around it may be more difficult. But now, as an assistant rabbi, I really think that you'll get a job." His confidence gave me the courage to apply as an out lesbian.

During my last two years in rabbinical school, I had the extraordinary opportunity of serving as rabbinical intern at Central Synagogue in Manhattan, where I worked with Rabbi Peter Rubinstein. When I came out to him, he was extremely supportive and unflinching. Much to my surprise, a few months before interviews, Rabbi Rubinstein offered to create an assistant rabbi position for me. However, because of lack of funding, for the first couple of years, at least, I would receive a salary about 80 percent of what was usual. Also, because of temporary structural issues, my responsibilities would be more like an expanded internship than like a assistantship.

I had a true dilemma. On the one hand, this would be a dream come true. Working with Rabbi Peter Rubinstein, my friend and hero, would have been wonderful. I remember that my parents advised, "You will never work for as great a man again. He is the best." At the same time, due to the circumstances, it would have felt like a sellout; taking the low road. There were no guarantees that this position would grow into a normal one, and I would always have wondered whether I took the job out of fear. Would I always feel that because I am gay, I am really "worth" only 80 percent of what my peers were "worth?" I did not think that I could live on that salary in Manhattan. Also, it was almost too comfortable. There is something to be said about flying the coop. Were I to stay, I might always be the "kid," the rabbinic student.

So I entered the job search like everyone else. The only difference was that, because my odds were so low, I was going to apply for every job and take every call-back (a second interview at the site of the synagogue) that I might be offered.

I became obsessed with strategy. I knew that if I came out too quickly I would never get a job. I was aware of the painful truth that the more interviewers could know me as a straight person first, the higher were my chances that they could overcome their own homophobia.

When classmates and rabbis in the field said that I would never get a job because no one in the Reform movement had ever been placed in a mainstream synagogue as an out gay man or lesbian, I would comfort myself my saying that it had never been 1994 before. I gave President Bill

Clinton some credit. The almost daily news coverage of gay issues at that time, over the course of about a year, was partially a result of his (failed) efforts to help gays and lesbians in the military.

I approached my search with the dual philosophy that I would not lie, and that sexual orientation was a nonissue. The practical result would be that I would be as natural as possible, without perceiving the first five minutes of an interview as an opportunity to cure a homophobe. Therefore, I would not say, "Hi, how are you, I am a lesbian." But when asked, and I almost always eventually was, if I was married, or if there was someone special in my life, I would say "Yes, and her name is Rachel." I remember that I also kept in mind that some people's homophobia is triggered by the word "lesbian." So I would say "My partner's name is Rachel," instead of "I am a lesbian." Today this sounds like self-loathing, but at the time I thought I was very clever.

There was something philosophical about emphasizing a partner instead of an orientation. If I genuinely believed that sexual orientation ought to not be an issue, then why dwell on it? It was Rachel who was important to me.

Then there was the question of what to wear to my interviews. I am what they call a lipstick lesbian. Is this the real me? I don't know. The real me would probably dress up lipstick on one day, butch on another, and the rest of the time just dress comfortably. But professional life demands costume. I joke that my mother would probably rather have a gay daughter who "looks straight" than a straight daughter who "looks gay." I told her this once, and she responded, "That is probably true."

Does being a lipstick lesbian rabbi help me to be accepted in a straight congregation? Definitely yes. Is it a costume? No more than a man's suit. Does it reflect self-loathing, or is it just feminine expression? I hope the latter. Do lipstick lesbian rabbis box themselves into a role? Yes, but not any more than lipstick straight rabbis, who would love to show up in jeans just once.

I and others who cared about the issue of gays in the rabbinate knew that I was a litmus test of homophobia in the Reform Jewish community. I had all of the "right stuff." I was the right age, young enough at twenty-seven to not intimidate any senior rabbis who wanted a younger and moldable assistant who would be humble enough to do any grunt work. I was the right gender. At that time, since all senior rabbis were men, it had become desirable to hire women in the second or third post. This suits a sexist society that doesn't want to appear to be sexist. We could have a woman leader, but she would be appropriately subordinate to the male leader who was really in charge.

I had the right résumé. As I had been the rabbinic intern at Central Synagogue of Manhattan, in a position considered to be a prestigious internship that always resulted in top job choices, it would be obviously egregious were I to be offered no job.

Interviewing as an out lesbian seeking a position as assistant rabbi in a mainstream congregation was indescribably painful because of the blatant homophobia that I encountered along the way. I felt like Rosa Parks walking to the front of the bus, but with people poking at me, undressing me on my way there. I was honest about my life and I consequently believed that I had to be open to answering questions. Some people, laypersons on search committees during call-backs, took advantage of this to mean that they could ask anything. More than one person asked during an interview if Rachel was my first female lover. I was asked if Rachel and I dance together in public. I answered that one with, "If you're asking if we have the dream of pioneering lesbian Jewish dancing at B'nai Brith affairs in Miami, the answer is no."

One rebbetzin said to Rachel, who was flown in by the congregation for my interview, "My problem with you and Karen is not that you are lesbians, it is that you are living together unmarried." When Rachel reminded the woman that marriage is not possible between women or men in this country, she said, "Well, whatever; that is neither here nor there."

In three cases, rabbis broke protocol and offered me a job during the first interview. When I told them I was gay, in all three cases they became flustered and revoked the offer. "I am sure you understand," they said.

In the end, three pulpits listed me as their first choice, and two as their second. I was amazed that I was able to choose among Denver, Atlanta, and Great Neck. Rachel and I decided on Temple Beth-El of Great Neck, New York.

After placement, I typed up a record of my experiences at each of the synagogues. I went to meet with Rabbi Sher, to thank him and to fill him in on what had happened. I was hoping that my experience might help future candidates. I gave him two documents, one with the names of the rabbis blacked out. His support was very moving: "Why are you protecting them? If anything, you should block out your name. Let theirs be known."

Out of the eighteen congregations to which I applied, I received eleven call-backs. Out of the seven congregations that did not call me back, all except one or two knew that I was gay. I calculated that about 75 percent of those who knew I was gay did not call me back. Between 82 and 100 percent of those who did not know I am gay did call me back. In other words, my worst fears were confirmed. Many straight people will reject a gay stranger if they know of their orientation at the outset. But if at first they believe the stranger is straight, and later discover the truth, they are confronted with an ethical dilemma. Some follow their conscience in the right direction. Others accept their own homophobia and reject the stranger.

Whether this is different today, I am not certain. But I can say that each year since my ordination, gay and lesbian ordinees have called or met with me to find out all they can about interviews. Their confidence in their ability to get a job and their calm willingness to be out of the closet tells me that circumstances have definitely improved. The year 1999 was even better than 1994.

Serving at Temple Beth-El of Great Neck

There is no question that the interview at Temple Beth-El of Great Neck was the most professional and warm that I experienced. My interviewers were kind, sophisticated people who did not ask anything about my personal life. This created a quandary for me. I loved these people and thought they might offer me a job, but they didn't know that I am a lesbian.

I decided to have the then associate rabbi tell them after I left the interview, and to let the president, and Jerome K. Davidson, the senior rabbi (who was on sabbatical in France), know that they should call me if they had any questions.

I later learned of a rather ironic and charming misunderstanding that occurred after I left. I specifically conveyed the message as follows: Please tell the committee that my significant other is a woman named Rachel and that we are engaged to be married next summer. This was misinterpreted by the committee as, "She wants to be married at Temple Beth-El." The committee then engaged in a discussion not of whether they could hire a lesbian rabbi, but whether they could hire a lesbian rabbi who needed to be married in the synagogue. They were not sure if the community was ready. They also ironically needed to decide whether they were ready to hire another woman. This would mean that two of their three rabbis were women, and they were not sure whether the community would accept this. In the end they decided to take their chances on both counts.

While I was on the road with call-backs, I spoke with Rabbi Davidson on the telephone. I remember the conversation well. "Do you have a gay agenda?" he asked. Others had asked me this around the country during interviews, but somehow Rabbi Davidson's query was different. He did not really seem suspicious or worried, but seemed to feel that he just had to ask. "I have a Torah agenda," I said.

The question "Do you have a gay agenda" was quite reflective of that time. Again, today I do not think it would be asked. The words meant, "Are you coming here to be a rabbi or are you coming here to further the political rights of gays and lesbians?" At the time I was sympathetic to the question. A senior rabbi is hiring an assistant for some help. He wants to know whether you are going to do your job, or whether you are going to make his job harder. This was legitimate in my mind. Little did Rabbi Davidson or I know that a year or so later, he would be the one with the "gay agenda," teaching me what it means to fight for self-respect and dignity, justice and fairness.

Cognizant of the reality of homophobia and of the power of a straight first impression, I wanted my homosexuality to be revealed to the congregation in a natural, steady flow. I did not want it to be the first thing that they learned about me. It would have slowed down my ability to have a peaceful rabbinical beginning.

So when the Jewish Week caught wind of my hiring, I pleaded with the reporter to hold off. "I am appealing to your Jewish conscience," I said to him. "Wait a year, and I will give you a full interview." Simultaneously, a friend who is a professional documentary filmmaker wanted to follow me around the first year and make a film of my experience. She felt it was critical that it was the first year of this first lesbian rabbi experience. I asked Rabbi Davidson, certain that he would say no to having a camera following me around. But he said yes. So the decision was mine. Very conflicted, I said no. I wrote these words in my journal: "I am an undercover revolutionary, teaching Torah instead of handing out pamphlets, holding a pen instead of an *uzi*, singing prayers instead of shouting orders."

My first year went well. The information about my sexual orientation leaked out at a comfortable pace. Because the straight woman rabbi that I worked with happened to have short hair and I happened to have long hair, many people thought that she was the gay one. We all thought that this was pretty funny.

A Simple Blessing before the Wedding

Shortly after I began serving at Beth-El, Rachel and I began to plan our wedding, which would be held in Calilifornia during my second year at the synagogue. A couple of months before the wedding, Rabbi Davidson said that he would like to offer us a wedding blessing on the Shabbat before our departure for California. I was touched but reluctant. Things had been going so well; I had been out of the closet for a year with no problems, so why rock the boat? Rabbi Davidson felt that it wouldn't be a problem. People had already accepted me and would be happy for me. Besides, the aufruf would take place at a summer service, and many people would be away. The Sisterhood offered to have a cake at the oneg Shabbat. I could not decline the oneg, but turned down the cake, wanting the atmosphere to be as low key as possible.

Around that time, a past president, Stephen Limmer, told me that he would not be satisfied until Rachel and I would feel comfortable kissing each other Shabbat Shalom at an oneg Shabbat after services. Deeply grateful for his compassion, I wrote these words to him in my journal, based on Numbers 11:17:

> "*Lo tisa ata levadecha*: You shall not bear it alone": I climb and
> am certain that I have reached the top of the mountain, not
> because the view is so clear, nor because there is nothing above,
> but because of the simple reason that the climb has been so tir-
> ing that this must be the top. I can go no further. And then you

say, "You see that peak, my rabbi, my friend? It is not beyond
the realm of possibility. You can go there." And I say, "But the
wounds are already so deep. Can't you see my bruises, my
scratches? Several times I almost lost my footing." And you say,
"You have forgotten that you do not yet feel whole. Come, go.
We will be with you every step."

I was surrounded by "righteous gentiles," and I felt gratitude. I have
a friend who is a person of color. She considers it terrible that we are
grateful when people simply don't oppress us. I don't agree. To not
oppress when others do is to be like Noah: "ish tzadik b'dorotav". And
people like the past president, the president who hired me, and the
president who now serves the congregation, and Rabbi Davidson were
not just not oppressing, they were advocating on my behalf. Rabbi
Davidson's wedding blessing was stunningly beautiful. I will remember
that moment forever.

After a fabulous honeymoon in Hawaii, Rachel and I returned to
New York. I walked into Temple Beth-El and saw depressed faces. People
could hardly look me in the eyes. As it turned out, the aufruf had hit the
newspapers, and congregants were furious. Angry letters and phone calls
were coming in, mostly for Rabbi Davidson. It was the first time I had
ever really seen hate mail.

In my absence, Rabbi Davidson felt that a decision had to be made,
so he wrote a now famous "Dear Friends" letter to the entire congregation. In the letter, Rabbi Davidson wrote of the aufruf, our wedding, and
why he was in support of them. Though the letter was designed to calm
people down, it instead spread the news to absolutely everyone, even the
most uninvolved members who did not know me. This led to a thun-
derstorm. Most of the rage came from people with intermarried children,
children for whom Rabbi Davidson had not officiated because he did
not, at that time, perform intermarriages. These people could not com-
prehend how Rabbi Davidson could marry us (he hadn't, he had done
the aufruf, but rumors contort the truth) but not officiate at their children's "normal!" wedding. The local newspapers reported that one-third
of the congregation was leaving.

I was devastated and became clinically depressed. One night, I
couldn't stop crying. I told Rachel that if I didn't stop by 3 A.M. that she
should take me to the hospital. I would have taken a leave of absence if

a congregant who was a confidant and friend hadn't said to me: "If you leave, then they win. And if you leave, you will not come back."

It was such a difficult summer, because I spent about six to eight hours a day speaking with congregants about my sexual orientation. As during congregational interviews, I felt that I had to make myself available to teach. I had to give them the words with which to respond to their friends, words to offer to their questioning children, words that would begin to answer the deep, troubling questions each of these congregants posed to themselves.

Opening up this way was wonderful and terrible. It was wonderful because supporters were in training to become advocates. I became very close with some people, and felt touched by their sensitivity. Many would share with me stories of their own homosexual experimentation, or speak about a gay brother or a lesbian niece. But the other side was hearing the painful comments. I went to lunch with one very vocal homophobic congregant, with the dream of convincing him. He tried to convince me that there is a gay agenda to take over the world. He paid for the lunch and kissed me afterward and said that we should do it again.

One group, which we came to jokingly call the "satanic chavurah," organized against me and demanded that Rabbi Davidson come home from vacation and meet with them. He did. They never directly attacked me. They attacked him, saying that he "shouldn't have done this" to me, that everything was going all right, until he put me in a position of "flaunting it." They knew that they could not say, "We're not comfortable with the lesbian," so they attacked my straight colleague.

The storm began to subside after Rabbi Davidson gave a powerful sermon on the rights of Jewish homosexuals that Rosh Hashanah, which touched all, and changed the minds of many. In the end, we lost about a dozen members, but we gained at least that many.

Though I was engaged in many conversations and small meetings that dealt with the issue, I never addressed the topic of sexual orientation in public. This was a deliberate strategy. I would break stereotypes by being out, but not making a public issue of it.

After a while, though, the silence was suffocating. For two years, Rabbi Jerry Davidson had spoken for both of us. During the year after the wedding, due to the press coverage, I had numerous invitations for speaking engagements. I turned down most of them, but took some. I was conflicted about how much to take on the issue. Having survived the storm, I wanted to be a rabbi, not The Lesbian Rabbi. Couldn't I just live and make a difference by being seen?

During my third High Holy Days at Temple Beth-El, I spoke to the congregation for the first time about being a lesbian rabbi. I didn't set out to speak about it. What occurred was that for the first time, I didn't edit out the reality of my life. The sermon was about Jonah and shlichut, having a mission in life. In it, I wrote a letter to God about what happens if you try, like Jonah, to run away from your shlichut.

> During this year, God, I have contemplated what it means to be like Jonah. And what it means to be a coward. And what it means for me to sit by while homosexual teenagers and adults commit suicide because they choke from being in their closets. And what it means for me to remain silent while thousands die of AIDS and I protect my career. And what it means for me to turn down speaking engagement after speaking engagement on this issue in the name of wisdom. In the name of prudence.
>
> And they die and I go to sleep each night. On a soft pillow in a home that is heated in the winter and cooled in the summer that I might be comfortable.
>
> Except for the nights when I cannot sleep, God. Because my conscience is bothering me. And I feel like a victim. And I feel like Jonah. You know Jonah. The expert victim. Fantastic at running away. Fantastic at doing nothing because he is so terrified of doing something. . . .
>
> And the saddest thing of all God, if I can open my heart and tell you the truth. If I can open my heart and tell me the truth. The saddest thing of all is that I know Jonah. I am Jonah. I have been running so fast and so hard that I haven't been able to catch my breath. Running away from part of my mission, my shlichut. A responsibility that torments me. Colleagues and friends and mentors have courage to speak out on this, the civil rights movement of our time, but I am silent. Because I am mainstream. My hair is long and I wear makeup. I wear suits which are feminine and sometimes I accessorize. And I pass while others drown. And sometimes I say, "What am I?"
>
> You see, God, Carl Jung put it best when he said that "the achievements which society rewards are won at the cost of a

diminution of personality."[2] Society rewards behavior which denies a person's mission. Society rewards behavior which advances your reputation, which advances your financial port-folio, which advances your career, but shrinks you as a person. . . .

I don't want to be Jonah anymore.

I was stunned by the reaction I received from this sermon. My con-gregants applauded, and then they hugged me. Perhaps in part they were hugging and applauding themselves for the progress they had made. Like parents, they had moved from rejection to acceptance. Our Tem-ple community had grown and healed the way a family grows and heals.

Delivering this sermon offered me "permission" to speak on gay and lesbian matters whenever I wanted to. And so I did and I have. Speak-ing at Parents and Friends of Lesbians and Gays (PFLAG) and other gatherings was once like breathing from an oxygen tank. Then it became more like the inhaler my brother uses to control his asthma when he plays basketball. Resuscitating. Now it is just fun.

Not all stories have a happy ending, but this one does. Through alternative insemination, I became pregnant in the fall of 1997. Our baby daughter was born on July 1, 1998. The congregation was not only supportive, but excited. Everyone loves a baby. Mothers with small chil-dren, a population that had not been particularly drawn to me and was perhaps even afraid, suddenly came to me. "Can I lend you our stroller?" "What week are you in?" If the wedding had made me into a lesbian, the pregnancy made me into a woman. It was almost as if they had said, "I thought she was a lesbian, but apparently she is a woman."

We named our daughter Josie Bender Bernstein. Bender is her middle name and Bernstein is her last, to honor Rachel's beloved father z'l. In Hebrew her name is Yosefa Pnina. Pnina was my wonderful and altruistic grandmother, and Yosefa means "to add." Gay and lesbian fam-ilies can add a great deal to our world.

I recently went to the mikvah to celebrate having weaned our daughter. I laughed and cried and said, "Modah ani, modah ani": thank you, God.

At the time of the writing of this chapter, Josie is fourteen months old. She can say "more," "uppie," "doggie," and she can say, "Mommie o Mommie," which means, we think, "Mommie and Mommie." She calls us both Mommie. Life is magical and joyful, and we can't wait to give Josie a little brother or sister.[3]

Notes

1. I am exceedingly grateful to the following rabbis and loved ones for their courageous support and activism for justice and equality: Rabbi Jerome K. Davidson, Rabbi Harold Schulweis, Rabbi Sue Levi Elwell, Rabbi Peter J. Rubinstein, Rabbi Arnie Sher, Shelley Limmer, Roger Tilles; my parents, Ilan and Adina Bender; my mother-in-law, Sylvia Bernstein; and my wife, Rachel Bernstein.
2. Harold Kushner, *When All You've Ever Wanted Isn't Enough* (New York: Simon and Schuster, 1987), 23.
3. Joshua Bender Bernstein was born on September 20, 2000.

Chapter 9

SYDNEY MINTZ

Ger V'toshav

Member and Outsider

I WAS ORDAINED BY Hebrew Union College-Jewish Institute of Religion in New York City two years ago. When I applied to rabbinical school at the age of twenty-four, I included the fact that I was a lesbian in my autobiographical essay. I came out of the closet in my psychological evaluation and calmly told the interview committee that I wasn't choosing the rabbinate as a soapbox for my sexuality. I think that I was more than a little naive about how profound the mutual impact of the rabbinate and my sexuality would be. Being out in rabbinical school was an amazing experience for me at Hebrew Union College. I entered the rabbinate at a time when gay and lesbian rights were at the forefront of our world politically, culturally, and religiously. I felt comfortable enough to be outspoken and to encourage dialogue about the presence of gay and lesbian rabbis.

At the first joint dinner between Reform and Conservative rabbinical students in Los Angeles, we ventured into difficult and tentative territory. As the dinner began, a young man from the University of Judaism (the local Conservative seminary) seated next to me asked if the woman across the table was a rabbinic student. I told him she was not. He asked who her husband was. I explained that she did not have a husband. He looked at her wedding band in disbelief and whispered to me: "Is her husband dead; did he desert her?" I told him that the reason she didn't have a husband was because she was my spouse. "What do you mean?" he asked incredulously. "I mean we're lesbians," I said. He left the table, I think to go bang his head against the bathroom wall or to splash cold water on his face. When he returned we had a long discussion. My Reform classmates were leaning so far over in their chairs to hear my responses to his questions that one fell onto the floor.

Since I entered the rabbinate, I have been very open about the pride involved in my identity as a woman, a mother, a lesbian, a Jew, and a rabbi. I feel fortunate to live in the world at a time when I do not have to hide. There were times when I would have liked to do so, but the responsibility I felt toward the college and the Reform movement weighed heavily on me. Both in rabbinical school and in my first position at Congregation Emanu-El in San Francisco, I felt I had a responsibility to be as out of the closet as possible.

Being out as a lesbian in school and in my present position is not only a responsibility, but also a gift. I entered the rabbinate because I felt that the Jewish community and my Judaism had given me so much. Having grown up with a strong feminist consciousness, in a family led predominantly by strong, independent Jewish women, I felt that it was only right to go on carrying that mantle in the Jewish world. I felt a need to give back, and I knew that as a lesbian, I could bring benefit to the Jewish community through my presence as a leader and an educator. These are the reasons I felt so strongly about being out of the closet as a rabbinical student and out in the rabbinate. I know that my sexuality and my interest in the rabbinate are intertwined, but I did not become a rabbi to be a "lesbian rabbi." I became a rabbi because of my love for the Jewish people, my desire to teach Torah, my own wrestling with our tradition, and the fact that my career as a stand-up comic was limited. I often say that the rabbinate was the next obvious step for me; I love to make people laugh, and the bimah seemed the best way to involve humor to educate the Jewish community.

At the end of my third year in rabbinical school at the Los Angeles, my partner, Deborah, and I were married. Our wedding was the first same-sex union that many of my classmates attended, and I believe that the ceremony itself and my ensuing senior sermon that year had a profound impact on my classmates and on the faculty of the college.

Our wedding was the first time Rabbi Peretz Wolf-Prusan was only m'sader kiddushin . I say "only" because it was the first time that he had ever officiated as a rabbi without functioning as an agent for the State of California at a wedding. Like most clergy members, he officiated at weddings as a religious figure and as a representative of the government. But this wedding wasn't legal. It wasn't illegal; it just wasn't recognized by the state, by the government, by most of society, and by many other Jews.

As I wrote in my senior sermon:

On October 9, 1994, I was married. Or maybe not. I wear a wedding ring, I signed a *ketubah* and I ate cake, which should make it easier to discern my status, but I still struggle with this identity. It is not only new to me; it is new to the Jewish people. Like Abraham in the Torah portion of Chaye Sarah (Genesis 23–25), I am *ger v'toshav*, both a member of our Jewish family and an outsider, permanently dwelling in no-man's-, or no-woman's-land. How can this be? Don't I feel accepted, loved, and supported by our community? Of course I do. Don't I also feel neglected, compromised, and excluded from our community? Of course I do, because I married a woman. I can legally marry people as a rabbi, but my own marriage is still not legal.

In *parashat* Chaye Sarah, Abraham calls himself "ger v'toshav," which has been understood in many different ways by our commentators. Abraham is expressing a duality of belonging and existing as an outsider. In Chaye Sarah the concept of *ger* is brought into focus twice. Once as Abraham buys the portion of land called "m'arat Machpelah" from the Hittites to bury Sarah, and again as Eliezer goes in search of a wife for Isaac. In Abraham's identification of himself as ger v'toshav, he tells the Hittites, I dwell among you, but I am a stranger to you. My flocks graze in the next pasture, but I still need to buy this land in order to assume true ownership of it. He forces them to recognize his plight and his difficult existence as ger v'toshav. Although Abraham wasn't gay, this expression is parallel to the reality of lesbian and gay Jews. We ask for equal status as human beings, and we also ask for our uniqueness to be recognized. Like Abraham among the Hittites, we, as modern Diaspora Jews, are aware of our own precarious position living in a land that is not ours. And in our midst, with our communities are people who may seem strange, maybe different, and are definitely the Other.

At the conclusion of Rosh Hashanah services at my first student pulpit, the president of the synagogue and the two ritual committee chairpeople were the last people to shake my hand and wish me a "shana tova" before I left the synagogue. As they shook my hand, one of the women noticed my engagement ring. They asked me if I was engaged and wanted to be introduced to my fiancé. My heart began to race; my palms became sweaty. In that moment I knew that I could not tell them what they wanted to hear. And, since my very female fianceé was standing right behind me, I took a deep breath and introduced her to them. Two of the three lost their ability to speak, and their expressions turned into contorted smiles. The other woman emphatically pumped my hand up and down while crying out, "Mazel tov, mazel tov; I know two lesbians that just got married." I was the rabbi to this congregation. I was the representative of the College-Institute and the Reform movement. In one revealing moment I moved from member to stranger. And that was the result of someone noticing a not so obvious engagement ring.

Many people later asked me whether the rabbi who officiated at our wedding was gay. His wife had assured us that he wasn't. But still, people assumed that because we were having a lesbian wedding, we would obviously have a lesbian or gay rabbi officiate. The reason that we decided that Rabbi Wolf-Prusan would officiate was because he told us that he wouldn't do a commitment ceremony, he would only officiate at a kiddushin. He said to us, "Every marriage ceremony that I do between two Jews is a kiddushin." He explained if every lesbian or gay couple were married by a lesbian or gay rabbi or called their wedding a commitment ceremony, these couples would continue to be marginalized and their status would continue to be that of ger, not toshav.

Under the chuppah, the rabbi reminded us that every Jewish act is a political act. Every time we perform a Jewish ritual, we are being political. We are making the statement that we exist to a world that in many ways would rather forget our existence. But it wasn't under the chuppah that I felt the most political. It was at our egalitarian Conservative synagogue the day before our ceremony. Our synagogue had a great deal of difficulty granting us permission to have an aufruf. When we did finally stand at the Torah together, it was not in front of a completely welcoming congregation. Standing at the Torah with Deborah, chanting a double aliyah, I was more nervous than I was at my bat mitzvah, my first sermon, and standing under the chuppah all rolled into one. I felt as if I was standing in front of the Jewish community and saying, "Hello, I'm a lesbian Jew; I'm your daughter, your sister, your friend; I exist; don't pretend I am invisible." How many times have we heard the terms "yid" or "kike"? How many times have I heard the words "dyke" or "faggot"? The one pervasive difference between being lesbian or gay versus most other minorities is that we do not share our minority status with our clan, with our family. Most of our parents are straight. Most of our children are straight. Most Jews have Jewish parents and children; most African Americans have African American parents and children. In some way sharing this minority status with your family gives you strength and resilience. After all, they have experienced the same discrimination as you.

In my last year of rabbinical school in New York, I had to answer the important question that all rabbinic students pose before they are ordained: "Pork, pork only in Chinese food, or no pork at all?" Then the second most important question: "What am I going to do next?" I struggled with the idea that the gay and lesbian community needed more gay and lesbian rabbis as their leaders. What I realized for myself was that the gay and lesbian Jewish community needed less help being educated about the gay and lesbian community than did the community at large. I was very drawn to the pulpit, but I had also been made aware of the ramifications of being an out lesbian in a mainstream congregation from my colleagues who had already braved that challenge.

During the placement process, Congregation Emanu-El in San Francisco, California, listed an opening for an assistant rabbi. My partner, Deborah, and I had been living in the Bay area prior to rabbinic school, and she had taken a one-year sabbatical from her position as director of Camp Tawonga, a Jewish community center resident camp in the Sierra mountains outside Yosemite National Park. We knew that we were going back to the Bay area for her to resume her work, and Congregation Emanu-El seemed to be a great match for me.

Congregation Emanu-El is the oldest and largest Reform congregation in Northern California. This coming year we will celebrate our 150th anniversary. We currently have seventeen hundred member families. I was no stranger to large Reform synagogues, as I had grown up in Glencoe, Illinois, attending North Shore Congregation Israel, a large suburban synagogue the same size as my current pulpit. But here in San Francisco, I am the first openly lesbian rabbi in the area, a place that most people identify as the gay and lesbian mecca in this country. It is indeed the land of milk and honey for the gay and lesbian population, but my congregation is more than a few blocks away from the predominantly gay neighborhood of the Castro, both geographically and metaphorically.

When I arrived in San Francisco, the entire congregation received a letter introducing and welcoming the newest addition to the clergy at Congregation Emanu-El, Rabbi Sydney Mintz. The letter went on to say that: "Rabbi Mintz will be joined by her partner Deborah Newbrun, and their 18-month old son, Elijah." In a large Reform congregation with deep historical roots, the idea of a lesbian rabbi was a stretch for some of the members. I was very fortunate to have the complete support of our senior rabbi, Stephen Pearce, who smoothed the rough spots during my transition into my new job. With his support, as well as the support of the entire staff, my first years at the synagogue have been an enriching, rewarding, and very enlightening first experience in the rabbinate. Initially, I received a few letters that were critical and harsh. A noncongregant responded to my first sermon with a letter that stated: "Perhaps your attitude and swagger on the bimah would be better suited at another congregation." The week before I began my new job, the *Jewish Bulletin of Northern California* ran an article about me. They had called me in New York before I was ordained and conducted a phone interview. They wanted a front-page article with the title "New Lesbian Rabbi at Emanu-El." I told the reporter I would do the interview only if that wasn't the title and if the article wasn't on the front page. So the article appeared on the second page of the *Jewish Bulletin* with the title "Emanu-El's New Role Model: Lesbian, Woman, Rabbi, Jew." I was shocked!! I had always assumed that to be a rabbi you had to be a Jew, and to be a lesbian you had to be a woman. I reiterated in the article that the congregation hadn't come to interview for a lesbian, they had come to interview for a rabbi, and that my sexuality had very little to do with my being hired for the job.

Another place where my lesbianism has been dealt with in a straightforward way that is both educational and groundbreaking is at Camp Tawonga, where my partner is the director. When Deborah became pregnant in 1995, she addressed her board of directors frankly about the potential impact of our family on the camp community. She and the other directors wanted the issue of our family dealt with in an honest way. I think that it is very significant that with the support of the board of directors, a prominent Jewish Community Center Association resident summer camp in Northern California took the lead in honestly educating young adults and children about the diversity in Jewish families. Each summer the staff is taught how to respond to questions about our family from campers. We teach both the staff and the campers about the acceptance of diverse families in our community. I know of no other camp in this country that has dealt with a gay or lesbian director and family who are out of the closet in this way. It is a wonderful feeling to be educating Jewish families and children in a concrete way about the possibilities for diversity in our community.

When I was asked to write a chapter for this anthology, I questioned whether or not I truly fit into the definition of a "first generation" lesbian rabbi. Lesbians have been ordained for many years, and I believe that my predecessors have paved the way for my acceptance and my own ability to serve the Jewish people openly and honestly. Without their efforts, I would not be here today, continuing the work of opening the doors and eyes of our community.

I know that I would not be in this position at a large mainstream Reform congregation and be living completely out of the closet if I had been ordained a decade ago. My life as a lesbian, living in the Bay area, and working in the Jewish community as a rabbi is extraordinary because at no other time in history would I be afforded the freedom and acceptance that I have today. Because the Jewish community has come this far, I am hopeful that gay, lesbian, bisexual, and transgender Jews will gain greater acceptance in the Jewish world. I am still at the beginning of a long journey. I will never take for granted the fact that I can live my life openly as a lesbian, a Jew, and a rabbi.

I look forward to the day when I will look back and say that I remember when registering at Macy's as two brides was a big deal. I remember the advice I received not to come out of the closet during my rabbinical school interview. I remember the first time that a straight Episcopalian minister, in solidarity with her queer brothers and sisters in her community, vowed not to perform another civil ceremony until she could perform one for any couple that wished to be married in her church. I remember when the Central Conference of American Rabbis refused to vote on the issue of same-sex marriage. I look forward to the day when all of those battles will be a thing of the past. When those obstacles to freedom are breached, we will all be closer to olam habah, the world to come.

Part III

Serving Gay and Lesbian Congregations

Gay and Lesbian Synagogue as Spiritual Community

Chapter 10

SHARON KLEINBAUM

I NEVER WANTED to be a congregational rabbi. I certainly never thought I would want to serve the gay/lesbian, bisexual, transgender communities. I thought the first was an empty, dying form. And the second, well, that was too narrow, too isolated from "real" Jewish life. I now serve as rabbi of New York City's gay and lesbian synagogue. How did that happen?[1]

Growing up, I never experienced congregational life as vibrant, passionate, or world changing. Even after eight years of three-day-a-week Hebrew school in a Conservative synagogue in Rutherford, New Jersey, I knew almost nothing about Judaism. I didn't even know that Hebrew verbs were conjugated, and I had never encountered Jewish texts in their original languages. When I applied to the Orthodox Frisch Yeshiva High School of Northern New Jersey as a ninth grader, the rabbi who interviewed me asked me to read the first verse of Bereshit. I could read it only haltingly. When he asked me if I could at least point to the Hebrew word for "created," I just picked a word at random and by sheer luck my finger landed on the word "bara." He let me in. To this day I am grateful to him.

I'm not sure what I expected when I applied to Frisch, but what I found was a home, even though I had to become a kindergarten Jew while my classmates were functioning fluently, expertly, comfortably in the ancient texts of our people. I was surrounded by adults who were passionate about issues of meaning, questions of purpose. We teenagers were treated as intelligent, thinking young people. There were high expectations of us. It was intellectually thrilling. Nothing would make a teacher more excited than a student who asked question that he could not answer. We were rewarded for thinking. And yet I started struggling with Orthodoxy. As I learned more, I became increasingly uncomfortable with aspects of Orthodoxy. And I now understand, from the perch of a couple of decades later, that I was struggling with what it meant to be a lesbian.

I went to Barnard College thinking I might escape the dilemmas Judaism presented to me. When I entered college, I thought that Orthodox Judaism was the only legitimate form—all other Judaisms were watered down. My time at Barnard opened me to the possibility that I could be Jewish and still be me, that there was a Judaism that shared my enthusiasm for the world of politics and social change. All of that remained separate as I came out during college.

There was a foreign language requirement then, and I decided to meet it by taking Hebrew and Yiddish, which was pretty esoteric in the mid-1970s. In my senior year I took Paula Hyman's seminar "Jews and Revolution." She was an extraordinary teacher. She showed me that the socially active, the politically engaged, the prophetic tradition of Judaism had not ended with the prophets but had continued through to the nineteenth century and on down to the present day. Dr. Hyman herself lived a life that was both passionately Jewish and deeply committed to feminism and politically progressive values.

Throughout the political activism of my college years, whether it was urging Columbia to divest itself of stocks in corporations that invested in apartheid South Africa; protesting nuclear power and weapons; fighting for racial justice; or practicing civil disobedience sitting in at the Pentagon, I was struck by the number of Jews who were leaders and yet rarely identified Judaism as an ongoing source of that activism. By contrast, many of the Catholic activists I knew proudly drank from their faith traditions to nurture and support their political work.

Sometime in the summer of 1981, I was hitchhiking through Massachusetts with a girlfriend and a large Labrador retriever. It was a rainy afternoon, and the three of us were grateful when a beat-up old van pulled over on Route 9 to give us a lift. The driver said he was going to Florence and could take us to Northampton. He apologized for the fact that there was no place for us to sit except on the boxes in the back, but we were so glad to have the ride we didn't care about that. The boxes weren't sealed, and I was curious about what was in them—they were so heavy and so solid. When I looked, I discovered that they were filled with books in Yiddish, some by the same writers I had studied at Barnard. I was astonished, and I asked the driver, shouting over the noise of the rain and the van, what he was doing with boxes full of the books by the writer Mendele Moykher-Sforim in his van. He turned around and asked me, with equal astonishment in his voice, how I could read Yiddish in the first place to even know there were books by Mendele Moykher-Sforim in his van! So I told him.

That was how I met Aaron Lansky. A year later I moved to western Massachusetts, and for the next three years I worked with Aaron as the assistant director of the newly founded National Yiddish Book Exchange (later changed to Center). It was a real cultural rescue operation. Someone's mother or father or grandfather or aunt would die, and the children or grandchildren or nieces and nephews would find themselves with a whole library of books written in a language they didn't know—Yiddish. Or Yiddish speakers would anticipate their own death, or a move into a home and want to protect their yerusha and want us to take the books. Once a month we got up early and drove the empty van into Brooklyn, Manhattan, or the Bronx, and at the end of the day we drove it back to Amherst again filled with boxes and boxes of these unwanted books that otherwise would have ended up as landfill on Staten Island—as so many others no doubt did. Aaron had rented an old elementary school in Amherst—not far from Emily Dickinson's house—and when we got back we just piled the books up on the floor and then spent weeks sorting them out and cataloguing them. Nobody else seemed very interested in these books, but to us they were a treasure, the legacy of a culture that had been destroyed in Eastern Europe a generation earlier and that was seemingly being forgotten everywhere in our own generation.

In the 1960s, the area around Amherst, Massachusetts, had become a haven for young Jews who wanted to drop out of the urban religious culture in which they were raised, many for politically motivated reasons. By the 1980s, there was a vibrant lesbian and gay community in the region. Many were looking for some way to be Jewish without the Judaism in which they had grown up and that they rejected every bit as much as it had rejected them. When the National Yiddish Book Center began to offer classes in Yiddish and Yiddish literature, they came, and then I discovered that I was a teacher and that I loved it. What I also discovered was that it was nearly impossible for my students to appreciate the literature I was teaching if they didn't know Jewish liturgy or the laws of Pesach, if they had never struggled with the legal conundrums of the Talmud's goring ox or worried about carrying a pen in their shirt pocket after sundown on the Sabbath. I was excited about being a bridge for my students. I was challenged to think through my assumptions that as an out lesbian I couldn't live an actively Jewish life. Once I rejected that dichotomy, I wanted to study more. I knew that however much I had learned at the yeshiva, it wasn't enough, and that I had to learn more, I had to go back to the texts, the debates, the discussions of my adolescence and take them on as an adult, as a lesbian, and as a progressive Jew.

After three years of working with Aaron Lansky at the National Yiddish Book Center, I left to enter the Reconstructionist Rabbinical College. I first encountered RRC as a site in Philadelphia that was designated as a depository for books until we arrived in the beat up van to shlep them back to Amherst. Aaron and I had many stimulating discussions about Jewish life with then president Ira Silverman z'l. He encouraged both of us to consider rabbinical school. I went to RRC not to become a rabbi but because I wanted to study the texts of our tradition in a way that I knew would only be possible in a seminary setting.

It was 1985. Sixteen years after Stonewall, not one rabbinical student—anywhere in the world—was officially out to the faculty or administration of his/her seminary. HUC-JIR's official position was to reject any candidates known to be gay. One student who had come out to selected students and faculty at HUC-JIR was sent to a psychiatrist. The Jewish Theological Seminary's position, then as now, barred any openly gay candidate and refused ordination to any openly gay rabbinical student. One RRC faculty member, Linda Holtzman, who had to leave her pulpit in order to be open, was out. I was totally closeted. Although RRC had passed a policy of nondiscrimination on the basis of sexual orientation—mine was the first class to be admitted under the policy—there was no awareness of the changes that it would necessitate. Those of us who were lesbian or gay met in secret caucuses in private homes. I moved from a world in which I had been basically out to being very closeted. I was overwhelmed by the heterosexual assumptions and biases I found in my first encounter with so-called mainstream Judaism.

In the fall of 1986 word spread that a conference was being called for lesbian and gay Jewish professionals working in the Jewish community. Although such caucuses had been secretly meeting at various professional organizations, there had never before been an attempt to call us all together across movement lines and professional categories. The meeting place was kept secret. We were told which city to fly to and given a number to call when we arrived to the airport. Only then were we given directions to the conference. Some of us were so scared to be there that we had long discussions about confidentiality agreements: No printed lists of participants would include last names, or even the name of the conference. No one could refer to the conference by its location—lest our congregants hear about it and know that their rabbi was in that city on that day and come to the right conclusion.

The meeting was transformative for me. I had the experience of being Jewish without sacrificing or hiding who I was. When I returned to RRC, I had strength to do things I had been too closeted to take on before. I started the "What now?" Committee, a group of three faculty and administrative staff (Rabbis Jacob Staub; Linda Holtzman, and Rebecca Alpert) and three students (Sharon Cohen; Daniel Kamesar z'l; and myself) who met weekly to work through issues of transforming this Jewish community into a welcoming one for and lesbians and gays. The next year, Rabbi Rebecca Alpert, then dean of RRC, asked me to fill in at the last minute as the High Holiday rabbi for Bet Haverim, the gay synagogue in Atlanta. I had never wanted to do congregational work and I had never wanted to do "gay" Jewish work. But I had tasted what it was like to be completely out, and knew I could only be a deeply spiritual leader if I didn't suffocate such a deep part of myself. I also felt that I had a debt to pay to those members of the organized gay Jewish community who had been willing to be visible. My fears about being perceived as a gay rabbi, I realized, were somewhat disingenuous. It was at that wonderful congregation in Atlanta that I realized the potential of congregational life. It was there that I began to develop an appreciation for the radical transformative possibilities of a gay/lesbian synagogue as spiritual community.

That newfound appreciation has turned to a conviction in my eight years as rabbi of Congregation Beth Simchat Torah. I do not experience this GLBT Jewish community as fringe or ghettoized or narrow. I saw and felt the tremendous possibilities of people, many broken and hurt by a destructive world, deeply searching, with great passion for real meaning in Jewish life.

If you celebrate Kabbalat Shabbat often enough at CBST here in New York, sooner or later you will hear me say that I believe in cosmic influences, and I do: I believe that we ourselves influence the cosmos, that we influence the world. I believe that what you do, what I do, what *we* do, matters; our lives, our actions, our words, even our thoughts can make a difference. I believe that we are all here—every one of us—for the sake of what we can do together. Together, we can change the world.

If I didn't believe this, I could not do the work I do.

When Jacob Gubbay and a handful of friends started a synagogue in a room in a church annex in Chelsea in the winter of 1973, what they had in mind was a place where they could be both Jewish and gay together. What they did was change the world. Every fall now—twenty-seven years later—thousands of lesbian, gay, bisexual, and transgender Jews, their families, and their friends from all over our greater metropolitan area gather together at New York's Jacob Javits Convention Center to observe Yom Kippur at services sponsored by that synagogue, CBST. Everyone who joins us there is changing the world.

With us on any given Friday night may be some who remember CBST's first Kabbalat Shabbat on a cold, rainy, nasty Friday night in February twenty-seven years ago—they were there. With us may be some who are entering a synagogue for the first time since leaving home or since their bar or bat mitzvah. Others may be coming into a synagogue for the first time in their lives. For some, coming in means coming out, openly acknowledging their sexuality, for the first time. They too will change the world.

In the eight years that I have been CBST's rabbi, I have officiated at the funerals of leaders of both the New York and the national gay movements who, following in the footsteps of the Jewish union organizers of a century before, believed they had an obligation to change the world—and they did. I buried the son of an Orthodox rabbi who refused to come to his son's funeral. I comforted his partner as he was grieving his beloved and being excluded from the family as a mourner.

I have married couples who understood that such a ceremony was not only an expression of love but also a political act of defiance against a society that still does not accept relationships between same-sex couples as equally valid to those of heterosexuals. These couples are changing the world. I have given blessings over newborns and newly adopted infants of same-sex couples who believe that raising a family is a part of the Jewish heritage that is legitimately theirs, even if the racial and gender makeup of their family does not reflect the larger Jewish community around them. These parents are changing the world; their children and their children's children will change it even more.

One of the very greatest and best-known of our many rabbinic legends tells us that the first primordial light God created filled many vessels. But this first light was so strong that it broke the jars and got away, leaving behind only their scattered shards. These broken shards are our world, and our job is to mend it. The great rabbis of our tradition tell us we are not obligated to complete this work—tikkun olam—but we are not excused from it either.

How do you mend a broken world? How can we live through the brokenness? How do we get past the feeling that we are caught in the midst of a second mabul, a second Flood, whether we experience it as lesbians or gays or women or Jews or as African Americans or people with AIDS or Kosovars—or even as ordinary middle-class Americans with a nagging sense that we've gotten just about everything we could ever really want in life except the sense of meaning and purpose that would make it all worthwhile? How do we get past the feeling that God has forgotten the covenant with Noah, has forgotten the promise of the rainbow, has forgotten us? We can only do what Noah did: we can build a tevah, an ark to help carry us through the Flood of our times, both in a personal sense and also in the larger sense of our lives, the historical and global sense. This ark is community, and I believe that the synagogue can be such an ark, a spiritual community, in every sense of the word.

Ironically perhaps, I think, a gay and lesbian synagogue has the potential to fulfill the best and deepest vision of what synagogue life could or should be. This is not to say there are not profound problems

embedded in the very structure of synagogue life. But I believe the position of outsider provides perspective and passion which often makes the
questions of purpose and meaning come alive in a synagogue setting.

Some say that a synagogue is not a place for politics but a place to
go deep inside ourselves and to forget the world outside; some say a synagogue is a place to find comfort for our own pain, not to expose ourselves to the pain of others. If this were true, then I would say we should
close our synagogue doors and do something useful like make the space
into a parking lot. The vision of being Jewish which compels me is not
just about taking care of our individual souls. The Children of Israel who
entered into God's covenant at Sinai did so as a people, a community,
not as a collection of individual souls, and every Jew's relationship to
God is mediated by the community. From the moment we are named,
however, we are also, as Jews, a part of the covenantal community itself.
And this covenant means that there is obligation from the side of the
individual to the side of the community and back again. This doesn't
mean that we don't constantly try to deepen our internal lives as individuals, because, after all, if we don't have a rich religious life of our own,
we aren't likely to find the energy and the commitment and vision for
the very hard and often discouraging work of mending the world.

The life of lesbian and gay Jewish spiritual communities is a political challenge to the mainstream of our society; it is also a moral challenge to the mainstream of our society's religious discourse. In a society
that tries to ignore us and would prefer to exclude us, lesbian and gay
synagogues are an increasingly visible and undeniable social and religious
reality. In a society that does not recognize same-sex marriage, our
couples marry. In a society that considers homosexuality a threat to traditional family values, our congregants are raising children, and raising
them in one of the world's greatest religious traditions.

In a spiritual landscape that has been largely divvied up among the
religious right, New Age searchers, and the prevailing secular culture,
lesbian and gay synagogues represent a vital religious alternative, putting
forward the model of thriving lesbian and gay communities transforming traditional values of organized, institutional religion. In the face of
the religious right's vigorous efforts to co-opt and dictate the terms of the
dialogue within organized religion in America, our communities are living proof that the spiritual resources of traditional religion are not the

exclusive preserve of one particular segment of society or of one particular view of the nature of religion and the religious life.

Like all my openly lesbian and gay colleagues, I am constantly called upon to give advice and support to my heterosexual colleagues both in other synagogues and in Christian churches as they grow in their determination to acknowledge, celebrate, and honor the life cycle events of their homosexual congregants. Not long after I first arrived at CBST I received a call from a colleague in a liberal synagogue in the northeast. Why, he wanted to know, did no one call their hotline for people with AIDS? Why did no one utilize the services of a rabbi willing to talk with dying PWAs? I asked him, "What do you do for gay/lesbian Jews who are living? How welcome would they feel in your congregation? Not just one individual—but what if a group of gay people joined; how would your synagogue respond? Do you celebrate with equal joy the smachot of gay people? If not, why would a gay person who is sick or dying seek solace from you if your community has not embraced us as we live?"

Recently, I have participated in a national round table of liberal religious leaders sponsored by the National Gay and Lesbian Task Force to address the religious right. As one of a growing number of lesbian and gay rabbis who are finding our voices and the forums in which we can be heard, being the openly lesbian leader of an openly gay religious community reinforces my individual efforts to address the political and religious challenges facing our community. Lesbian and gay synagogues such as CBST are a constant reminder to the world at large that being gay is not a passing fad, that being openly homosexual and connected to traditional religious practice is not a contradiction in terms, and that a religious community can be something altogether different from what either the secular society at large or the religious right would lead one to believe.

I now believe that a synagogue could create an entirely different kind of religious experience. People don't join CBST in order to impress their grandmothers, bar mitzvah their child, or increase their prestige at work. People join CBST for the sake of participating in a hardworking, volunteer driven, active and activist religious community. At CBST, we come together to worship, and to determine the best way to send relief to the Kosovars. We pray, and we wrap packages of holiday food and other things and take them to people who are homebound and hospitalized and who could not possibly get to a Passover seder or who would not otherwise have a menorah for Chanukah or dreidels, groggers, and hamentaschen for Purim. We study Torah, and visit people with AIDS who have been disowned by their families. We learn Talmud, and support programs for the elderly. We make music, and campaign against discrimination in the workplace. We learn Yiddish, and attend vigils in memory of Matthew Shepard. We educate ourselves and our children.

This work comes from a deep spiritual commitment, felt individually and acted upon communally, that being Jewish means more than attending High Holy Days services and that being an out lesbian or an out gay man means more than watching the annual Pride Parade. The depth of this commitment is what makes CBST the community that it is: a profoundly spiritual community that is at the same time highly engaged with the world around it.

When CBST celebrated its first Kabbalat Shabbat on that February night twenty-seven years ago, fifteen people showed up. The following year, about a hundred came to our first High Holy Days services. This year, over three thousand people attended our Kol Nidre and Yom Kippur services. It is our long-standing tradition at CBST to offer all of our services, including our High Holy Days services, at no charge, either to our members or to the members of our wider community, whether lesbian and gay and Jewish or not. Our commitment to this open-door tradition is deeply rooted in our personal experience of the many closed doors—family, school, work, synagogue—that we have encountered as lesbian and gay Jews, and we are determined that no one shall ever find CBST's doors closed to them. Many of us only began to accept our own sexuality after we walked through the doors of CBST on Rosh Hashanah or Yom Kippur or on some Friday evening during the year. Many of us have found CBST to be a profoundly Jewish community; many have stayed, and now call CBST their spiritual home.

We are an unaffiliated, nondenominational synagogue for lesbian and gay and bisexual and transgender Jews. This is where we began, this is who we are, and this is what is and must always be the cornerstone of all our work. Yet the spirit of CBST attracts heterosexuals and non-Jewish people to our congregation as well. We welcome them in the same way we welcome everyone else: Whatever your sexual orientation and whatever your relationship to Judaism, you are welcome to join our community.

In a larger sense, the issues of our lives as lesbian and gay Jews—the issues of healing, of purpose, of meaning, of community, of holiness—are also the world's, which we lesbian and gay Jews only experience a little more acutely, perhaps, than other people and into which we thereby maybe gain a little special insight. This insight is not only a gift but also a special obligation: It is what we bring, by virtue of who we are, to the greater task of tikkun olam, of mending the world. *"Even ma'asu habonim haitah l'rosh pinah,"* said the Psalmist: The stone that the builders rejected has become the cornerstone.

I did not become a rabbi in order to sell Judaism. I became a rabbi because I believe in the meaning and power of prayer and the presence of God in our lives. I did not become a rabbi in order to be a politician or a social worker. I became a rabbi because I believe in the power of religious community to overcome the culture of despair, a culture devoid of meaning and values, in which we find ourselves. As an openly lesbian rabbi of a lesbian and gay synagogue I have learned through my own life, and through the lives of my congregants, the power of a synagogue as a spiritual community.

Note

1. As CBST's rabbi I owe far too much to far too many people to be able to thank everyone as I should, but here in particular I would like to thank my partner, Rabbi Margaret Moers Wenig, who saw the potential of the shidduch with CBST and urged me to apply; and our children, Liba and Molly, without whose love and support I cannot imagine my life as an out lesbian rabbi of an openly gay synagogue; Richard Howe, kindred spirit and a writer without whom this and other papers would never be written; and our entire congregation, without whose extraordinary efforts over the past twenty-seven years there would be no CBST spiritual community to write about. I would like also now to remember two people, Mel Rosen *z'l,* whose vision and leadership made it possible for CBST to hire its first rabbi; and Irving Cooperberg *z'l,* whose still lively and wise spirit continues to sustain my own.

Chapter 11

Why I Choose to Be a Rabbi at a GLBT Synagogue

LISA A. EDWARDS

Wʜᴇɴ ɪ ᴀᴘᴘʟɪᴇᴅ ᴛᴏ the Hebrew Union College-Jewish Institute of Religion in 1988, guarded calls were made on my behalf to discover how out it was safe to be in my application process. Once accepted, my partner, Tracy Moore, and I were told by the powers that be that we were the first lesbian couple to ask the College-Institute for spousal privileges.

Although only a dozen years have passed, this all sounds like ancient history these days, with open admissions firmly in place, and so many queer rabbis around that this anthology of essays by lesbian rabbis easily found a publisher. But we shouldn't take our progress for granted, and we shouldn't assume that we've yet arrived where we need or want to be. When the editors asked me to contribute this essay, one of them wrote: "A number of contributors have written about their decision not to seek work with a g/l/b congregation. I think it's really important to hear from folks like you who are working within the community."

It saddened me to think that so many of my queer colleagues hold this opinion. I've long known it, though, for back in rabbinical school some of my queer classmates said they considered gay/lesbian congregations as their "safety" jobs, where they'd go if no one else would hire them. It seems I've managed to join yet another minority within a minority——a lesbian rabbi who chooses, who wants to be rabbi of a GLBT congregation.¹ I entered rabbinical school with that career goal.

Becoming rabbi of Beth Chayim Chadashim (BCC), the world's first synagogue founded in 1972 by gay, lesbian, and bi Jews was the fulfillment of a dream for me, and it continues to be a great blessing in my life.

I put this peculiarity—my minority status as a queer rabbi who wants to be in a queer congregation—up against another: not long ago one of BCC's oldest members sadly said to me, "I realized recently that if I were to come upon BCC today, not having ever been part of it before, I wouldn't join." The explanation offered was that BCC is "no longer cutting edge, that there's no longer the sense of excitement there once was of doing something deeply radical."

Certainly there is truth in that statement, and I can understand the sense of loss, the "thrill-is-gone" feeling. In the early days, BCC was profoundly radical at many points: back in 1973, for example, when BCC fought to be accepted into the Reform movement's synagogue organization, the Union of American Hebrew Congregations (UAHC),[2] or creating what was probably the first gender-sensitive prayer book in the history of Judaism, or educating the Jewish community about homosexuality, or even hiring a rabbi—Janet Marder—who had a different sexual orientation from the majority of synagogue members. But the word "radical" comes from the Latin meaning "having roots." "Radical" has two main meanings, one of which sometimes surprises people. The familiar definition of "radical" is "favoring extreme change; specifically, extreme change of the social structure." But the surprise is that radical also means "fundamental, basic, foundation, the source of something," thus its etymology: "having roots."[3]

Change or the possibility of change is fundamental in Judaism. Change in Judaism today is no longer (if it ever was) surreptitious or inadvertent, or something we notice only after the fact (like the huge change between Torah Judaism and Rabbinic Judaism). Change is approved of now, expected, in a way it never was before. This is true certainly in liberal Judaism, but I suspect it may even be becoming true in certain Orthodox circles as well. As a case in point, Judaism's first out gay Orthodox rabbi, Steven Greenberg, is currently speaking and writing radical, yet Orthodox, interpretations of sacred texts and the matter of homosexuality.

Certainly the original Reform Jews sought change, and indeed, Reform Judaism is based on radical change. Several of the early Reform changes could be described as bringing extreme social change: little or no Hebrew, no kashrut, the bringing of musical instruments and choirs into the prayer service, Shabbat services held on Sunday mornings, kippot and prayer shawls banned in the sanctuary. Even the shofar was banished from the first Reform Rosh Hashanah service in Germany in the mid nineteenth century.

Such changes do sound radical to us—and not really much like the Judaism practiced at our Reform synagogues today, not at BCC, and not at most others either. If you look inside most liberal synagogues today, including BCC, you'll find firmly in place most of what was removed by the early Reform Jews.

This might indeed lead one to think that liberal Judaism is less radical than it once was. But I think that the way Judaism is being practiced[4] more and more today by liberal Jews, especially Reform and Reconstructionist Jews, is, in actuality, far more radical in both senses of the word; it is more radical in the sense of being rooted, fundamental; and in the sense of being revolutionary, moving toward extreme change. For while serious liberal Jews increasingly take back the trappings of a more ancient Jewish practice, they do so for profoundly different reasons than our ancestors had for such practices. It may be more accurate to say simply that we do so with much reason, rather than out of unquestioning habit or blind tradition as so many of our ancestors practiced it. We look more traditional than Reform Jews used to look because we have studied the traditions and the reasons they were established. Even more important, we have begun to transform some of those traditions by grounding them in new understanding.

For example: who would have imagined, twenty-five years ago, a Jewish wedding between two women or two men? And yet in increasing numbers such couples are choosing to make a public declaration of our fundamental and revolutionary—that is, our radical—desire to join one soul to another, to choose, though others would deny us the right, to create a loving relationship filled with caring and commitment to the mate we have found, even against so many odds, the one to whom our soul is drawn. And these weddings are not copies nor parodies of Jewish weddings between a man and a woman. Rather, the couples take each symbol of a Jewish wedding, study it, seek out what is at its heart, and transform it into a symbol that speaks to their relationship, their commitment to Judaism, and to God. The power of these ceremonies is their transformational nature: They transform the couple's relationship into a sacred one; they transform Judaism into a radically inclusive religion; and they often transform witnesses from skeptics, even homophobes, into passionate supporters of the couple's relationship.

So if it is true that some Jews today are transforming some Jewish traditions by grounding them in new understanding, from where does this new understanding come? It comes from the kind of radical challenge that late-twentieth-century Jews were willing to bring to Judaism. It comes from a happy and still evolving equation. The first half of the equation is that radicals, the fringe, the previous outsiders, including women, queers, feminists of all genders, radical thinkers of all sorts, even some non-Jews, became suddenly interested in Judaism, interested enough to want to explore its possibilities in our own lives.

The second half of the equation has been a willingness on the part of the liberal Jewish establishment to open the door, albeit sometimes just a crack, to the outsiders. Although this revolution's beginnings date back at least to the late sixties (the *First Jewish Catalog* was published in 1973), it is far from over. And while it's true that BCC was in on it near the beginning, that BCC was born out of this revolution's start and quickly became a leader in its continuation, it's not true that we've settled down into being some sort of mainstream, establishment Jewish institution. There are few congregations in the world today where you can have the kind of conversations about Torah, about God, about Judaism, about prayer, about ourselves, that we have at BCC. There are few places where Judaism is examined through so many different lenses, and where everyone's lens is equally valued. There are few places where diversity is a mainstay, is the mainstream. And BCC and our sibling congregations are among those places.

We've barely begun, I think, to break open the possibilities Judaism holds for us. Barely begun, but hardly ready to stop. Though I wasn't there in BCC's early years, I don't doubt that it looks different in many ways now from how it looked then. But I don't think one should mistake that kind of change for changing back, or backpedaling, or standing still.

One of the benefits of a GLBT synagogue is the support, the foundation, it offers its members, who then feel safe enough to operate as activists elsewhere in the world. Here is a sampling of what some BCC members are engaged in: biphobia education in gay/lesbian and hetero-sexual Jewish communities, queer biblical scholarship, confronting the Conservative movement on their homophobia, writing books that embrace GLBT people (including a novel for adolescents about a teacher rumored to be gay), writing a masters thesis on the effect of AIDS in queer congregations, editing an oral history of Israeli lesbians, being out judges in superior courts, leading a speakers' bureau on gay and lesbian equality, running an organization for children of gays and lesbians.[5]

BCC's former rabbis have also helped pave the way for many of us. Rabbi Janet Ross Marder, BCC's first ordained rabbi, became an out-spoken and influential ally within the Reform movement for gay and lesbian Jews. Rabbi Denise Eger was out to most of the faculty at HUC-JIR in the years before a policy was in place, and then from the pulpit at BCC became one of the first lesbian or gay rabbis to speak to the press when the CCAR did vote on an open admissions policy,[6] and is now hard at work on same-gender marriage issues (among other issues) from her pulpit at Congregation Kol Ami. Rabbi Marc Blumenthal, by being an openly gay rabbi with AIDS, has brought many Reform Jews a new understanding of AIDS. Before any ordained rabbis came to BCC, sev-eral student rabbis shaped their rabbinates in large measure through their training at BCC. All of BCC's former rabbis, and their presence at BCC, helped me become more the rabbi I want to be, a rabbi who advo-cates diligently, in a variety of ways, for the rights of people to be who they are and to become more the people and the Jews they want to be.

The rabbis who have occupied BCC's pulpit are of course not our only models or mentors. Like so many other gay, lesbian, or bisexual rab-bis, I benefit from all the gay, lesbian, bisexual rabbinic and cantorial stu-dents and rabbis and cantors. Because they were brave in all sorts of ways in the years before HUC-JIR and other schools had any policy stating whether they could even stay in school, I was able to be open and unafraid my whole time at HUC-JIR. Although it didn't help me get a job anywhere except BCC, I was able to be the first ordainee to be totally out from the first interview on. And those who are in school or in the field now continue to help create a safer world for all of us. If the Jewish world is still far from perfect for gay, lesbian, or bisexual rabbis or cantors, we can at least see change happening and can be optimistic that a time will come when queer rabbis and cantors will be able to find work without experiencing discrimination.

The list of activists and their activism above is not comprehensive by any means. I know BCC members, friends dear to BCC, and members of sibling congregations, will be living lives—parenting, volunteering, publishing, teaching, running for office, engaging in all kinds of endeavors—that will help change the world and Judaism too. And for all of them, BCC and its sibling congregations provide a radical base: a safe home, a firm foundation, from which to go out into the world and bring fundamental change to the social structure. I would also venture to guess that the queer Jews (rabbis and cantors included) who choose not to affiliate with a GLBT synagogue still feel safer, more firmly grounded, in the world knowing that such institutions exist.

For some of us, though, it's not our congregations or communities alone that provide the firm foundation. The Reverend Elder Nancy Wilson of Metropolitan Community Church (MCC), Los Angeles, speaks of the queer people who push the envelope, who instigate change. She suggests that certainly in the past, and often still today, coming out lowers your class status, stigmatizes you, limits your career options, so that in our history the ones who tended to come out in a big way were the ones with nothing to lose. They were the ones already thrown out by their families, the ones who already had few career options, or the ones who couldn't have stayed closeted, couldn't hide, no matter how hard they tried. Thus, for example, it was the drag queens who fought back first in the Stonewall riot. "They could fight because they had no fear of losing," said Reverend Wilson; "they had nothing left to lose."[7]

There is another group of people (and I count myself among them) who can afford to stand up, who can push the envelope, because we too have nothing to lose. With this group, however, it's not that we have nothing left to lose because we have already lost everything. We have nothing to lose, because no matter what we do, we won't lose what's most important to us—we won't lose our families. We won't lose them because we come from families, bless them, who love us, no matter who we are, what we do. We come from families who respect our difference, who appreciate our needs and desires, who are willing to see us for who we are. They give us what we need; they give us a safety net to go out and seek radical change.

Those of us with the good fortune to have the love of our families behind us—surrounding us—have nothing to lose. But given that, we, like the drag queens and other queer heroes who came before us and are still at it today, have a role, we are change agents. I take this seriously. Even when we move slowly, we move. Determining how to do so, how to make change (or know when not to change) is a never-ending, always challenging task. It's far from a new task, however. Here too, we stand on the shoulders of the ones who came before us.

There are two phrases used frequently in the Talmud: One is "Get up and do" and the other is "Sit and don't do." The first is used thirteen times; the second, fourteen, so you might guess from the count that "Sit and don't do" wins over "Get up and do!" But I think such a close count suggests that the two axioms are of equal importance. There are times when the appropriate action is to sit and not do; and there are times when we must get up and do. The challenge for the rabbis of the Talmud was in determining which was the appropriate action in any given situation.

Both actions can be radical: "Get up and do": Think of the founding of Beth Chayim Chadashim, where Jews who might otherwise have left Judaism have instead become leaders in the Jewish community, helping both to preserve and to change Judaism. Think of liberal Jewish leaders who might have ignored these queer Jews, but have instead embraced and encouraged them to be part of the Jewish community and its leadership. "Sit and don't do": Think of the teachers and study partners of queer Jews who might have followed a so-called Jewish line of thought that would encourage them to cut off their queer colleagues, but who choose not to do that, but instead to sit and study with them. Either action—standing up or sitting down—can be radical, for either one can keep us rooted, tied to our foundations, to our principles, even as it allows us to challenge directly the status quo.

Although Judaism right now is in a time of profound change, it's important to remember that change is not new to Judaism. We do follow in a long line of revolutionaries, the rabbis of the Talmud chief among them. From where we sit in the scheme of things—close to thirty years after the first woman rabbi was ordained and the first gay and lesbian shul (BCC) was founded—it can sometimes feel like it's taking forever to arrive where we think we should have been long ago: at a totally "unqueerphobic," truly feminist and egalitarian Judaism, in the best senses of those words. Especially after what seemed like such a promising, fast-paced, jump-up-and-do beginning (as when BCC was accepted into the UAHC within just two years of its founding, making it the first gay/lesbian congregation in any religion to be accepted by its mainstream religious organization). When you start out quickly, not quite three decades can feel like forever if you're still not there. But consider the several thousand years Judaism in some form has been around. Or consider the few hundred years, at least, it took for Jews to go from biblical to rabbinic Judaism; or the more than nineteen centuries it took to get to Reform Judaism.

The rabbis of the Talmud knew what we would do well to learn, if we haven't already: that not all change comes quickly. Some requires a lot of sitting—maybe it needs time to hatch. Part of our task is to determine when to jump up and when to sit, and when to do some combination of the two.

I suppose that learning when to sit and when to jump up is among the hardest tasks we face. When we want so much, it's hard to be patient; it's also hard to know exactly what to do. Our ancestors took this challenge seriously; so should we. None of us has to do it alone, though; we have each other. And that is why I am so committed to serving a queer synagogue, where I am blessed to have so many partners to sit and study with, as we seek to understand God and Judaism and our relationship to both. That is also why I am so blessed to have BCC as the firm foundation from which to go out into the world both to help repair its many ruptures and to enjoy its many wonders.

Notes

1. A note on my use of terms. "GLBT" stands for "gay, lesbian, bisexual(bi), transgender (trans)." I'm trying to be historically accurate here, as well as politically correct. At the end of 1999, our congregation was just beginning to add the word "transgender" to the list. It was not yet on our letterhead, for example. We added "bisexual" to our list officially a few years ago. When our congregation was founded in 1972 it was called a "homophile" community, then "homosexual," then "gay" and not long after that "gay and lesbian" (the favored descriptor until the mid-1990s). I also use the term "queer" interchangeably with GLBT, although in truth I prefer the term "queer" because it casts an even wider net.

2. This occurred in 1974, making BCC the first gay and lesbian congregation to be admitted into any mainstream religion's umbrella organization.

3. See *American Heritage Dictionary of the English Language*, ed. William Morris (New York: American Heritage Publishing Co. and Houghton Mifflin, 1969), 1076.
4. "Practice" is a good word for it, for "practice" means "to do regularly in order to become proficient," and it also means "to put knowledge into practice." (*Webster's New World Dictionary of the American Language*, college edition [Cleveland and New York: World Publishing Co., 1960], 1199).
5. In the order of the list above, these are the names of BCC people (not all of them gay, lesbian, or bisexual) doing this important work: Fran Magid Chalin, Amy Sapowith, Rabbis Benay Lappe and J. B. Sacks-Rosen, Ellen Jaffe McClain (now Gill), Jeannette Vance, Tracy Moore, Jerry Krieger and Donna Groman, Rebecca Weinreich, Tara Weinreich.
6. The CCAR (Central Conference of American Rabbis, the rabbinic arm of the Reform movement) voted on the acceptance of gay and lesbian rabbinic students and rabbis in 1990.
7. Private conversation, May 1999.

Chapter 12

Ten Years
and Counting . . .

DENISE L. EGER

I NEVER INTENDED TO serve the lesbian and gay community. I didn't even think I would be able to integrate my sexual orientation with my life's work. I thought I would have to sublimate or hide a significant part of my essence to serve God and the Jewish people. At least that is what I told myself and tried to convince myself I would do. Being Jewish, I was taught, was about marriage, family, and children. I was taught that anything outside of this paradigm was somehow less than perfect—dare I say, less than holy. Without the familial trappings, a person steps outside of the center of the Jewish people and remains forever on the periphery.

But the view from the periphery isn't so bad after all. My work these last ten years since ordination has been serving as rabbi in Los Angeles' lesbian and gay community and as an openly lesbian rabbi in the Jewish community. My rabbinate has been about *shlemut*—integration and wholeness. It is about moving from the periphery toward the center.

These are the very things I thought I would never be able to achieve. Yet I believe that God called me to work through these concepts for myself and hence for others as well. I feel that I have moved too, from the periphery to a more central place, a more grounded place. For during my service, I have learned important lessons.

When I came to serve as rabbi of Beth Chayim Chadashim, the first gay and lesbian synagogue, in 1988, following my ordination, the rab-

binical powers warned me to stay away. "Denise," they urged, "you'll
never work again. Don't take this job." I had already experienced the
very real hand of job discrimination both as a woman and as a lesbian.
Several positions had disappeared when it became known that I was a
lesbian. But I also knew that for my own sense of well-being and inner
peace, I should accept the position at BCC. I could not live a lie, and the
only way for me to live honestly at the time seemed to me to be as the
rabbi of a gay and lesbian synagogue. I would become its first rabbi of
the same sexual orientation as the majority of the congregation. Founded
in 1972, the congregation had been served by student rabbis and rabbis,
but none who were openly gay or lesbian.

My very presence in serving in the first synagogue with outreach to
the lesbian and gay community was a new hallmark for the congregation
and for both the lesbian and gay community and the Jewish community.
I was not the first openly gay or lesbian rabbi to serve a gay congregation,
for both Allen Bennett and Yoel Kahn had already served Sha'ar Zahav,
the gay and lesbian synagogue in San Francisco. But for Southern California, the first place in America where gay men and lesbians had created religious homes, this was a turning point. Reverend Troy Perry,
founder of the Universal Fellowship of Metropolitan Community
Churches, recognized my arrival as an important step in the gay and lesbian spiritual movement. At the Fellowship's twentieth-anniversary celebration, I gave the opening benediction. The idea that Troy Perry had
that God loved gay people too, affirmed for me that full inclusion of lesbian and gays within the Jewish world was not only a dream but must
become reality. The creation of gay and lesbian synagogues would open
other doors for gay and lesbian Jews throughout Jewish life. The members of the UFMCC understood that the movement they began was
maturing in a variety of ways, including the appointment of a lesbian
rabbi in the congregation they had helped to found. Thus one of the first
lessons I learned was about the power of symbols in our movement. Just
as we were learning to build our own political base, the gay and lesbian
movement was also expanding its own religious and spiritual base. I
have been blessed to a part of that task.

I had no guide, no rabbinic role models. I had no textbook to tell me
how to do the work. I had to figure out how to make a go of being Jewish and gay for myself and now for my congregants. How would I bring

together these identities in a setting that would allow for growth, creativity, holiness, and happiness? How would I refute the notion that gay and lesbian Jewish life is peripheral to or outside of the communal Jewish tent? When I returned to Los Angeles as the rabbi of BCC, I began to see that my rabbinate must bring a Jewish consciousness to the gay and lesbian community. When one of the tougher gay bars had a uniform night and decided to hang a Nazi flag over the bar, I along with several others interceded and explained how that flag symbolizes hate not only of Jews but also of gay and lesbian people. I know my involvement helped those responsible understand the ramifications of their actions. They removed the flag from the bar.

My rabbinate has also challenged the Jewish community by demonstrating that gay and lesbian Jews are not some fringe group but rather their own sons and daughters, sisters and brothers. I have always tried to teach and show by example how gay and lesbian Jews are real people, with real lives who have much to offer our Jewish community. I always say we don't have a Jew to waste.

In 1992, a prominent "modern" Orthodox rabbi, a past president of the Southern California Board of Rabbis, called me in an article in one of the Jewish papers " the lesbian pig rabbi." I knew then that there was still much work to do within the Jewish community. I now treasure my own involvement with the Southern California Board of Rabbis as a way to open up the boundaries of the Jewish community at large. I have had the privilege to serve as the first woman officer of that organization.

My career has been spent reaching out to those gay and lesbian Jews who for many good reasons had left or distanced themselves from our Jewish community. Many gay people have been wounded by Jewish communities that have ignored and excluded them. And so some gay people rejected all that was good within our system of worship and ethics and community alongside that which was hurtful. Gay and lesbian oppression was often internalized and manifest as a self-loathing that undermined the self-images of many within the community. How do you help Jews find the joy of Torah and the uplifting message and spirituality of our history, stories, ethics, and music, when some won't even cross the threshold of the synagogue? My task became clear: Meet these Jews where they were. So I took my rabbinate beyond the walls of the synagogue into the community where people worked and played and lived.

I went where my congregants went. I participated in the communal organizations in which my congregants were involved. Their rabbi shared their concerns and their struggles. I tried to bring living Torah into their midst at every turn. Soon after the establishment of the Gay and Lesbian Alliance Against Defamation (GLAAD), there was an organized attempt to get the Anti-Defamation League of B'nai B'rith to include issues of homophobia in its "World of Difference" curriculum for the public schools. I was able to help the process along by meeting with Jewish judges involved in ADL and with gay judges and lawyers (all who were Jewish as well) involved in GLAAD. The ADL didn't come around on this issue. But we were able to get the Los Angeles Unified School District to accept a companion curriculum that included lesson plans on the effects of bigotry toward gay people, those with disabilities, and the effects of gender bias, issues that were omitted from the ADL's original curriculum. That early dialogue helped the ADL in later years recognize that GLAAD was an important ally in their work, and since then the ADL and GLAAD have worked to form strong alliances, especially concerning hate-crime legislation on the federal level.

The prophetic messages of justice and hope, and the tradition of confronting those who teach hate, provide powerful inspiration for gays and lesbians, for whom civil equality and justice is often a mirage. Jewish texts teach about a God of justice who challenges all people to seek justice. I realized that part of my task was to help the Jewish community recognize how treatment of sexual minorities is an issue of justice. Representatives of the liberal Jewish community had marched in Selma, and many understood the struggle for freedom and equality in that context. One of the lessons that I learned was to demythologize gay and lesbian life to the heterosexual world and most specifically in the rabbinic community. Then I believed I would have some allies who could help me focus on the real issues of equality and acceptance.

My participation in the larger gay and lesbian community showed the Jews how Jewish they really were, and how their Jewish values were embodied in their communal work. Jews were involved in every social cause and concern in the lesbian and gay community. Often they were not able to understand their commitments in Jewish terms because their own Jewish education was lacking. One tactic of working toward integration and wholeness became identifying how Jewish values were manifest by individuals and within their work in the community. I hoped that as they identified the values that supported the work, these Jews would come to want to explore these Jewish ideas. In conversation with someone who raised money for social services in the gay community, I would identify their work as tzedakah—an act of justice, and a mitzvah—a God-given command. I would name the Jewish values that applied. In meetings of other organizations in the gay community, especially when I noticed that most around the table were Jews, I would speak about the concept of tikkun olam—the repair and healing of our world through acts of justice and reconciliation. By going beyond the walls of the synagogue, into the community, the message of integration became part of people's lives. Judaism and Jewish values were also a part of our everyday lives, not part of an annual visit with relatives or evident only during a religious service. This pathway toward shlemut allows each person to begin the process of removing internal walls that continued to keep sexuality and spirituality compartmentalized.

I remember one occasion vividly. In the early spring of 1990 there was a retreat of local gay and lesbian activists. It was the first time in the history of the Los Angeles gay and lesbian community that all of the leaders of the various organizations had come together. Many in that group wouldn't even speak to one another at the beginning of the weekend because of various turf wars or other political clashes. It was a monumental weekend. There was much healing, and there were many opportunities for personal growth and coalition building. There were many Jews at this weekend who had never had anything to do with the Jewish community. It was their first contact with me. In discussion groups and activities, I was able to put their work in a Jewish context. For most of the Jews present, it was the first time they had considered this possibility. I knew I had succeeded the following High Holy Days when many of them attended services for the first time in years. I believe I was able to rekindle the possibility that Judaism, the Jewish community, and even God blessed their work for equality and blessed their work in bringing comfort to those with AIDS.

When I joined coalitions to work on stopping antigay initiatives, I helped to reframe the discussion for many. So often when there is an antigay ballot initiative or antigay marriage initiative or legislation, the Christian Right claims to be the only religious voice and sole moral arbiter of the discussion. The Christian Right's vast network of churches and infiltration of the Republican Party often took these civil and secular debates out of the arena of secular and civil dialogue and into the realm of religious discourse. I helped our coalitions, formed to combat these measures, rethink their strategies and reclaim the moral high ground not by excluding the message of the Bible or religion but by speaking about prophetic justice. My work with these coalitions also encouraged them to reach out to other religious groups who shared this philosophy and were our natural allies.

My participation and involvement was a statement to the entire gay and lesbian community that the Bible still has important lessons for us, even though there are clergy and religions who misuse the text to justify discrimination and even violence against us. From 1993 through 1996, through our Coalition for Personal Freedom, I led training sessions for activists to enable them to take on the religious radicals. In those sessions I described how the Bible can support the message of a loving, caring God who created all people in the Divine image.

As our congregation grew, AIDS was decimating our community. In the first years of my rabbinate, I officiated at countless funerals and spent most of my day driving from hospital to hospital to visit the sick and dying. I would make the circuit between hospitals across the vast landscape of Los Angeles. The largest Jewish hospital had not yet created an immune-suppressed floor. The Jewish chaplain on staff would not visit Jewish AIDS patients. Back then, a diagnosis of AIDS seemed a certain death sentence. Many died. I felt, and still feel, as if I walked on a march with the dead. I still remember their names and I recite kaddish for them. Each time I visit a local cemetery, I visit the graves of those who died from this plague. Some, I know, haven't been visited since their funerals.

AIDS hasn't gone away, but it is different now. We do know more about the disease and manage it differently. People still get sick and die of complications of AIDS, but not in the sheer numbers of those years. No wonder we felt damaged. We were. We lost a great part of ourselves. Yet in many ways the AIDS epidemic helped us translate the humanity in our lesbian and gay lives to the nongay world. We were not demons and monsters that prey on children, but real human beings who belonged to families. We had mothers and fathers and siblings. We had lovers and dear friends who nursed us and cared for us and mourned for us. We showed ourselves that compassion was a part of our own makeup. We were able to defy the myths about ourselves that even we had sometimes come to believe.

While the horror and reminders of AIDS is still with me daily, there are many lessons I have learned from my friends with HIV and from the course of the epidemic itself. Perhaps the greatest lesson is the wisdom of Judaism that teaches us to visit the sick, accompany the dead, care for the living, and above all to choose life. The AIDS crisis, even in our brokenness, brought about completeness and sometimes a reconciliation between family members and even sometimes between gays and God.

Some remained angry and filled with rage at a God who inflicts such suffering. At times, I too was angry, but my own spiritual practices helped me through this difficult time. As other lesbians and gay men turned to spiritual questions to look for comfort and balance in their lives, I found kindred spirits. I am fortunate that I have been able to study with them and to point them toward the Torah that provides us with a sense of awe and speaks of covenantal love. It is this search and study that continues to teach me about the positive power of integration of my spirituality and sexuality. This foundation allows me to challenge those who would continue to exclude me or other gays and lesbians, Jew and non-Jew alike, from the religious traditions that are our inheritance.

In the now more than eleven years since my ordination and in the beginning of my service to our community, I have seen our politics grow and change. I believe that my participation in a variety of political and justice demonstrations has been an expression of my spirituality and my belief in tikkun olam. I have participated in radical ACT-UP demonstrations, as well as the spontaneous marches and vigils that took place when California's then governor Pete Wilson vetoed at the last moment a statewide bill that would have provided protection from discrimination in housing. I have spoken at rallies protesting DOMA (the Defense of Marriage Act), on the streets of West Hollywood, and participated in town hall meetings on gay and lesbian marriage. I have been arrested during protests against AIDS funding cuts, and worked with police to identify the attackers of lesbian and gay youth. I have worked with Russian immigrants in West Hollywood to decrease their homophobia and have listened to many gay candidates running for office. I have blessed busloads of protesters off to the state capital, Sacramento, and have marched on Washington.

All of these issues: funding for AIDS, marriage, protection from job discrimination, the freedom to associate, adoption, and school board sex education curricula, protecting the worker and the stranger in our midst, caring for the dying and bereaved, concern for our environment, comforting and visiting the sick, issues of welfare reform and poverty, all are matters of justice. I believe my involvement in political and social issues, from women's rights to immigrant rights, has brought Torah alive. For me, these issues are not mere politics but issues of the spirit and issues of chayim, life. These are the ways that my spirituality is realized. Social justice has become the foundation of the congregation I helped found in West Hollywood, Congregation Kol Ami. I believe that the challenge for Judaism in the future is to heed this call for righteousness extended to all people.

My belief in the integration of spirituality and sexuality also led me to believe that while there would always be a need for gay-only groups, the real challenge for me would be to continue to try to bring reconciliation between gays and nongays. I also strongly believed that it was important to throw off the shackles of internalized homophobia. Thus in the spring of 1992, I joined with a small group of other people to create Kol Ami. With our strong commitment to social justice and our belief that we must reach beyond our gay ghetto, we formed a new kind of synagogue, one that would indeed celebrate gay and lesbian life but would seek out our nongay family and friends who simply couldn't imagine their lives without us. We wanted to create a congregation that was diverse and presented a vision that would include heterosexuals and gay and lesbian people together. We wanted to create a community that would be there in the next generation for our children, for the children we were birthing and adopting, and for the children who would one day come out as lesbians or gay men.

Our death experiences during the height of the AIDS crisis and our advances in reducing discrimination against gays and lesbians around the country helped to bring about a baby boom in the gay and lesbian community. Lesbians and gay men are having and adopting children. It is no surprise to me that once again Jewish lesbians and gay men are very much a part of the gay parenting movement. Jews who grew up with an emphasis on family life now wanted to create their own families. They often turn to the synagogue as a place of support during the challenges of adoption or pregnancy, as well as after the children are born. At our congregation, we hold family services once a month and are not too many years away from building a religious school. It is a relief to be involved in as many baby namings as funerals. The joy I get from our son, Benjamin, adds to my own understanding of the challenges yet to come.

My Reform Jewish upbringing provided the foundation for my social justice work in the lesbian and gay community. Throughout these years politics and spirituality have been intertwined for me because of the Jewish view of justice. One of the most important lessons for me about integration and wholeness has come through the continuing struggle for equality and civil rights for lesbians and gay men. I guess I have learned that you indeed can be Jewish and gay and even a rabbi and a lesbian at the same time.

Lesbians and gay men have much to teach our Jewish community. They have much to teach about the meaning of family at a time when the Jewish community is in flux and when Jewish families, like other American families, are in turmoil. Jewish gays and lesbians serve as a reminder to the Jewish community that oppression still exists, even in our own communal midst. My work and my commitment will continue because lesbians and gay men have yet to know full equality in society at large and in the Jewish community. I hope my work has helped us find a better place to be seen and heard.

Working with Jews "at the Margins" and on Campus

Part IV

Chapter 13

On Being a Rabbi at the Margins

REBECCA T. ALPERT

MOST RABBIS ARE KNOWN by some defining characteristic. For some, it's as simple as geography, as in the Lubavitcher rebbe. Others come to be known by some dimension of their personality, not unlike the seven dwarfs—the grumpy rabbi, and so on. For some, it's a physical characteristic—the large rabbi, the short rabbi. For still others, it's an identity they have—women rabbis, lesbian rabbis, black rabbis come under this rubric. For many, their defining characteristic is their passion for something—the dancing rabbi, the meditation rabbi, the social justice rabbi. At this time in my life, my rabbinate is characterized not so much by who or what I am, but by where I am: I see myself, and I think others see me as well, as a rabbi at the margins. To me, the margin is a fine place from which to be a part of, as well as apart from, the Jewish people.

Looking at the World from Different Perspectives

I have been aware for a long time of the significance of perspective. When I was in high school, reading the works of Martin Buber completely changed my life. Buber's psychological recasting of Hasidic tales is crucial to my understanding of how important perspective is, and of how each of us sees the world from a different one. Buber tells the story of the Hasid who searches around the world for buried treasure, only to discover it in his own home. The story can be mined for many lessons, but Buber calls it "The Place Where One Stands." This was my first realization of how an individual's perspective determines her or his worldview. Things look different depending on where you are.

This insight came to me in a more complex way in my adulthood through the teachings of feminism. Feminists focus on the politics of perspective. Where you stand determines both how you see things and how you are seen by others. Women, feminists suggest, have a particular standpoint. Kept outside the circles of patriarchal power, women have a different view of the world, a view from the margins. This view gives them a particular way of seeing reality, but the reality they see is often ignored. Women of color, lesbians, Jewish and Muslim women, women with disabilities, and working-class women gave the argument nuances, suggesting that there were multiple ways in which people stood at the margins, and therefore multiple vantage points from which to view the world, and multiple ways in which their insights were not taken seriously by those at the center. One of the goals of the feminist and other liberation movements of the seventies and eighties was to shift the balance so that marginal perspectives would at least receive public attention and, more significantly, the center itself would change and incorporate their vision as well.

In many ways, those liberation movements succeeded. Women's viewpoints are now taken seriously, and women's voices have been included at the centers of power. This has certainly proven true in the Jewish community. Although the situation is far from perfect (women really don't hold significant positions of power in Jewish circles; issues like domestic violence and reproductive freedom are not at the top of the Jewish agenda), it certainly can no longer be said that women hold the same marginal place in Jewish life they held two decades ago when I entered the rabbinate. Why, then, do I find myself at the margins today?

The World from the Center

In truth, I did not always see myself as a rabbi on the margins. My perspective was that of Buber's Hasid after his return from the journey: I stood at the center of my world. Raised in Brooklyn, New York, I grew up with the view that Jews were everywhere. I never imagined that we comprised under 3 percent of the population of the United States—Jewish institutions, people, and products were wherever I looked. Public schools closed on Sukkot and Simchat Torah. Local politicians were Jews, and so was Sandy Koufax of my beloved Brooklyn Dodgers. It was not until I went to college that I discovered there were people who had never met a Jew and others who were openly anti-Semitic. I came from a perspective in which Jewish life was clearly at the center. So it made sense to me that when I became a rabbi I would take a position in the center of the Jewish community.

Of course, there was much evidence to the contrary in my life. I went to graduate school at the same time as I was attending rabbinical school, and noticed for the first time how rarely Jewish topics came up in the course of secular study. I was among the first six women in Jewish history to attend rabbinical school, and certainly noticed that I was not in the majority in any of my classes, which, after I had attended a women's college, was a bit of a shock. And I chose to attend the Reconstructionist Rabbinical College (RRC), which was small and new and was considered marginal by the majority of the Jewish community. Yet I never defined myself as marginal in those days. If anything, I viewed those in the Jewish community who opposed the Reconstructionist movement or women rabbis as peripheral to the future of the Jewish people as I understood it. I was convinced that Jewish feminists would succeed in making women's issues and perspectives part of the center of Jewish life. And I was sure that Jewish history would also become less marginal to the broader educational framework in American schools. After I graduated from rabbinical school and completed my doctorate, I became the dean of students and taught at RRC. During those years, I also functioned as a spokesperson to new congregations, wrote articles, and coauthored a book about Reconstructionism. I saw myself as central to this movement that nourished me. I lived at the center of a self-contained universe, feeling very much part of an important enterprise in Jewish life. That was the place where I stood.

Moving toward the Margins

What changed all that was coming to terms with the fact that I had been living with a lie. As I saw it, my status at the center of Reconstructionist Jewish life was predicated on my being heterosexual. It is certainly the case that had I announced in my 1971 application to rabbinical school that I was more attracted sexually to women, I would not have been accepted. But I had lived for most of my life with the knowledge that although I could form close relationships with men, my deepest erotic attractions were toward women. I did everything I could to avoid that part of myself, from self-deception to psychotherapy to heterosexual marriage to becoming a rabbi.

But my strategies failed. I thought involvement in the Jewish community would protect me from dealing with the issue of my sexual orientation, assuming that one couldn't be both a lesbian and a rabbi. It was my intention to avoid lesbianism through my connections to Jewish life. It worked for a while. No one raised the issue of homosexuality in the Jewish world at all. When I spoke about the issue at a synagogue in the 1970s as a part of a series on Jewish ethics, it seemed theoretical to most of the congregants, who had never met anyone who identified as gay or lesbian. But things were shifting. In 1979 an openly gay man applied for admission to RRC. I was the one dissenting voice in the faculty decision not to admit him. But I was afraid to speak out, knowing that publicly supporting gay rights in the Jewish community would change my life drastically and put me at risk. It was true in those days, and is true even today, that people who take a strong interest in gay issues wind up suspected of being gay themselves. At the same time I listened to the stories of the closeted gay students then enrolled at the school. Their presence also served as a reminder about how painful it was for them and for me to be living a lie.

Being part of the courageous decision of the rabbinical school faculty in 1984 to begin admitting openly gay students was a turning point for me. When several openly lesbian students appeared at RRC, my world began to unravel. I saw others identifying as gay and lesbian and becoming rabbis, forming what were then secret organizations, finding ways to be public. And I knew I was one of them. I left my marriage and began the process of coming out, of identifying as a lesbian. These actions were crucial to my sense of self and my well-being. But this process changed my perception of where I stood in the Jewish world, and even in the world of Reconstructionism.

Because I was in such a visible and important role, the college's leadership at the time was concerned that my coming out could have made the movement vulnerable to attack. By 1987 there was already an openly gay faculty member. RRC was the only place openly gay and lesbian students could apply at that time. (Although Hebrew Union College-Jewish Institute of Religion, the Reform rabbinical school, had many closeted gay and lesbian students and would change its policy within a few years, RRC was then the only place to be out.) While today being gay or lesbian would be considered unremarkable either as a student, staff, or faculty member at RRC, in the early years of the open admissions policy the implications for inclusivity had not been fully worked out. The senior college leadership at that time made it clear that I could not come out publicly either in writing or to the Reconstructionist community. It became increasingly obvious that I could no longer serve effectively as the dean of students. It was time for me to move from the center and to reinvent myself as a rabbi on the margins.

It is reasonable to wonder why if being a Jew, a woman, and a Reconstructionist rabbi did not deter me from seeing myself at the center of the Jewish community, why being a lesbian was different. My upbringing as a liberal Jew in Brooklyn in the fifties and sixties, and participating in the feminist revolution in the seventies, made my role as a Reconstructionist woman rabbi a valued one. But being openly gay was another story. It might be courageous, it might be important for me psychologically and morally, but it would diminish my ability to serve. I did not want my defining characteristic to be "lesbian," which at the time was inevitable. I had worked too hard as a feminist, a Reconstructionist, and as a progressive Jew committed to social justice to be perceived in that way.

But despite what I knew I would lose, ultimately I felt that I had no choice in the matter. My life depended on it. And the chance I took was well worth the risk. I discovered that the view from the margins suited me fine. I found a place from which to say things I never could have said as a spokesperson for the center. And I had a chance to work with people who wanted to connect to being Jewish, but who also saw themselves as marginal to the Jewish community.

Working as a Lesbian Rabbi on the Margins

After I left my position at RRC, I chose not to look for work in the Jewish community. In the mid-eighties there was no place as welcoming for lesbians as the Reconstructionist movement. I would have been typecast there, and congregations were not entirely ready for the change. I did get a chance to serve as a rabbi for the High Holidays, but the congregation was really concerned that I would use the position as a platform to talk about lesbian and gay rights. They were very relieved that I didn't raise the issue until my third year there. And at that point they and I wondered whether they ever really got to know me. But elsewhere it could only have been worse, as gay and lesbian rabbis were still losing their jobs.

I welcomed the opportunity to try out a new vantage point. I redefined my rabbinate as moving from center to margin and not working professionally in the Jewish community. In this move, I experienced a strong sense of freedom from the constraints of working in the Jewish world. But I never saw myself as an outsider, only as someone who had changed her perspective.

This was the difference: I would compare Jewish life to a page of Talmud. In the center, we find the text of Mishnah and Gemara. But in the margins we find the commentary of later thinkers and scholars. The commentary explains the text, and in the process gives new perspective to the meaning. It stands apart from the text, but it is a part of what is going on there, contributing to the overall meaning. That is how I see my role as a marginal rabbi. I am no longer in the center, but I am still on the page, and can provide a valuable perspective from which to view what is going on.

Over the next years I defined my new role. Part of that redefinition meant finding ways to integrate my Jewish and lesbian identities. I helped to found a congregation that, although comprised of mostly heterosexuals, was truly welcoming to gay men and lesbians. I gave sermons and taught adult education classes about lesbians in Judaism. I performed numerous lesbian commitment ceremonies. I began to write about Jewish lesbian issues: dealing with difficult biblical texts, creating ceremonies for coming out, thinking through gay marriage and inventing a gay awareness week. These essays culminated in a book about how Jewish lesbians can transform Judaism. That publication gave me opportunities to speak about those insights in many different Jewish contexts, although most Jewish book fairs declined to invite me, and many Jewish bookstores chose not to put my book on the shelves.

My freedom as a lesbian also made me free in other ways. I felt more courage to criticize Israeli policies, and to work for peace with the Palestinians. I began to get involved in causes that were not of great concern to the Jewish community, but in which it mattered to other religious leaders to have a Jewish presence. I worked with interfaith groups supporting an end to the conflicts in Central America and promoting democracy in Haiti; I spoke out publicly against the death penalty, and in favor of abortion rights. I did all of this as a rabbi. There is no doubt in my mind that I was invited to speak at rallies, visit elected officials, and publish articles as much because of my status as a rabbi as on my personal abilities.

Working with the "Unaffiliated"

I also began to serve a population the organized Jewish community likes to call "the unaffiliated." These are people who may identify strongly as Jews, contribute to Jewish causes, observe at least some Jewish holidays, but do not belong officially to the Jewish community by virtue of synagogue membership. This group accounts for about half of the Jews in the United States today.

While their needs for a rabbi are sporadic, like other Jews they want a rabbi to participate in their life cycle events: weddings and commitment ceremonies, baby namings, funerals and occasional b'nai mitzvah ceremonies, conversions and divorces. I have never advertised my services to this population—there are unscrupulous rabbis who make nice livings doing that sort of thing—but they find me nonetheless. I hear from them through friends, through work, through networks of gay and lesbian Jews. They come to me because they are not religious or spiritual, or because they are not interested in communal involvement and don't want to join synagogues or chavurot. They come because they are gay or because one of them is not Jewish or has disabilities or because for whatever reason they think they will not be welcome in the organized Jewish community. They are often more comfortable with me because I am a lesbian. They see me as one who, by virtue of that identity, lives at the margins of Jewish life, as they do themselves. It is a perspective to which they can relate.

Working with this population has been deeply rewarding for me. I have had the great rabbinic privilege of seeing some of them through multiple events and across generations. Sometimes they go on to greater contact in the Jewish community; sometimes they do not. I do make them aware that at least in a Reconstructionist setting they may find a community that welcomes them. But my goal has not been to convert them; I don't do outreach. If I worked for the Jewish community I would experience pressure to bring them in. I want the people I work with to be able to choose how much contact they want to have with Judaism beyond their connection to me. I understand and respect their perspective on the margins, their lack of interest in belonging to a group as an expression of being Jewish. Synagogue life is not for everyone. This freedom is another advantage of my position.

Coming out as a lesbian was the point of departure for my new rabbinic role. I would never have found the courage to remake my rabbinate without finding the courage to come out as a lesbian. I have incorporated my lesbian identity into my rabbinate, but I have also gone beyond it to a new location as a rabbi on the margins. Many lesbians have had the opportunity in recent years to choose a different path, to become central to the larger Jewish enterprise. Their lesbianism for them is much like what my Reconstructionist and feminist identities have been for me. So it is not the lesbian identity itself, but the perspective it brought to me that made the difference in bringing me to where I stand today.

Chapter 14   My Piece of Truth

JULIE GREENBERG

Many years ago, I sat at the "Medieval Thought" seminar table, knowing that this was the day for announcing my big news. Around the table were my fellow rabbinical students, people with whom I had studied intensely for three years and would study with for three more years. Then we would be colleagues, rabbis, for the rest of our lives. These were not people I wanted to hurt or offend, yet I knew some of them would be shocked and troubled by my joyful announcement.[1]

Gladly would I have avoided telling these folks my precious and wondrous news, knowing that they had no context whatsoever from which to understand a single, never-married, lesbian rabbinical student intentionally getting pregnant. But unfortunately pregnancy isn't so easy to hide. I had agonized over how and whether to share my story. Now, in my fourth month, the secret couldn't be contained much longer.

I wondered whether my life experience, my understanding, would be embraced by anyone else there. In my Jewish women's community I was surrounded by love and support: Susan altered clothes into maternity fashions; Merle prescribed raspberry tea and brought ice cream; Joanna promised to pay for child care when I needed it, she and Moon and Elana would be at the birth, Felice was already hunting for the right teddy bear for the baby. My mother and sisters were solidly supportive, and my father rose to the occasion after an initial panic. Just months before, I had helped plan a conference that brought together colleagues who I knew would rejoice at hearing my news.

In the fall of 1986 I helped organize a top-secret, national Jewish conference. The public was not to know the date, location, or content of the conference even though its attendees would be rabbis, cantors, Jewish educators, and other professionals working for the Jewish community. The thirty-two individuals who ultimately attended the conference came from a broad spectrum of the organized Jewish world. We were all gay, lesbian, or bisexual.

Although we had a range of Jewish religious identities and practices, one thing we all shared was the intense homophobia we faced in our professional lives. At that time there was not a single "out" gay or lesbian rabbi in a mainstream congregation. Intense and pervasive job discrimination, including periodic witch-hunts against suspected gay or lesbian leaders, ensured that dedicated Jewish communal workers lived in fear and conformity. By gathering together for purposes of support and strategy, we hoped to change the situation. We hoped to open Jewish communities to the full, enriching reality of diversity.

Change was already happening at lightning speed in the rabbinical school that I attended. When I had applied to the college in 1982 there was one closeted upper-level student and a closeted lesbian faculty member. I was coming from an activist milieu in Berkeley, California, where I had been living for a few years after college. With a group of friends I had organized Dyke Shabbos, which collected unaffiliated Jewish seekers, many of whom had been wounded by the Jewish community, for celebration, study, and life cycle ritual. The experience of running Dyke Shabbos was so inspiring that all of its early leaders went on into advanced Jewish study and organizing within the next few years.

When I applied to rabbinical school I considered whether to come out as a lesbian. I knew that if I were asked directly in my interview, honesty would mean certain rejection, but I was not willing to lie about who I was. What a relief that the interviewers asked me what they probably considered to be a screening question:

"Do you expect to have a family?"

"Yes," I answered honestly, even though I knew that their concept of a family required a husband, while mine did not.

I was accepted.

In the following years, a small group of us—mostly lesbian activists and our feminist allies—worked bravely to challenge heterosexist assumptions in the Jewish world. In 1985 at the P'nai Or Kallah, an international gathering of Jewish Renewal folks from all branches of Jewish life, some of us held the first-ever Jewish coming-out ceremony. During the Torah service, gays, lesbians, bisexuals, and allies publicly pinned on pink triangles, pledging to act in the name of our tradition to end the hostility against loving.

By 1986 the Rabbinical College had instituted a historic nondiscrimination policy stating that applicants and students would not be discriminated against on the basis of sexual orientation. While almost none of the deep educational work that would truly erode homophobia had been done yet (in fact, even after passing the new, inclusive policy, the college administration was not willing to publish it), nevertheless we were extremely proud of the hard-won principle that gay and lesbian Jews should have equal opportunity to prepare for the rabbinate.

As we organized our national gathering, eventually known as Ameinu, we intended to take the process of education and change one step beyond a mere legalistic tolerance of gay and lesbian people. We wanted our people to be welcomed and recognized as leaders in the Jewish community. When the conference was being planned, its working name was Aron HaKodesh (the Holy Closet), which in Hebrew creates a play on words; "aron hakodesh" is also the name of the cabinet that holds the Torah in a central place in every synagogue. A heated discussion about the name of the gathering resulted in a new name, Ameinu (Our People), because as one rabbi insisted, "I refuse to be part of any closet. A closet can't be holy."

To raise money for the conference we sent out a fund-raising letter that called on the whole of the RRC community:

> As the only rabbinical school that has a non-discriminatory
> policy toward gay and lesbian students, RRC has taken an
> important step in confronting discrimination and prejudice
> within the Jewish community. But this is just a first step. Much
> more needs to be done. Issues concerning the professional
> *futures* of our lesbian and gay students now arise. . . . The issues

which will be addressed at this conference *are of concern to the WHOLE Jewish community, regardless of personal orientation or lifestyle*. Matters of equality, justice and freedom transcend the boundaries of "gay and straight"—and go to the core of our work in the Jewish community. . . . Please support our efforts. (Letter dated Nov. 10, 1986)

A substantial response from the college community helped fund three students to participate in Ameinu. We met at a Christian retreat center in Southern California because we felt that it was too dangerous to meet in a Jewish space: If the gathering became public there was the real danger of people being thrown out of rabbinical school, losing jobs, scholarships, and colleagues, and of being banned from work in the Jewish community.

Ameinu represented connection and promise, an opportunity to share stories, laugh together, address common concerns. We also enlightened each other because there was, of course, enormous diversity within our group. The gay men raised my awareness of the AIDS crisis, which was barely brushing the nation's consciousness at that time. The Conservative and Orthodox participants gamely joined in an experiential feminist session that I led, experimenting with colorful ribbons in place of tefillin (as we were bedecked in our bright garlands, giving each other blessings in dyads, the Sisters who ran the Christian conference center walked by; I remember wondering what they thought about Judaism!) Questions of language were also discussed as the word "queer" offered a broader identity, one that I have come to appreciate and claim, than one based simply on the status of one's sexual orientation.

Ameinu conferences were organized three years in a row: the first in Southern California, the second in the Philadelphia area, and the final meeting in Toronto. Each year the networking, empowerment, and recognition strengthened individuals who were working in isolation against enormous oppression. One Conservative rabbi was on a commission about homosexuality, serving as a supposedly straight man studying the issue. An Orthodox rabbi who had been outed was allowed to continue serving his congregation as long as he promised to remain celibate. All of us were told that we damaged society by undermining the family, yet when we tried to build families through same-sex marriage and baby-making, we were told we damaged society by being in families.

After three years, we decided to continue the work in our own denominations for change was happening at the grass-roots level, and we felt that our energy was needed there.

During the time before and after the Ameinu conference, I was beginning to come out about being pregnant. One of my professors, a dedicated Jewish mentor who only wished his students would follow in his footsteps, called me into his office to say, "You've got to help me with this pregnancy."

"I've always felt family was important," I responded.

"Well, I hope you aren't going to make a political statement out of this."

"Lesbian lives aren't necessarily going to look exactly like heterosexual lives," I tried to explain.

"You could be blacklisted," he warned in a well-meaning way. "It could be that you never find a job in the Jewish world. You can't be political about this."

"I'm not trying to be political. I'm just trying to make a family. It's just that it is kind of political, isn't it, in this context? It's the heterosexism that makes it political." He and I never did reach a good understanding.

The board of the congregation where I worked devoted most of one board meeting to a discussion of whether to fire me for being pregnant. They finally concluded that I was an excellent educator, having built their school from the ground up into a thriving, successful endeavor, and "we hired her to be an educator, so we won't fire her."

One parent, who one week earlier had filled out a questionnaire raving about the wonderful Hebrew school that I ran, rebuked me by saying, "I can understand how an ordinary person could be in this situation. But you are supposed to be a moral and religious leader!"

"I am a moral and religious leader," I said.

In the end the congregation rallied and presented me with a stroller as a new-baby gift. Looking back, I think I had a lot to learn about fitting into, let alone leading, a mainstream suburban congregation, and its members had a lot of growing to do to embrace me. Considering everything, we really didn't do too badly with our mutual learning curve.

The thing I think most people didn't understand was that including queer people in the rabbinate meant opening up to new wisdom that would come from our life experience. In my life as a woman and as a lesbian, during my first decade of serving as a rabbi, my perspective on Jewish issues has not been the same as that of the heterosexual mainstream. In any system there is a center and an edge; I see things from the vantage point of the edge. The margin is where I feel at home. As Jews have been marginal throughout history in terms of the dominant society, I relate well to the "Jews" of the Jewish community, that is to the marginal ones: same-sex couples, interfaith couples, small-town Jews, uneducated Jews, diverse family-builders. My ministry has been to these people.

Just as sometimes the edge becomes the center, I think in some ways my practices and beliefs augur the future norms of Judaism. Then there will have to be a new edge. If we are truly an evolving religious civilization, we can't always do the same old same old—or how will we evolve? There has to be some creative tension, some dynamic disagreement, some experimentation in response to the stuck places.

So, for instance, I, along with a handful of colleagues, was one of the first rabbis ever in history to perform weddings for same-sex couples. As society evolves, I hope this won't seem very radical to many younger people reading this. But coming from where we were coming, this was radical. Most of us grew up never hearing the words "gay" or "lesbian" mentioned. Ever. We never saw public images of same-sex couples loving each other, let alone being celebrated. For me to use the power of the rabbinate, standing under the chuppah in my formal white rabbinic robe, draped by the ritual prayer shawl, facing a congregation of family and friends and say, "We are here today to celebrate the creation of a new lesbian (or gay) family,"—that is momentous.

These ceremonies are life-changing experiences; they are an example of how ritual can create social change. They work because they take place on strong moral ground—it is right for people to sanctify their love in the context of a committed relationship. They work because they enact a vision of justice. Just as Susan B. Anthony went to the ballot box to vote before there was any law allowing her to vote, we create reality by sanctifying same-sex relationships even in lieu of legal privileges for the couple. These rites help create rights.

Besides working with same-sex couples I also work with many interfaith couples and with other non-Jewish clergy. The kinds of people I work with and the kinds of ceremonies I do are controversial in the organized Jewish world. Most rabbis won't marry an interfaith couple, and only one or two other rabbis I know will stand with a non-Jewish clergyperson in a ritual role. There's a connection between my lesbian perspective and my commitment to working with this disenfranchised population. I don't do this work without questions. I ask: How can we make Judaism welcoming, meaningful, relevant so that people will want to be part of it? How can interfaith families enrich Judaism? I don't think we have the answers yet but an important part of my rabbinate has been devoted to exploring these questions through my work with the Jewish Renewal Life Center.

The Jewish Renewal Life Center was a dream born of necessity. By the time I finished rabbinical school, I had a two-year-old daughter and was pregnant with my second child. When I applied to education positions within a grand radius of my home, despite a stellar résumé of classwork, experience, and publications, no one would hire me. Congregations were on the alert for deviant rabbis, because the word was out that RRC was now prepared to graduate lesbian and gay leaders. Each congregation wanted to make sure that it did not end up with such a leader. Their procedures were somewhat subtle. The search committee chair would say, "Why don't you bring your husband to dinner before the interview?"

Realizing that there was no job for me, I decided to take the leap into founding a project that I had fantasized about ever since I had been a part of a social change group called Movement for a New Society (MNS), which was a network of activists committed to making a better world through nonviolent organizing. Many of its founders had come of age in the civil rights and antiwar movements. They wanted a way to live the revolution, to live in a way that respected the earth and each other and that liberated energy for doing good work in the world. Thus they created a life center where people from all backgrounds lived in community, sharing child care, cooking, housework, and political projects. The early creators of MNS were mostly radical Quakers and Catholics. I had dreamed of building a life center within the Jewish world where people could work together to nourish the heart while healing the world.

Born in 1990, the Jewish Renewal Life Center attracts an extraordinary group of seekers each year for training in Jewish spiritual community-building. Our graduates move on to build vibrant, inclusive Jewish communities around the world. In my own little way I hope I am leaving my children the legacy of a Judaism that will be more alive, authentic, and welcoming. This legacy has come to be because all along the way I was fortunate enough to be part of an upsurge of Jewish lesbian and gay liberation throughout the land. My own experience took place in the context of an exhilarating and revolutionary fifteen-year period in which we succeeded in putting issues of respect for diversity on the national agenda. There is still a tremendous amount of work to be done before every Jewish community respects and includes a variety of sexual identities, life choices, and family structures. But every step along the way matters.

Years ago, as my "Medieval Thought" seminar came to a close, I faced my peers, almost as if they were a rabbinic court sitting around the table. I drew a deep breath and offered my news. "For many years I've been planning a family," I said, "and now I am happy to announce that I'm expecting a baby." After a moment of stunned silence a round of "mazal tov"s, some feeble, some whole-hearted, resounded around the table. Together we continued a journey of understanding that has opened the parameters of what is called normal. These days there are openly identified gay and lesbian rabbinical students, rabbis, parents, and Jewish leaders. These days it is almost not news for a single, unmarried, lesbian woman to become a mom.

Looking back over the journey, I have a number of reflections. When I was a rabbinical student I felt sad that I couldn't please my teachers the same way that a heterosexual male traditional rabbinical student could please them. It gave the teachers joy to raise up another generation in their own image, an image I could never fulfill. When I was a young rabbi in a very heterosexual, suburban congregation, I felt sad that my understandings and my ways were troubling to the folks; they feared me. When I was a more experienced rabbi establishing my own practices and standards, I felt sad that my actions caused pain to leaders of my rabbinic association, that I was often seen and treated as a traitor.

But when I look at the good that has come from my being who I am—the mind-stretching opening up of the Jewish community, the space made for people, dialogue, ideas that wouldn't have been welcome, I see myself as a gift to the Jewish community. Now, in the middle of whatever gut-wrenching battle is going on in the synagogue or in the rabbinic association, when I'm saying, "Oh God, does it have to be me again who organizes the community because the board just fired the gay youth director for being gay?" I remember that we are all standing at Sinai together and my piece of the truth can't be left out. For the future of Judaism, for the sake of us all, my piece of the truth, along with yours, is essential. Each one of us a gift, each one of us a speaker of truth. Together, we enrich the Jewish world.

Note

1. Thank you to all the allies and friends, of various different sexual identities, without whom this life and this work would not be possible: Felice Yeskel, Jane Litman, Merle Berman, Joanna Katz, Jeff Roth, Susan Saxe, Moon Smith, Arthur Waskow, Phyllis Berman, Leila Berner, Marcia Prager, Rebecca Alpert, and Drorah Setel.

Chapter 15

My Language Is My Country

SHIRLEY IDELSON

WHEN I WAS A kid, I was a T-O-M-B-O-Y. I know that because my parents and my grandparents used to spell out words to each other when they didn't want me to understand. One time when we were all in the living room and I was sitting in the middle of the floor playing, my grandmother announced to everyone, "Shirley's a T-O-M-B-O-Y." I'd learned to spell by then, so I jumped up and said, "I am not a tomboy." I was a tomboy and I knew it, but I needed to resist this exclusionary practice of adults speaking secrets right in front of me. That was the last time they used that spelling trick, but my grandmother, whom I adored, would still exclude me from conversation whenever she felt like it by speaking in Yiddish to my mother. My mother understands Yiddish, although she cannot speak it fluently; I don't even understand it.

When I was a little older, the story of the founding of the State of Israel captured my imagination. Countless nights I'd spend lying on the floor in my room with the lights out listening to Arik Einstein singing "Eretz Yisrael hayshanah vhatovah" (Good Old Land of Israel) dreaming—I should say fantasizing—about the chalutzim draining the swamps in Palestine in the 1920s. I'd seen pictures of the women on those kibbutzim, the ones who worked all day and then sang and danced all night. They were strong and they were beautiful and I really think I would have done anything to be one of them. But it was the 1970s, not the 1920s,

190

and I was stuck in Newton, Massachusetts. So, since I couldn't yet be a part of that enterprise called the Jewish state, I used my imagination to carve out a territory of my own. I kept a journal all in Hebrew, which no one in my family could understand, and I immersed myself in study not only of Hebrew but also of Jewish history and literature, classical and contemporary. The territory of language and study that I carved out for myself when I was sixteen is in many ways the place where I dwell today, having embraced the concept of exile as a rabbi—a lesbian rabbi—and in that sense part of a different group of chalutzim.

Now when I look back at this sixteen-year-old who decided she had a right to claim the land of Israel as her own, I understand something I knew only subconsciously then. Ever since I was a little tomboy I wanted to be strong and powerful, and Zionist ideology had me convinced that land equals strength and power. Unable to actually live the physical reality of which I dreamed, through the use of language and study I created a place in my imagination where I could be strong. In a way, although I wasn't really aware of this, that was a very Jewish thing to do. For centuries, when Jews were landless and stateless, Jewish communities constructed language and study and text as territory to be conquered and controlled, to be passed on as an inheritance through the generations. Following in that tradition, as a senior in college, I decided to become a rabbi.

Traditionally, study of Jewish text has centered around teaching and expanding Jewish law. For me, as a first-year rabbinic student, learning the halachic system was integrally connected to questions I had about how I wanted to live a Jewish life. I found halachah compelling because it offered the possibility of living an ordered life, within a system proven and tested through time. Its practitioners, men and women alike, seemed strong—not unlike the chalutzim of my childhood dreams. Their lives were rooted in tradition, and their guiding principles and legally mandated practices gave them a map for how to live. Early in my rabbinic studies I spent a year studying in an Orthodox yeshiva in Jerusalem. I hoped my life and Orthodoxy might fit together.

But that year, while one side of me tried to live according to Jewish law, another side rebelled. Living in an Orthodox community, I saw how much power my male classmates gained from the halachic system. One weekend, we went to a West Bank settlement for a Shabbaton.

Friday night the mood was joyful as we entered the synagogue to welcome Shabbat. As the men took their seats facing the holy ark, we women were shuffled over to seats cordoned off by a hanging sheet, the mechitzah. We could barely hear the service, and could see even less. The next day, despite the yeshiva authorities' disapproval, a few of us conducted our own women's service. And I wondered . . . would my male classmates have been willing to sit behind that mechitzah? Would *they* submit to a system that denies them the honor of leading services, of blessing and reading from the Torah? Would they worship in a place where they are prohibited from saying central prayers without ten women present?

Had I been a man capable of enjoying the privileges of halachah, I might have become Orthodox. But I could not accept a system that privileges the other sex. I could not accept a system in which I could not participate as an equal among equals. I still wanted to be strong and powerful. I returned to rabbinical school in New York.

It was 1987, and AIDS activism was at its peak. ACT-UP and Queer Nation were demonstrating in the streets, and at Hebrew Union College we held debates. Is it acceptable to be a homosexual Jew? A reductive argument ensued between two ostensibly legitimate rabbinic stances—one claiming it is all right to be gay, and the other arguing homosexuality remains unacceptable. It was during these debates that I was finally willing to notice something about myself. I was, and always had been, afraid to make eye-contact with, talk about, or be near lesbians.

To confront that fear, I did what I knew how to do: I studied. More than anyone else, Adrienne Rich helped me understand my fear. I read "Diving Into the Wreck" and I leapt. I came out as a lesbian and a feminist.

More than I ever could have imagined, coming out brought me the strength and power I sought in Zionism—without the trappings of any state or institution. As a third-year rabbinical student, I regularly went to the Dutchess, a lesbian bar in Greenwich Village, and there I read Maimonides. From my table in the back corner of the dimly lit bar, I tried to focus on the text before me, occasionally peering at the patrons from the corner of my eye. Over time my eyes adjusted to the light. I saw a space controlled by lesbians, where no man could enter unaccompanied by a woman. The Dutchess became my beit midrash. My vision, once unable to include lesbians, focused clearly on the beautiful women clad in leather jackets, smoking cigarettes, dancing together. Meanwhile Maimonides beckoned from the page. Since I was not responding, I knew it was time to return to the library. I was a changed person.

My gay and lesbian classmates formed a group, and we announced ourselves to the community at Passover time, the season of liberation, with a flyer that said Hinenu—we are here. Married classmates, our allies, stuffed the mailboxes. The prevailing fear in Hinenu was that years of study would culminate in our being ostracized from a Jewish community unwilling to share pride in its gay and lesbian members. This, I decided, I could live with.

I knew I wanted to work on a college campus, and in my last year of rabbinical school I was offered two positions that interested me. One entailed working with a Hillel rabbi on a large state campus. I came out to that rabbi, wanting to know whether he could support me knowing I was gay. Absolutely, he said, adding just one caveat: "You know I would not feel comfortable having you and your partner in my home, in front of my *children*," he said. The other job offer was from Vassar College. Vassar did not agonize over my gay identity; to the contrary, the college administration offered unambivalent support. My choice was clear.

Working with college students, I get a glimpse of the future. A generation of Jews has grown up with lesbian, gay, and bisexual rabbis serving in their synagogues, on their college campuses, in hospitals, and in social justice organizations. Many in this generation proudly identify as queer. Some, still very young, have already fought courageous battles against homophobia in their families, schools, and jobs. They go into the world out, assuming they will be treated with dignity and respect in all their religious, political, and cultural milieus. Many continue the practice of constructing language, study, and text as territory to be explored and passed on to future generations. Some of these young queer Jews are headed for the rabbinate.

When I was a child, I could not imagine a woman rabbi—I never saw one until I was in rabbinical school. As a student at HUC-JIR, I knew of few out gay and lesbian rabbis, and it was unclear whether or not our small group would find a professional place in the Jewish world. But now it is clear a paradigm shift has taken place. What distinguishes this new generation from all those who came before are their assumptions— that *of course* women are rabbis, and *of course* rabbis can be queer.

Part V

Lesbian Rabbis and Conservative Judaism

Chapter 16

Saying No in the Name of a Higher Yes

BENAY LAPPE

THREE DAYS BEFORE ORDINATION, the dean of the rabbinical school called me into his office at nine P.M. and told me that an anonymous caller had phoned the seminary to inform them that I was a lesbian. He said that if I told him it was true, I would not be ordained. "What do you have to say?" he demanded.[1]

This was a scenario I had carefully planned for and had played out in my mind over the previous six years of rabbinical school. Just in case. I knew I could be called in at any moment and had rehearsed what would be my instantaneous response the way soldiers are trained to react in battle without having to think, to automatically do what is necessary to save their lives and the lives of their fellow soldiers. It is a kind of learned instinct, and one never knows whether it will actually stick until that moment when one is under attack. For me, that moment had arrived.

Just as that soldier's first instinct may be to respond to fear by getting the hell out of there, but whose life may depend on short-circuiting that gut reaction and instead fighting back—it was now time to see whether I would listen to that voice deep inside me that said, "Lying is wrong," or instead act in self-defense and lie in order to do what was right. I sat there in the frozen but eerily calm silence of the proverbial deer-in-the-headlights for what was at least a full minute as I mentally fast-forwarded through each of the possible responses I could have given and their resulting outcomes.

I never set out to be a rabbi. I was simply looking for God. I wish someone had told me that rabbinical school was the last place a Jew was likely to find God. But then again I probably wouldn't have listened. I had to find out for myself.

I figured every tradition had its Wise Men (I didn't know of any that had Wise Women—except maybe Native American—but I figured the principle would be the same in either case), its keepers of the tribe's wisdom. If anyone knew the Jewish way to God, I thought, it must be the wisdom-keepers of the Jewish tradition. And who were our wisdom-keepers? Rabbis! Well, OK, that's what I thought, anyhow. So I decided to go where rabbis went to learn whatever it is that rabbis know: rabbinical school. And that's what I did. (One thing I learned along the way, and most painfully and disappointingly so in the two years of fall-out after the dean's little interrogation, was that rabbis, as a whole, are no wiser than the rest of us—they just know more Jewish stuff, because that's what a rabbinic education is mostly about. And some rabbis turn that Jewish stuff into wisdom and some don't.)

I was born and raised in Skokie, Illinois, a predominantly Jewish suburb of Chicago. We considered ourselves Conservative although we might more accurately have been described as "unobservant Orthodox" (we knew what we were supposed to do, and though we didn't do it most of the time, at least we felt guilty about it).

I loved Hebrew school and going up on the bimah to drink the grape juice kiddush at Friday night services. But as I grew up and competing worldviews—feminism, gay rights, and American you-can't-tell-me-what-to-do-ism—entered the picture, I dismissed Judaism as irrelevant.

It wasn't so much that I ever actively rejected it; it just simply never came to mind when, at the age of twenty-two, while I was living in Japan for what would turn into seven years, I went in search of a spiritual path. I still felt proudly and deeply Jewish, went to shul on the high holidays, fasted on Yom Kippur, attended family seders, wouldn't think of eating chametz during Pesach, and lit Chanukah candles every year (always in the right order and in the right direction). Judaism had just never popped up on my mental radar screen as having anything to do with the spiritual endeavor, and so, when I went looking for a way to find

God, it never occurred to me to try the Jewish way, whatever that might have been.

I realized I was a lesbian at eighteen, in my sophomore year of college. As I had never personally known a gay man or lesbian (that I was aware of), it was a lonely and scary experience. But at nineteen I fell in love for the first time, with a woman, and realized that love is love, regardless of the gender of the ones doing the loving, and that I was going to be all right after all. In my early coming-out years of the late seventies and early eighties, I was blessed with lovers and close lesbian friends for whom being gay was so natural that I absorbed their ease with it all, and my early shame fell away as pride and a confident matter-of-factness took its place. I discovered a loving, exciting, and intellectually challenging gay subculture in which I remained immersed for the next ten years. I lived in a gay world, disregarding the institutions and assumptions of the straight world "out there." The larger world didn't belong to me, but that was OK—I was the citizen of a privileged, special world that provided constant proof in the form of the outside world's violence against us that it was *we* who "got it" and they whose behavior belied an obvious misjudgment.

This confidence in the rightness of my sexuality would prove indispensable when my lover at the time (who was bisexual and had been quite at home in the larger heterosexual world up until the time of our relationship) convinced me that the larger world really did belong to me, too, and that I was cheating myself and it by living only in the sheltered world of the gay and lesbian community. My first act in claiming my rightful place in the larger world would be to apply to the Jewish Theological Seminary.

I had gone to Japan after graduate school and encountered, for the first time in my life, sincere seekers of every sort—mostly Westerners born Protestant or Catholic or Jewish who were searching for God and following spiritual practices of one kind or another in traditions other than the ones they'd grown up in. These young people had, like me, found themselves far from home for any number of reasons—mostly sad, some mundane—and while they wandered in exile in a country in which they were profoundly "other," were moved to search for a kind of meaning that had eluded them in their own homelands, within their own families, or in their religions of birth.

This very Jewish paradigm of one who is called to leave home or is in exile for fear of his or her life and finds God in the wilderness did not occur to me then, as I did not even know my own Jewish story well enough to see how thoroughly I was typecast within it. Whatever I did know, I didn't dare imagine applied to me as a lesbian, so alienated did I feel from its message. Had I been able to see my own life within the mythic stories of my tradition, I might have been better able to navigate my way through, or at least feel less crazy, in my process of searching for God, for a sense of wholeness, meaning, and contentment in my life.

As I felt my own "otherness" as a caucasian lesbian woman in a male-dominated, fiercely heterosexual Japanese culture—and by no small accident living half a world away from my family, which was having a very hard time adjusting to the reality of having a lesbian in it—I realized that, like the seekers I saw around me, my own life's questions were in serious need of some new answers. I soon stopped laughing cynically at the word "spirituality" and before I knew it, was on a spiritual search of my own.

Buddhism—specifically Vipassana meditation—became my path and my practice. Buddhism was accessible, made sense, seemed true, presented no theological conflict and compelled no Jewishly forbidden behavior and, quite simply, just worked for me. Probably equally important, it had no Leviticus. Or, more accurately, its "Leviticus" was not my Leviticus, so it was easier for me to take the good and not be so personally hurt by the bad. I sat in cross-legged silence in Buddhist temples for several weeks each year, learned to see the world in Buddhist terms, meditated every morning and evening, and was, quite honestly, a perfectly happy Buddhist.

Until that pintele yid popped up—that little, often dormant Jewish consciousness that most Jews have (at least those raised with or who acquire on their own a strong Jewish consciousness). The more I meditated, the more aware I became of thoughts and emotions that might otherwise have gotten lost in the background noise of life. And slowly I began to sense my own discomfort at having "unfinished business" with my Jewishness. Here I was, a Jew, living as a Buddhist, having learned Buddhism with an adult mind, and having rejected Judaism, which I'd stopped learning at the age of thirteen! I was simply no longer comfortable with that arrangement. I realized I had to go back and learn about

Judaism with my adult mind, and give it the same chance I'd given Buddhism. I fully expected, even hoped, to confirm my suspicions: that Judaism was as simple-minded and juvenile as my recollections and current practice reflected. I would read a few books, I figured, put my mind at ease at having rightfully ignored such a "pediatric" religion, and return to being a Buddhist, but this time in good conscience.

I went to the rabbi of the synagogue in Tokyo, and told him my story, and he gave me a book I'd never heard of before: *Pirke Avot*. It was a tiny volume packed with the kind of accessible Zen-like wisdom I'd found in Buddhist writings, and I started to realize that the Jews might just be as smart as the Buddhists after all, and were, in fact, onto the same truths as the Buddhists. Then he gave me an anthology of essays written by rabbis of the various movements, including Reconstructionism, which I had never heard of. I then realized that the Judaism that I grew up with was only one of many authentic Judaisms, and that what I believed about God and the way the world worked did not make me a bad Jew, just a bad Orthodox Jew. I saw that the circle containing authentic Judaism was much bigger than I'd thought previously and that I actually fell quite squarely within it, and not at all way outside it, as I'd imagined.

All of a sudden, the prospect that I was actually still "a good Jew" drew me back into the Jewish game as a player who hadn't fouled out, and I was now ready to play even harder. I realized that although Buddhist truths were very easy to understand and accessible, Jewish truths were simply more deeply encoded in ritual and required extra work to decipher. But they were there!

My next experiment would be Shabbos, and though my lover at the time wasn't Jewish, she agreed that, one day a week, without exception, no matter what, no phone, no electricity, no money, no shopping, no trains, no work, an immaculately clean house, fresh clothes, a beautiful dinner, telling stories, reading, leisurely walks, singing and lovemaking—was a pretty good idea. The magic we felt from the moment we lit those first Shabbos candles taught me that God could indeed be found in what appeared, on the page, to be a restrictive, even oppressive ritual. I realized then and there that if Judaism could come up with something like shabbos, then it had to have come up with lots of *other* places where God would be just sitting and waiting, as God was in Shabbos. I knew I would never again be able to casually dismiss out of hand what appeared to be archaic texts or rituals. I had experienced God in what happened when the Shabbos that as a child I had learned about on the page was lived out. Who knew where other seemingly archaic texts would lead me?

After seven years of combining Vipassana meditation and Shabbos, bamboo sukkahs and Sanskrit chanting, I realized that when I did Jewish things I felt more Jewish, and when I felt more Jewish, I felt more whole, and feeling more whole felt good. Like the wholeness and truths I found in the exploration and integration of my identity as a lesbian, I was now finding more wholeness and truths in my identity as a Jew. Although I didn't completely understand it at the time, Shabbos was the first Jewish "place" where I felt that I was completely present—as a woman, as a lesbian, and as a Jew. There was enough room in Shabbos for all of us, and during those twenty-five hours I felt that all the parts of me were one integrated whole. Shabbos was about a way of shaping time, and appreciating life, and doing so as a lesbian, with my lover, allowed it to work. It couldn't have otherwise. Shabbos wanted— *needed*—me to bring my whole self, sexuality included, to it. Shabbos was my first inkling that there was a path of wholeness for me—as a Jew, and as a lesbian. I was determined—passionately—to pursue this path to wholeness, to God, and would let nothing stop me.

It seemed that if I was going to get my whole self to God, I was going to have to do it in a Jewish way, doing Jewish things, in the Jewish "spiritual vernacular," as it were. Now I had to figure out what exactly that might be. What *was* the Jewish way to God? I knew Shabbos was part of it. But what else was there? I figured the answers were in Jewish text— the same texts that held the secrets of Shabbos—and I would let nothing and no one keep me from learning them.

I had no interest in the rabbinate as a career, but figured that if I did in fact find something useful in those texts, as a rabbi I might be able to teach whatever it was that I found to other people. I also knew it was conceivable that my hunch was wrong and that I might find, after six years of rabbinical school, that Shabbos was all there was. But that was okay, I figured; it would still be worth it, because then at the very least, I'd know a bunch more places where God wasn't, and I could check those off my list of places to look.

I felt pretty confident that the Jewish Theological Seminary was the place I'd get the best text education. And I believed the map that would lay out the Jewish path to God was in Jewish texts. Of all the rabbinical schools, it required of its students more semesters of study in Mishnah, Talmud, midrash, legal codes, and halachah than any of the other rabbinical schools that accepted women. I also knew I would come out of there "knowing my stuff"—I wouldn't ever have to feel insecure when confronted by anyone to my "right" who claimed to be more a real Jew than I. I would be able to hold my own when challenged, and as a woman and a lesbian I had good reason to expect that my knowledge and authenticity probably would be challenged quite a bit.

If I went to JTS, I imagined, I would never have to worry about being religiously railroaded out of access to God because I didn't know enough to know that I was being lied to, as had happened to me when as a child I was told that "Girls can't touch the Torah because they get their periods" or "Women aren't allowed to read from the Torah." When I learned enough to know that these were simply lies, I understood the truth to the claim that "Knowledge is power," and vowed to gain the knowledge that would at the very least keep me from losing whatever power the tradition actually gave me, and might even show me how to gain the power that the tradition had not yet given me but could.

I have always had a profound respect for tradition and mess with it very carefully, only where absolutely necessary, and only then after spending a great deal of time in debate, having given it a second, third, fourth, fifth, even tenth chance before I allow my gut to trump it. I feel strongly that you have to understand what you're changing before you change it. With a few obvious and glaring exceptions, overall I trusted the seminary to be as cautious as I was in dismissing parts of the tradition as "No, no God here," without careful study, struggle, and reflection first. Their beliefs about gays and lesbians notwithstanding, I was, deep down, a true Conservative Jew, and the Jewish Theological Seminary of America was the rabbinical school of my movement. On a simple emotional level, the seminary felt, of all the rabbinical schools, the most familiar and most comfortable in some very hard-to-quantify way. It was simply the place I felt most religiously at home.

I truly thought I would find the Jewish way to God in that place, and the fact that I would have to conceal my sexuality to take up residence in this "home" of mine for the next six years seemed at the time like a relatively small price to pay. (Though this may sound supremely sim-

plistic, and perhaps even silly, probably no student should apply to any
rabbinical school who does not feel that she/he will find a way to God
there.)

   Though I try to approach the tradition's claims with humility and
generally give them the benefit of the doubt until I've dug thoroughly
into the texts and my own conscience, I have never seriously doubted my
own gut on the issue of the rightness of one's sexual identity, whatever
one feels it to be. I know, with my body, with my life, that being a lesbian is good and right. So I have always seen the seminary's refusal to
ordain openly gay and lesbian rabbis as profoundly misguided, obviously
rooted in homophobia, and certainly not a prejudice that should be
honored. I never hid my views on the issue (a handful of my heterosexual classmates were also vocal in their disagreement with the seminary's
policy), and for a number of months in my first year of rabbinical school,
Rabbi Danny Gordis, then assistant dean in Los Angeles, and I had a
standing weekly meeting to explore "the gay issue" (in a theoretical
way) together. He was sincerely struggling with the movement's policies
and his own stance on the issue, and during those months I allowed
myself to be open to the possibility that I was indeed wrong, that there
was some reason, even if I couldn't understand it, for maintaining the
heterosexism of the tradition. We debated the ability of the halachah to
change as profoundly as would be necessary to uproot those verses in
Leviticus that have been seen to prohibit homosexuality. In the end we
came to the conclusion that, in fact, halachah did have the built-in
mechanisms to allow it to make such a radical change and in fact had
utilized these mechanisms numerous times before on other issues. But we
differed on whether or not we felt it should in this specific case. I concluded that it should. And, though I could not tell him why, it was
because I simply knew it from my life's experience. His gut sent him no
such overwhelmingly convincing messages. I realized that what really
separated me from those in the movement who advocated continued
exclusion of gays from the rabbinate was not whether or not Jewish law
could legitimately change on this issue, but whether or not one believed
deeply enough in the full humanity of gays and lesbians to think that it
should.

   I have every confidence that most of those who uphold the movement's current policy will one day realize their mistake; they will one day

feel the rightness of Jewish gays and lesbians being accorded the same rights and privileges as other Jews, and when that happens Jewish law will change as effortlessly as darkness leaves a room when the light switch is turned on. I saw no reason to allow them to live out their temporary ignorance on me. I certainly was not about to suffer from their ignorance in the meantime or to sit in the back of their rabbinic bus. I would seek admission to JTS and not reveal my sexuality to them for the next six years. If, as the tradition claims, we all stood at Mount Sinai, then those texts are the rightful inheritance of every Jew, I figured, gays and lesbians included. The seminary's motivation for keeping gays and lesbians from being interpreters and transmitters of those texts has always seemed to me to be rather transparent as just another form of good ol' American apple-pie homophobia.

Their claim that "gays and lesbians can't be rabbis" is a lie as halachically unfounded and sociologically motivated as the "women shouldn't touch the Torah" lie of my youth. (Tellingly, the Conservative movement's Committee on Jewish Law and Standards, which determines halachah for the movement, recently voted to allow access, for the first time ever, to lay Conservative Jews to the movement's responsa, including their legal rationales, textual sources, and the like, on any issue dealt with by the Law Committee, in order to encourage an informed and halachically literate laity—with one exception: No layperson will be allowed to request any responsum on any topic related to gays and lesbians!)

I had no illusions about or interest in obtaining a rabbinic position once I was ordained. I was fairly certain that I would be kicked out of the Rabbinical Assembly, the professional organization of Conservative rabbis, but didn't care much about that, since I never saw myself ever actually working in the movement anyhow.

Although I had felt certain of the rightness of my decision to go into the closet at the beginning of the entire process, I had vastly underestimated the emotional price that six years of living there would exact. I tried to maintain my resolve by imagining myself a hidden Jew, forced to hide my identity in order to protect myself from those who would unjustly persecute me merely because of who I was. I tried to maintain a sense of dignity by seeing myself as unjustly persecuted by Jews for being a lesbian, as Jews were by the Christians simply for being Jews.

Even still, slowly, imperceptibly, over the years I absorbed from the seminary atmosphere and from my own silence and hiding a sense of shame and guilt. My self-confidence and trust in my own perceptions eroded. Without realizing it, I started, not to believe exactly, but to be spiritually infiltrated by the heterosexist assumptions of the seminary and the tradition it conveyed in its own image. I began to lose the sharpness of my political and analytical voice. It was nearly impossible to keep my lesbian head above water, so to speak, with such an enormous tide of homophobia and sexism washing over me every day.

Social situations at school—even the few minutes spent waiting with classmates for a class to begin, or sharing a table with classmates in the cafeteria—were excruciating for me. There was so much I had to edit from conversation, so much life experience I couldn't refer to or convey in the most general terms. I had to be constantly vigilant about what I was saying, always steering clear of conversational landmines that seemed more numerous than the safe spaces around them. Of course, I could never refer to any personal relationship or attend seminary functions with my partner, and I must surely have come to be perceived as asexual, aloof, and private, none of which is true of me.

Davvening with the seminary community became impossible for me, and I soon had to accept the fact that my attempt to find God in prayer would have to be aborted. I realized that one needs to feel safe and relaxed in a prayer setting to have any hope of connecting with one's God-voice. Standing in a room surrounded by people who I knew certainly would do everything in their power to see that I got kicked out of school if they knew who I really was, was hardly conducive to prayer. (I got into the habit of davvening standing up in the back of the room while my classmates sat in the pews or chairs in front of me, to minimize contact with them.)

When I moved with my classmates from campus to campus (Los Angeles, Jerusalem, New York), I made sure I did not live in the "Jewish neighborhood" where the majority of students and professors lived. Living too far away to walk to their homes afforded me some privacy and gave me the perfect excuse for not accepting invitations to Shabbos lunches, a social situation that was always very difficult to negotiate given all the things I couldn't talk about. This process of constant conversational vigilance made me self-conscious, nervous, and awkward in social encounters. If I had been a private person by nature, it might have been easier, but I am not.

In my second year, I came out to my chevruta, Eddie, who became my soulmate, sanctuary, and lifeline to sanity. The chevruta relationship is an intense and very intimate one. For six years we spent four to six hours a day, three days a week, poring over Talmud volumes, sharing our personal and spiritual struggles—which, of course, are ultimately the same thing. Our study table became the one place where I did find God. Looking back on it now, I see that I shouldn't have been surprised. It had all the necessary ingredients: an intense personal relationship with someone whom I loved and who loved me, a place where I could be completely myself, and a sacred text. Of course God would be there! I had now found a second Jewish "place" where I was whole, as a lesbian and as a Jew. That the texts themselves rarely reflected my experience as a woman never made that much difference to me. It was in the process of learning the texts that I was able to be fully present—as a woman, as a lesbian, as a Jew—and that was more than enough for me. For me, God is in the process of learning Talmud even more than in the content of the texts themselves.

Although I will not disclose the number of gays and lesbians in my graduating rabbinical school class for fear of inadvertently outing those who remain in the closet—and if you're going down the roster, remember, marriage does not a heterosexual make—suffice it to say, I was not the only one. By far. We came out to one another slowly, cautiously, and were of immense support to each other, from glances of recognition at a homophobic joke or comment to just simply knowing that each of us was not alone. The most confusing and sometimes even comical aspect of our little "club" was negotiating who was out to whom (as we were each out to a different but inevitably overlapping handful of confidants within the seminary) and to whom each of us could make reference to the other in conversation.

Perhaps the only thing that got in the way of our being even more helpful to each other was the fact that each of us was in a different place in our figuring out the two questions: "How does this Jewish thing fit into my life as a queer?" and "How does this queer thing fit into my life as a Jew?" I had been an out gay activist for ten years before even applying to rabbinical school and had that whole issue figured out. What

I didn't know was how I was going to integrate Judaism into that life. I had no illusions about getting a job as a rabbi in the Conservative movement, so the question of how to do so was of no concern to me. Most of my gay and lesbian classmates came out during rabbinical school and, in addition to having to come to a positive understanding of themselves as gay or lesbian in such a hostile environment, had to deal with the enormous loss of knowing that their professional dreams would never come true if they were ever to come fully out of the closet. In the end, they all chose to remain closeted in their professional lives to achieve some semblance of the rabbinate they'd always dreamed of. I look forward to the day when none of us has to make such terrible choices.

In my first few years of rabbinical school, it was nearly impossible to take advantage of even the immense support offered by the Jewish gay and lesbian community. It was painful to let down my guard in those situations, because it only highlighted the necessity of my putting it back up afterward. Soon I also realized that I could not casually mention that I was a rabbinic student even at the local gay shul because, the Jewish world being what it is, word was likely to get around, albeit innocently. So I found myself in the unfortunate position of having to be in the closet as a lesbian in the straight Jewish world, and in the closet as a rabbinical student in the gay Jewish world.

In my fourth year, I came out to one professor who, word on the street had it, was safe. His advice to me was to "stay as far away from this building as you possibly can. Be here as little as possible for your own mental health. Just get yourself to ordination day." And that's what I did. With the exception of learning Talmud with Eddie, it was very difficult to learn any longer in that environment, so shut down did I have to be to merely be physically present there, which was heartbreaking for me as the whole point of my suffering through being in the closet was to be able to learn. Now, I remained in the closet without even gaining the thing for which I was making the sacrifice. But by that point, preserving my mental health was my primary concern. I was no longer even sure why I was continuing to persevere toward ordination, but I knew that there was some reason. I knew that, one day, I would know why I had done this and what greater purpose it served. I was sure that, someday, my being a rabbi was going to make a difference somehow, to someone, and that someday I would know it had all been worthwhile. It was a blind faith in this "someday" that kept me going.

Ironically, being in the closet presented an additional unexpected and painful experience: that of benefiting from the heterosexual assumption and all the privileges that come along with it (awards, prizes, speaking engagements, job offers, professional connections)—all of which I came to enjoy in the most bittersweet way (never having experienced the world as a presumed heterosexual "insider" before), knowing all along that "if they really knew me . . ." the offers would be withdrawn, and knowing that that day would inevitably come.

In my last semester of rabbinical school I began to plan the ordination party that I'd been fantasizing about for six years, the evening that would symbolize my return to freedom. I hired a caterer, a DJ, a klezmer band, an Israeli folk-dance teacher, rented the hall, and sent out the printed invitations in fancy plastic tubes. I was in the final stretch and was certain I would make it to the finish line now.

Then came that Monday night before ordination. I had just three days to go. Ordination was to be Thursday morning. The dean called me in and told me that he had something important to talk to me about. He said that someone had called the seminary, had spoken to several members of the administration, and had informed them that "they" (he didn't tell me whether it was a man or a woman) knew me to be in a lesbian relationship, knew that I had had a commitment ceremony with my partner, knew that I was having my ordination party at the gay and lesbian synagogue (to which "they" had received an invitation!), and wasn't it true that the seminary didn't ordain gay people?!

"What do you have to say?" he asked firmly.

I had had no idea how hard it would actually be to look someone in the eye and deny who I was. I couldn't bring myself to say, as I'd made up my mind to should it ever be necessary, "Of course I'm not a lesbian!" I sat there in silence, processing all of my possible alternatives. I could not bring myself to say that I was not a lesbian, and I knew (because he said so) that if I admitted that I was that I would not be ordained. I had only one option left, it seemed: I would refuse to answer him at all.

Though I reminded him that it was not the seminary's practice to ask students to reveal their sexual orientation, I did not have the wherewithal as I sat there being interrogated to actually remember the exact words of the seminary's written policy, which, it turns out, explicitly forbids "instigating witch hunts" against students or members of the RA, the Rabbinical Assembly. As Rabbi Elliot Dorff, author of the policy and vice chairman of the Conservative movement's Committee on Jewish Law and Standards later wrote, in my defense, "the whole point of the language forbidding witch hunts among rabbinical students or members of the RA was that we would not ask such people about their sexual orientation in the first place. Any questions posed by authorities in either the rabbinical schools of the Movement or the RA that would ask a student or member in good standing to divulge his or her sexual orientation would thus violate the explicit policy established by the Law Committee then."

"Benay, if you tell me this isn't true, this will be the end of it, and you will be ordained on Thursday," the dean offered. It was an offer I couldn't bear to accept. I was still hoping my strategy would work and that I would make it out of his office without having to inflict another, much more serious wound into a soul already ailing from six years of hiding.

Over the course of the next two hours, as calmly as possible, I made every argument I could think of to defend my right to refuse to answer. He resorted over and over to the "This-hurts-me-more-than-it-hurts-you" thing, and hid behind the old "You-know-_I_-think-this-policy-is-wrong-but-as-long-as-it's-the-policy-I-have-to-follow-it" defense, as he persisted in pushing me to give him an answer to the clearly implied but never actually articulated question: "Are you a lesbian?"

I couldn't afford to feel anything as I sat there. I had to think. And think clearly. Any show of emotion, I thought, would belie the truth and I would be expelled. And though my motivation had never been to become a rabbi at all, but simply to learn, at some point during the six years the title became important to me. I wanted the same recognition, the same access, that the title would afford my classmates once I was out of school. I not only wanted to learn the Jewish way to God; I wanted others to be able to teach it to others, and I knew the title would help me do that.

I offered Talmudic passages to defend my position and offered others the dean could lean on to support what I had hoped would be his decision to end the interrogation. He wasn't interested. Finally he went even further and told me that he would not ordain me if I continued to refuse to answer him. Though such a coercive threat was even more indefensible than his first question, I was too frightened to realize it at the time, and figured I had to say something.

It was obvious to me at this point that he knew the truth. As a friend of mine later put it, "It doesn't take a straight woman two hours to deny that she's a lesbian." In fact, I assumed he had suspected long before the night of the interrogation. He obviously just wanted me to be the one doing the lying and not he, so he continued to push me to answer him. I knew I had to say something. So I tried answering those parts that I could answer truthfully: "I have never had a commitment ceremony with anyone" (I hadn't), "and, yes, I am having my ordination party at the gay and lesbian synagogue. So? That's where I davven. It has gay and straight members, as I'm sure you know, and besides the seminary itself has a student there as an intern! My renting their hall for my ordination party is neither here nor there!" I hoped he'd leave it at that, and allow me not to address the third accusation. But he didn't. "The central question still remains," he said gravely.

I paused, knowing I'd have to answer his unspoken question and searching for the words with which to answer him in a way that didn't feel like an outright lie. Slowly I let the words come out of my mouth. "The answer to the central question . . . is no." Those were my exact words. He looked at me for a moment and then said, "Okay."

"So, is this the end of the matter?" I asked. "I don't know. I don't know if the caller is going to continue to pursue this. We'll have to see," he responded. That my fate should be determined by whether a vindictive homophobe was going to go to the newspapers or be more vocal did not even strike me as outrageous at the time. I simply prayed that he or she would let it go.

I left the dean's office at eleven P.M. and walked the three flights down to Eddie's dorm room in a fugue state. "It happened," I said. "I can't believe it. Someone outed me." For the first time that evening, I could let the feelings come, and I started to cry. I was scared. I was hurt. I was ashamed. Somewhere deep down, I know I was also angry, but I couldn't feel the anger, so full of shame was I at my own lying. I could only think of what I myself had just done, not what the dean had just done to me. I told Eddie the whole story, and he vowed, as he'd done many times before, to refuse his own ordination in protest if they denied me mine. I knew he would do it, too, though I would never have let him go through with it. The world needed people like him to be rabbis, not martyrs. But it was comforting to hear him say it again, just the same.

People ask me if I ever found out who the caller was. It may seem odd, but I've never been the least bit curious. The caller was not any one person. The caller was millions of people out there who hate and fear what gays and lesbians symbolize for them. It could have been any one of them. It makes little difference to me which one called the dean.

The next morning, I called Sharon Kleinbaum, my rabbi. I needed guidance; I needed perspective, I needed to know that they were the bad guys, not me, and I needed to hear her say that I had done the right thing. I'll always be grateful to her for being there for me then. She was outraged and helped me find some of my own rage. She talked me out of as much shame as I could manage to let go of. I spoke to other rabbi friends to get counsel and comfort. One of my gay Orthodox rabbi friends said, "You now understand more about what it means to be a Jew than that dean ever will." Those words meant a tremendous amount to me. And still do.

I realized that evening that even if I made it to ordination day, and crossed that dais to receive my tallis, I would still not have my diploma, the ordination certificate that declared, in black and white, that I was a rabbi. The diplomas had to be hand-calligraphed and were never handed out on ordination day, but were mailed out only months later. And suddenly that piece of paper became very important to me. If they should ever revoke my ordination, I thought, I at least wanted a physical reminder that, on one day, they thought I was qualified to be a rabbi, and the next they said I wasn't—only because I was a lesbian. Somehow, with that piece of paper framed on my wall, I thought, it would be easier to remember, myself, that I was really a rabbi, regardless of what anyone said. I canceled my ordination party for fear that the caller would show up and make trouble, my ordination would be revoked, and I would never get that piece of paper.

On Wednesday afternoon the dean called me at home. "Come see me in my office at nine sharp tomorrow morning." The ordination ceremony was to start at ten.

My entire extended family had come from Chicago and St. Louis to attend my ordination, and my parents had arranged a fancy dinner in my honor the evening before. My heart was heavy as I sat there, not knowing for sure whether I would even be ordained, and trying not to worry my family with the terrible possibility. I was too scared to be angry that, at a time when I should have felt so proud of my accomplishment, I felt like a criminal.

The next morning at nine I went to the dean's office, terrified. "Did you turn in all your papers?" "Yes, I did." "Is your family here?" "Yes, they are." "OK, I'll see you out there." Still too scared to feel much of anything but relief, I left his office to line up in alphabetical order with my classmates outside the auditorium doors. I was ordained an hour later, between the Ks and the Ms.

Once my diploma came in the mail, I was finally free to come out, but I did so quietly, without the fanfare I'd fantasized about. And though my classmates have long since hung their diplomas proudly in their offices, mine sits in a drawer, still rolled up in the cardboard tube it came in.

After ordination, I accepted a coveted position as a fellow at CLAL—the National Jewish Center for Learning and Leadership, a transdenominational Jewish think tank, and joined their faculty the following year. I was out from day one and traveled around the country teaching the leaders of the American Jewish community as an out lesbian Conservative rabbi, with the full support of CLAL's courageous leadership. I also took a part-time position as director of education at my synagogue, Congregation Beth Simchat Torah, the gay and lesbian synagogue in New York City, under the leadership of Sharon Kleinbaum. At CLAL I healed intellectually from my seminary experience, and it was at CBST that I healed emotionally.

I have regained my voice as a lesbian and have begun to integrate my identities as a lesbian, a Jew, and a rabbi. As I teach Jewish texts and Jewish law to gay and lesbian Jews, I am consistently overcome with gratitude to the seminary for teaching me the text skills and giving me the tools of halachic change that I can now bring to this community, which has been so long barred from learning them, tools we can now use to change the rules of the game that keeps us out.

A year after my ordination, a full-page article appeared in the Jewish press about me and the Gay and Lesbian Lehrhaus Judaica, a program of gay and Jewish studies I'd helped create at CBST, with the headline "Out of the Closet and Into the Classroom." The next morning, I received a call from the head of the Rabbinical Assembly. "Are you a homosexual?" he wanted to know. "What are the implications of this question?" I asked. "If this is true, you will most likely be expelled from the RA," he responded. "If you're threatening to take away my livelihood, this sounds like a pretty serious matter," I said, "so I'm going to ask you to put this question in writing, and I'll be glad to respond to you." I knew they'd be very hesitant to do that, especially since their policy didn't allow them to do any such thing. If they were going to act despicably, I decided, they would have to do so formally, and on the public record. And I told them that. I refused to allow them to expel me quietly, without subjecting themselves to public scrutiny for their actions. And I would not allow myself to be pressured into resigning.

Six months later, I received a letter from the RA's Ethics Committee charging me with violations of standards of ethics and honesty in "entering the Seminary under false pretenses," and "making intentionally false statements to the dean." With a tremendous amount of support from Rabbi Kleinbaum, a number of my Conservative colleagues, and numerous members of the feminist and gay and lesbian communities, for which I am deeply grateful, I have fought off the RA's attacks and threats of expulsion for the past two years. They have finally withdrawn all charges against me, though they continue to refuse to state so in writing. The struggle goes on, and I continue to push for permanent changes in policy so that, at least until gays and lesbians can be out in the application process, no gay or lesbian rabbinical student at JTS will have to fear being called in to the dean's office and confronted with the horrible dilemma: Be forced to lie or give up your career.

The Conservative movement is clearly in a bind. The world is changing, and the movement is slowly losing support for its position on gays and lesbians in the rabbinate. It is, according to the chancellor himself, not primarily a halachic issue but a boundary issue. It is what distinguishes Conservative Judaism, in the eyes of those on the right, from those on the left. It is the final remaining issue that keeps the movement from being lumped together with the Reform movement. It is what makes possible whatever legitimacy the movement is granted by the rabbinate in Israel.

But Conservative Judaism will not be able to morally defend its position to Jews here at home much longer. Their constituency is quickly realizing that there is no one behind the halachic curtain except a small, impotent man trying desperately to push and pull the levers that create an illusion of God mouthing their own will. The leaders can no longer even bring themselves to make their arguments publicly because they know how hollow they ring and how transparently homophobic they are.

Though I certainly do not recommend that any gay or lesbian person follow in my footsteps—the price is enormously high emotionally, and in retrospect, I frankly wish I had not been so fervently compelled to follow the voice that led me into that particular wilderness—I do not believe that concealing my sexuality in order to attend the seminary was morally or ethically wrong. Injustice, even injustice masquerading as halachah, must be confronted and resisted. In either case, I reject the fiction that the seminary's policy on gays and lesbians has one iota to do with halachah. If it did, the administration would be compelled to disbelieve even the confession of one's own homosexuality based on the halachic prohibition of self-incrimination, among other things.

I refused to walk away from the Conservative movement and pretend to be a Reform or Reconstructionist Jew. I chose to respond to the seminary with a form of peaceful halachic civil disobedience. What has upset them most is not that I purposely went into the closet to go to rabbinical school, but that I had the audacity to come out of it once I was ordained. (They don't bother the gay and lesbian Conservative rabbis—of whose existence they are admittedly aware—who continue to remain in the closet.)

I was asked to write this essay three years ago, but could not. It has taken me these three years to purge their shame, which I've carried around as my own. This essay is my first attempt to write about my experience at the seminary, and I know that I am still way too close to it all to see it clearly. But now I can finally begin to write. This is what I am able to write today. I know that, with the passage of time, I will be able to write about it with more perspective.

In the meantime, I think I'll take that diploma out of its cardboard tube and frame it.

Note

1. This title is taken from a line by Abraham Joshua Heschel, "To say no in the name of a higher yes," which appears in his book *Man's Quest for God: Studies in Prayer and Symbolism* (New York: Charles Scribner's sons, 1954).

Chapter 17

Notes from the Underground

DAWN ROBINSON ROSE

M<small>Y FIRST DAY OF</small> rabbinical school at the University of Judaism in Los Angeles, I saw a young woman with spiked white hair and a blue crocheted *kippah* bent absorbedly over her Torah lesson. The feeling I got was indescribable. My first thought was "I'm in love." My second thought after that first one was, "Damn! I'm at the wrong school" (The Conservative movement doesn't allow lesbians). That's how it all started.[1]

Shana and I became lovers almost overnight. She was an undergraduate. I was her first woman lover. Conditions were hardly right for her coming out. We had to be totally closeted, not telling even our closest friends. We spent a year at the UJ, and then, fearing on that restrictive campus our cover had been blown, we quietly transferred to the movement's main school in New York City—the Jewish Theological Seminary. It was 1987. We moved into a tiny, dingy apartment outside the seminary and tried to make it home. In some ways I was deliriously happy—just to watch Shana sleep was an exquisite delight; she had the purity sometimes of an angel. And we loved New York, escaping to the Village as often as possible. Shana was a punk and preferred the East Side, while I loved opera and preferred the more collegiate West.

Socially, however, at the Sem, we were totally marginalized. Afraid to let any one into our lives, we made virtually no friends. Not traveling on Shabbat, neither did we make connections with the gay and lesbian community meeting at the gay and lesbian synagogue Beth Simchat Torah.

The isolation grew as did the fear of discovery. But it seems it was already too late, and some people were already acting queerly, even meanly around us.

There was one student on campus who knew me from San Francisco. I heard through the grapevine that she was denouncing me as a lesbian to anyone who would listen. Another young woman from an extremely conservative background seemed terrified she would catch my gay cooties. Once, as I entered the cafeteria with my food tray, I saw her with her parents. When she noticed me, I could see the word "lesbian" formed on her lips. Alarmed, her parents sprang to their feet, their gaze following her pointing finger. They stared at me for an eternity while I tried to compose myself. Finally, the three quite literally ran away. I sat with my tray, my hands shaking too much to bring a fork to my mouth, fighting back tears.

But the worst hurt of those early days came from one who might have been an ally—another lesbian, not in the rabbinical program but "safe" in the graduate school. (There was no official law against homosexuals in the graduate school.) Shana and I knew of her. We wanted to get in touch, but, so conscious of our growing pariah status, we were afraid to make first contact. I ran into this woman in an empty hallway one night. She opened the conversation abruptly, and took the opportunity to make clear her position toward us: "Everyone knows you're both dykes," she said. "Stay away from me, you hear? I'm not risking my career to be associated with the two of you."

Her words hit me in the face like the flat end of a shovel. I went home and told Shana. We sat together silently in the apartment as if quietly considering joint suicide.

The one point of sanity in my life was my rabbinical internship at Congregation B'nai Jeshurun, a gay-friendly radical congregation on the Upper West Side. Shana and I were befriended by the rabbis, Marshall Meyer and Rolando Matalon. It became a bit of a haven. We ran the junior congregation there and received much pleasure out of the contact with children, the normalcy of interaction, the few hours a week of living free from suspicion. And slowly we gained a curious and tiny circle of friends, mostly foreigners. How it was that South American Jews more easily accepted us, I'll never quite understand.

That's when fate and the chancellor intervened. Some students invited a speaker from the gay synagogue, but to our horror, the program was canceled by the Student Life Office. People from "that synagogue" were not allowed to speak at the Sem. A few of us students were outraged. We wrote and circulated a petition—possibly the first ever at the rigidly apolitical JTS. It was not a petition in favor of gays. It was merely a petition that protested the administration's refusal to allow any Jew from any synagogue to speak at a program requested by students. The petition was enormously successful—over a hundred signatures, students and faculty. We ended up in the chancellor's office. Of course, he said, there had been a misunderstanding on the part of Student Life. The chancellor was cordial, conciliatory, blaming no one. We could have our speaker. While we were there, since we were on the topic anyway, the little devil in me spurred me on to ask, "By the way, Dr. Schorsch. I understand the prohibition against male homosexuality is found in the Torah. How is the prohibition against female homosexuality derived?" He flared a little in anger, saying that currently both were against the rules—that was all.

I learned later that with that one question I had sealed my fate. I think it is really important that at the Jewish Theological Seminary, even asking the question is dangerous.

Still conscious of the risk I was taking, but in no way aware how far things had already gone, I went ahead with the speaker program. It was wonderful. Many students along with two faculty and one vice president attended. The speaker was articulate and well practiced in the education of the extremely uneducated.

Soon afterward, however, I received a call from the dean of the Rabbinical School asking me to come in. Immediately, I was terrified. My fears were confirmed. "I've been ordered by the chancellor," he said slowly, "to ask . . . if you are in violation of the rule against homosexuality in the rabbinical school."

Before I answered he went on to warn me that the seminary lawyer had been consulted. I could be expelled with no possibility of appeal.

How easily I could deny it! I thought for a fleeting moment I could just end the thing with a single lie. But the dean went on: "I cannot remember anyone ever being asked this question before, not in all the years of the rabbinical school. In my memory, no one has ever been accused."

Suddenly, a whole new vista on the gay question opened before me. I saw a history, a silent history of men, all enjoying an old-boys' agreement: Don't tell and we won't ask. But now the seminary was reeling from the appearance of all these women, newly admitted into the school—just in this last decade. Some of us unmarried! Imagine. Over twenty. Alien. Acting like men with our studying Talmud and laying tefillin. Somehow out of control, out of our heterosexual boxes, whether gay or straight. And now there had been a petition and a program on homosexuals. I wondered who would be asked next.

I drew up all my courage and said, "I refuse to answer, I will not participate in any witch hunt." And then I said, far less bravely, "Will I be expelled?" He said he didn't know. Perhaps, he said, if I kept my head down and my mouth shut, I would be left alone.

I left his office planning to do just that. But it was an unnatural posture. I would not survive there long. I had come to seminary to battle God over AIDS, hunger, and homelessness. Instead, I found myself fighting the increasing fear that the longer I remained silent, the less I would remember how to speak. On one side I was tortured by the realization I was becoming someone I could no longer respect. On the other, I lived with the constant fear that one day there would be another call from the dean's office—perhaps three years later and $30,000 more in debt. It would all be over. I would have nothing, be nothing. Nothing but silent, permanently compromised.

So I kept my head down and my mouth shut for the next year or so, and my paranoia and self-loathing grew and grew.

Things continued to unravel all around. My chevruta and best friend of more than two years came to me one day to say she could not longer be my chevruta. More than that, she would no longer be seen with me, could no longer be linked to me in any way. She had heard through the grapevine that people were beginning to say she was a lesbian just like me. She couldn't risk ruining her career. She was sorry.

Everybody was sorry. On a pleasant walk through the park with me one day, one classmate said it was hard—he really liked me—but homosexuality was homosexuality, and Law was Law.

During these days, I had a recurring image, like a dream. I was a traveling merchant who had journeyed miles and miles over mountains and deserts. Now I spread my wares at the gates of the city—bolts of smooth silk and rich velvet, vials of sweet-smelling myrrh. All of these riches I offered free, but the gates remain closed to me. City dwellers stood on the walls, hurling refuse and insults that fell all around my tent, yet I sat on my stool, waiting patiently. I knew there would come a time when either the inhabitants of the city would accept my gifts, or I would gather my offerings and disappear into the desert once again.

The weeks turned into months. The gates would not open, and I would not leave. So I found a middle way.

One day I went to the dean and said I was done with rabbinical school. I wanted to finish the year, receiving the M.A. that is given after four years (with only two more to ordination). With the M.A. I would leave the rabbinic program on my own volition, and go into the graduate school. There, supposedly, I would be no one's headache. Although there had yet to be really out homosexuals in the grad school, there was no university law against it.

I finished the year and got the M.A. The philosophy department accepted me into its Ph.D. program. At this point I know I could have transferred out to another school to finish my rabbinic schooling, but I had a moral dilemma: *Leaving* is what every other homosexual at JTS is pretty much forced to do. This effectively has left the power structure unchallenged and the remaining gay and lesbian students just as fragmented and terrified. Shana and I felt we were in a good position to address the situation, but I could only do that if I stayed and went for a doctorate and not the rabbinate. If I left JTS, I could become a rabbi, but somehow I would feel less worthy of that title because I had walked away from a fight that needed to be fought. This was no martyr's stance, but rather part of how I understand the active and political role of rabbi in the modern world. (In the end, I'm not sure how hard a choice it was. I was totally scathed by my rabbinical schooling experience up to that point. As it turned out, the joy of pure academia—pure philosophy, no less—was balm to my mind and soul. And teaching has proved to be pure, unadulterated joy.)

Once I was safely in the graduate school, my lover and I went to Student Life and announced we were starting JTS's first gay and lesbian club. Technically, because it was graduate school, we couldn't be prevented from doing this. We made two things very clear: The membership wouldn't be restricted to grad students but rather would be open to anyone (even rabbinic students) who wanted to join; and, any member who wished to remain anonymous could do so. Shana and I would act as the coordinators dealing with the administration. We called the group the Incognito Club. We were very proud of that title, as I recall, envisioning the group as a social and support network. The school newspaper printed an announcement for the club, with our number as the contact.

Little were we prepared for our first call. A young man living in the dorm phoned in saying he was gay, neo-Orthodox, and suicidal. Suddenly Shana and I realized we were in no way prepared for the kind of contacts we might be getting. We made an appointment at the student mental health service to arrange for a crisis counselor to be on call.

The Incognito Club became a lot of different things to a lot of different people. To a small uneasy group of gay and lesbian students of various schools and departments at JTS, it was a connection to each other. To a couple of students, the club was a godsend. One student, recently diagnosed with HIV, was able to contact us and make friends, get some support. Another young woman, in the throes of coming out, likewise found us. For another, much larger group at JTS, the club was a powerful sign that there was finally a way for students to express their disagreement with school policy and support for gays and lesbians. Calling themselves the Friends of the Incognito Club, they began their own educational activities around the campus. It was extremely moving for all of us to see this groundswell of support. While there were many things the club itself could not do due to our small numbers and anonymity, the Friends could. We were very glad, for the most part. I think the most notable event was a Shabbos dinner put on by the Friends at which anyone gay or straight could come to eat together and show support for the club. It was an enormously clever idea—no one could tell who was who, so every one was safe. I did notice, however, that certain heterosexuals made an extra big deal about pointing out their opposite-sex dates or mates.

I think many members of the silent faculty were in support. For other members of the administration, the club held a certain grim fascination. All the time, I was asked how many students, in which schools, were members. We had a strict rule about never giving any information at all. Our policy was: "Let their imaginations go wild."

For a number of reasons, perhaps including the existence of the Incognito Club and myself, the Law Committee of the Conservative movement found it necessary to deal with the issue of homosexuality in the rabbinate. A very prominent legal authority for the movement wrote an extensive responsum proving that, despite all social and psychological arguments to the contrary, homosexuality was still forbidden by the Torah. He wanted not only to forbid homosexuals to enter the rabbinate but also to deny them teaching positions in Hebrew schools and any other leadership position in which they could serve as role models. This responsum was a devastating volume.

The Law Committee hearings were horrible for all of us gays and lesbians on campus. Every day, these rabbis from all over the country would gather and display their profound ignorance and hate. Deciding the fate, the educational and career possibilities, the very lives of so many, they were for the most part so incredibly steeped in bigotry. We heard them seriously discussing such "facts" as "Every gay man has over two hundred sexual partners a year." Our guys laughed at that one; they should be so lucky. But behind the laughter was a rip in the universe. How could these rabbis, leaders in the community, believe these wild statistics and base their decisions on them? We were dumbfounded again and again.

I wrote a letter to some of the rabbis involved, describing the air of paranoia and the ostracizing of homosexuals caused by their legislation. One rabbi responded with legislation of his own: It's against the law to mistreat homosexuals, but they still can't become rabbis. The connection between discrimination in one area and discrimination in other places just never penetrated.

And still the hearings continued. We listened day after morbid day, so depressed we of the Incognito Club were on suicide watch for each other. Some mornings I would wake up crying, so afraid was I to go to school again that day. And each day I would gather myself together and go. Why? So that the hearing would not be in the abstract—that all those horrid accusations of pederasty and lewdness should have a familiar face connected with them—mine and those of my friends, we who were here standing before them as members of their community. It was a Gandhian form of nonviolent protest that unfortunately was lost on most of the committee. Even though they didn't know who most of us were (being incognito), we sustained blow after blow and kept coming back. We would not be driven away.

The hearings ended. Nothing had changed, except that the Law Committee voted forthwith to conduct its hearings behind closed doors.

Shana left me soon afterward. At the time it was a horrible blow, but I later understood it was a step out of death into life. Shana moved out and took on another lifestyle entirely, far from Torah and tefillin. The Jewish community had driven away yet another young, enthusiastic, and willing participant—perhaps a future rabbi or scholar. But she remained a most faithful friend. A few months (or was it weeks?) later, when the fissure finally opened in my granite facade and I crashed, she was there. I left campus for a month or two.

While I was recovering, I read for my Ph.D. exams, and soon afterward finished my dissertation, "Resources in Jewish Feminist Theology." Soon after, I started teaching at the Reconstructionist Rabbinical College. At this gay-friendly school, I can be completely out. I dress in my chosen professional attire: men's suit and tie. At this very casual college, people laughed to see the only two people in ties were myself and the (male) president.

Amazingly, Dr. Neil Gilman, chair of the department of Jewish philosophy, hired me to teach my dissertation as a class at JTS. The lesbian who had been rejected now was openly teaching at the very same seminary. It felt to be an act of tikkun, of reconciliation, of healing. I wore my suit and tie there too. It has become my dyke trademark.

I know many students take my JTS class just for the breath of sanity in the homophobic and, yes, misogynistic atmosphere of the Sem. To them, I have represented hope, and I thank God for the opportunity to do that. I feel very committed to remaining a link, or at least a sign that they are not alone. Unfortunately, a certain population will never be caught in my class or even acknowledging my existence as we pass in the halls. Those are whatever homosexuals that might be still hanging on in the rabbinic program. It's painful sometimes. I'll see these people at parties or the gay synagogue, and they'll either chat with me as if nothing was up or turn from me in fear. The next week, however, I have to remind myself not to even nod hello. It is too dangerous for them to be in any way associated with me. I have made up my own private joke:

How do you pick out a closeted rabbinical student at the Sem? S/he will be the only one who *doesn't* say hello to Dawn Rose.

Note

1. This essay is dedicated to Shana Gerber and all the members of the JTS Incognito Club. In addition, I would like to name the following people who made survival at the seminary possible: Julie Blumenfeld, Lea Garret, Jose Badue, Gwynn Kessler, Anna Dancyger, Elaine Chapwick, Rabbis Chava Koster and Roderick Young, and all the Friends of the Incognito Club. Thank you, everyone.

Chapter 18   In Hiding

ANONYMOUS

RABBINICAL SCHOOL OFFERS A student a five- or six-year period of intense focus on spiritual development. It is a time to build, challenge, nurture, and enrich your soul and your spirit. Imagine being in hiding during this precious opportunity. Just as you are working to uplift and nurture your spiritual life, the pressure of hiding and covering your tracks takes over, and that soul that should be growing stronger every day is being attacked instead. Hiding is hurtful to the soul. It cuts away at the spirit. It is insidious. With each lie spoken, each name omitted for convenience or security, each half-truth offered, a little piece of your soul is torn away. Attending rabbinical school in hiding, living a life of half truths and lies, is harmful to the soul. I should know. I am a rabbi and a lesbian . . . and in hiding.

I applied to rabbinical school innocently enough. I was convinced that I would not need to constrict myself, to close off a critical portion of my life in order to attend rabbinical school within the Conservative movement. I did not believe that I would have to hide any beloved part of my identity (of myself) to get accepted. On the contrary, though I had been in relationships with women in college, I actually entered rabbinical school hoping against hope that this phase would pass, and I would find a way to become the good Conservative rabbi that I had wanted to be for as long as I can remember. Long before women were ordained at Jewish Theological Seminary, I imagined myself reciting prayers, giving divrei Torah, and teaching others the wonders I saw in Judaism . . . and doing all of this as a rabbi. And I wasn't going to let the fact that I was a lesbian (something I was then unable to acknowledge) keep me from this dream. I was young, naïve, enthusiastic, and full of internalized homophobia.

I entered rabbinical school with the intention that my personal desires would turn toward something that I and the school found more acceptable. But even as I fell in love with Rashi and Rambam, I also came to understand the depth of my attraction to other women. I realized then that my dream of rabbinical school was coming face-to-face with the harsh reality that the intellectual and spiritual wholeness I had expected was not to be mine, for I was in hiding. I had fallen in love with a wonderful woman and could not tell the extended seminary community. The very same community that honors and celebrates heterosexual relationships denied and condemned this most important relationship in my life. Though Judaism is a religion best lived in community, my rabbinical school community was limited to the few colleagues with whom I eventually shared my great secret. My partner and I had a rule during my rabbinical school years: Only those who knew about our relationship could come to share Shabbat, holidays, and other celebrations in our home with us. Home was my sanctuary, and sanctuaries at the seminary and elsewhere, while on the one hand comfortable and professionally welcoming, had become personally frustrating, unwelcoming, and hateful. As a rabbinical student, I was on the inside of the Jewish community; as a lesbian I felt alone, and unwelcomed . . . a stranger in the deepest ways.

It was a constant source of tension and confusion. The school honored me and gave me awards . . . and each time I would think that if they only knew my secret (the very secret which was beginning to allow me to find my true voice), they would be calling me forward to force me to leave rather than to be honored.

Because I finally came out to myself while I was in rabbinical school, my explorations as a lesbian and as a rabbinical student were continually intertwined. Each was tempered by the other. From early on, I was forced to confront the tension between myself as a Conservative rabbinical student and as a lesbian. During my first year, I had the opportunity to coordinate the Torah reading for the week of "Aharei

Mot/Kedoshim." I struggled for weeks with how to respond to this text. I knew we had to read it. After all, it was a part of the sacred text of the Torah. But how could I listen to this chanted when I knew how much hatred, violence, and bigotry had been drawn from interpretations of this verse? I finally decided that the text should be read, but it must be read differently. Since it is a part of the text that I do not want to emphasize, it should be read quietly, in a hushed tone (like curses in other portions of the Torah). I also knew that this text could not be read by one who actually believed that homosexual relations are "an abomination." And so, when the moment arrived, I picked up the yad, approached the Torah, explained what I was about to do, and proceeded to read this passage for all to hear. Somehow, I felt a little more control having found a way to respond to this tension. No longer did this text and the venomous interpretations that were being put upon it have control over me. This has become my practice every Yom Kippur afternoon, when we read this verse from the Torah. No matter who else is reading Torah, I am the one to chant this aliyah and to interpret it for our community.

For me, reading this passage the first time was an early moment of integration. It was the first time that my identity as a lesbian had deeply and consciously informed my actions as a rabbi. Through this action, the internal tensions that plagued me throughout my years in rabbinical school were put aside, and for a moment wholeness was mine. However, the questions, challenges and tensions I felt were not only internal; they came from many corners. It came first from those who believe that lesbians should not be rabbis. I also felt tension from my future colleagues in other movements who could not understand my decision to study within the Conservative movement. Most difficult for me were the challenges from those who, because they were gay, chose not to enter rabbinical school and who looked at me with jealousy and disdain for "passing."

These tensions weighed me down throughout school. I was not as involved as I had hoped and expected to be, and I can only imagine the joy and fullness that might have been mine during my years in school had I not been living half truths. Instead, my memories of Talmud classes and deep theological discussions are clouded by fear and anxiety and ongoing nightmares about a well-respected teacher at the seminary, standing on a balcony overlooking the courtyard, pulling out a gun and shooting me and others who did not belong at the seminary. I remember shaking years later when I first sat as a student in his class.

Each month for virtually my entire rabbinical school career, I would ask myself: Is this really where I belong? Can I ever be whole here? Am I violating some basic law by being here? Why am I staying in this school when I know how much it hurts? I know only that my commitment to the Conservative rabbinate and my identity as a lesbian are so central to my identity that to abandon one would be to cut off a limb, or to lose a soul, and I could not allow that to happen. I found support for this commitment in a talmudic passage I learned within my first weeks of school. It teaches that there are situations in which we can find value in ideas or practices that seem to be in direct opposition to one another. To paraphrase the text, "These and also these are the words [or in my case "the ways"] of the living God." I understood this to mean that both parts of my identity could and must live within me, because this combination is who I am, and it is the will of God that I have been created in this way. With this in mind, I was able to explain to myself and to others why I had to stay in rabbinical school at the seminary. Despite the nightmares, despite the fear, I knew I belonged in this place at this time.

If I ever doubted it, I only had to think of David, and I was sure again. David is a wonderful, enthusiastic young man I met at a retreat for gay/lesbian and bisexual Jews. We sat near each other Friday evening for Shabbat dinner, and he was singing zemirot with such enthusiasm that I felt compelled to join him. Soon, I let him know that I was not just a lesbian but a Conservative rabbinical student. (It was the first time I'd said that to anyone but myself.) David lit up with such enthusiasm when I said those words. Though he knew many Conservative rabbis and many lesbians, he had never met a gay Conservative rabbinical student, and it excited him to no end. We sang zemirot he had learned at Camp Ramah and in United Synagogue Youth (the Conservative camp and youth movement). He was thrilled. He had wanted to become a rabbi himself, but couldn't put himself into the closet in the way that being in rabbinical school demands. I have absolute respect for his decision and often thought that perhaps he was the wiser of the two of us. Through my interactions with David, I gained the strength to remain in rabbinical school despite the tension. David explained that in meeting me, he could begin to see himself finding a place in the Conservative Jewish world again. I represented an opening and an acceptance and a hope for a future of inclusion that he had not felt for many years. I thought of him often as month after month my relationship with JTS became increasingly tense—as I became more secure in my identity as a lesbian and as a rabbinical student. Whenever the tension seemed overwhelming, I just had to close my eyes and remember David's face when he met me and the hope he expressed that perhaps one day it would be possible for him to go home to the movement that raised him. Simply because I was created with an ability to love other women, a commitment to the ideology of Conservative Judaism, and a desire to serve the Jewish community as a rabbi, I was able to touch this man and to serve as a symbol of hope for someone who had given up the possibility of returning home.

I was alone with my conflicts until a dear friend and colleague taught me the importance of "being seen" by another, that is, to have another person know my story, my struggles, and my joy. It changed my relationship to rabbinical school. I sought out a few colleagues and entrusted my secret to them. To my surprise, instead of being shunned, I was embraced. For the first time there was a possibility of building a community within the extended world of JTS. I didn't know how powerful this (smaller) community could be until one day, Chancellor Schorsch came before the rabbinical students to explain the decision of the Committee on Jewish Law and Standards not to ordain gay men and lesbians. I vividly remember him telling us that a gay man or lesbian could not serve as a proper role model for the Jewish community. What I heard that day was not a speech about an abstract idea nor about some "others" I did not know. He was talking about me! I was the abomination! I was the poor role model! I should be denied the wonders of Judaism! This is what the chancellor said that day. But to me, it wasn't just the chancellor who spoke those words. In my eyes, he represented Conservative Judaism as a whole, and when he spoke, I heard not only his voice but that of all of Jewish tradition telling me I was evil. Suddenly, the institution that was sharing with me the secrets of Torah and Jewish life was stating clearly that I was not welcome within its walls. And now, Judaism itself, the ideals, precepts, community, and way of life that had always provided me strength and comfort, that had always been my home, was condemning me. I wanted to run away and hide. I wanted to scream and yell—but for better or for worse, I simply left the room and walked away, ready to walk out of those walls for good, ready to turn my back on my dream, to step away from the only form of Judaism I had known. I felt completely abandoned by the people and the institution and even the religious system I had grown to love and respect, and I was ready to separate myself from it before it could do any more harm. But as I headed toward the door, resigned to the fact that my dream was over, that I would not become a Conservative rabbi, my way was blocked by four special friends, classmates, and colleagues who knew what Chancellor Schorsch's talk represented to me. They stood there and one by one, without saying a word, put their arms around me. After that, I knew I couldn't leave. There was work to be done—and maybe, just maybe, I wasn't alone in this struggle.

These friends and colleagues provided a tremendous support to me during our rabbinical school years and beyond. They allowed me to see the importance of being present for another person, for they were there for me. Equally important were the moments when I realized that simply by allowing them to know me, to talk with me about being a lesbian and a rabbi, my colleagues, my friends changed their feelings about the possibilities of gay/lesbian inclusion within the Conservative rabbinate. They were able to put a personal face on something that once had been so strange to many of them. I'll never forget the day a classmate asked me to tell her about Congregation Beth Simchat Torah, a gay congregation in New York. Having spent many hours talking with me about sexuality and Judaism, she decided to explore this community and learn how she could better serve the Jewish GLBT community as a straight rabbi. Another told me that when Chancellor Schorsch announced that gay men and lesbians could not be Conservative rabbis, he agreed with this statement. Years later, at the end of our rabbinical school training, my friend knew how wrong he had been. "You need to be a rabbi," he told me, "not just in spite of but maybe even because of your sexuality. We don't need to wait until the seminary changes its mind. The seminary is just dead wrong on this." My friend is now preaching tolerance and support for the Jewish GLBT community; he is asking me how to make himself more accessible to his GLBT congregants. So many of my straight classmates are now strong advocates of the complete inclusion of GLBT Jews in general and rabbis in particular. I know that many fac-

tors brought them to this point in their own lives, but I would like to
think that our conversations and our ongoing relationship during rabbinical school and beyond helped them along the way.

It is now years after rabbinical school. I work as a rabbi in a nice city,
and I have discovered that it is still through personal contact and openness to conversation that I am able to be most effective in helping to
interpret and transmit something about the gay/lesbian community to
rabbis and suburbanites for whom this world and these issues have
seemed odd at best and more often goes completely unnoticed. For so
many people where I live, there is a genuine ignorance of the issues facing gay and lesbian Jews. It simply is not "on the radar screen" for most
in this city. For many who are aware, it is simply too different to understand or too shameful to acknowledge if it touches one they love. This
is a wonderful place to raise a family, and a town where people don't
want to talk about one's sexuality. As long as it is not "in their face," it
is acceptable. But for those who are themselves gay or who have children
who are gay, it is a real struggle to find a place to be open and to share
experiences. Though there is a welcoming community of gay men and
lesbians who support each other and are searching for ways to help the
rest of the community understand the needs of the Jewish gay and lesbian community, the community at large is still reticent to deal with
these issues. There remains a sense of shame and fear among many, especially those whose children have come out. Well-respected members of
this Jewish community have let it be known that their children have
died of AIDS. What is left unspoken is the fact that those same children
were gay men. Somehow the perceived stigma in the Jewish community
is so strong that even its leaders cannot "admit" that their children are
gay.

Many people in this community know that I am a lesbian and a
rabbi. In fact, just as in rabbinical school, I feel like it is the best kept
secret in town. Because they have grown to know me, I have become a
safe and manageable first step for many people. They trust me and can
understand me. I can speak their language—and help them understand
mine. They trust me to respect where they are—even when it is far
from where I wish they could be.

I will never forget the day a rabbinic colleague asked me if we could
discuss rabbinic officiation at same sex ceremonies. "Of course we can

talk," I responded. We talked for hours that day. Other rabbis have since joined this conversation and are willing to ask me the questions they are afraid to ask others and to reveal their fears and the realities of their situations that they cannot share with congregants.

Moments like this remind me of the role that I can play in this world, as does the student who seeks me out to try to understand for herself how she can integrate her identity as a lesbian and as a religious person; the young adult who comes into my office with tears and questions about his own sexual identity, with whom I have a conversation about trusting journeys; or the person who can barely pick up the phone and call (afraid to give me his name) because he is gay, from an Orthodox home, and heard that I might be able to help. It is the man who trusts me and asks how to take on a Jewish name during a transsexual change, and it is the parent of a child who died of AIDS coming up to me in tears at an AIDS seder in their synagogue. These are the moments when I know I am whole, and that I can help bring wholeness to others who are themselves feeling torn and lost.

When I completed rabbinical school, a small group of friends came to my house and joined me in a ritual of completion and release, honoring my ordination as a rabbi and celebrating that the confinement of JTS had been lifted. I am acutely aware, however, that this release was incomplete. I am still not ready to stand up to the Conservative movement and its Rabbinical Assembly and state that I am a lesbian. I have neither the security nor the courage to add my name to this page. I do hope, however, that in my own quiet way, perhaps even by adding my story to this collection, I will help to bring about the day when no one will have to feel alone or torn during rabbinical school, and that no one will have to hide who they are to discover the richness of Judaism, to dedicate their lives to the task of teaching, counseling, and inspiring the Jewish people.

Glossary

All words are from the Hebrew unless otherwise indicated.

Aharei Mot/Kedoshim   The portions of the Torah that contain the prohibition against male homosexual behavior, Leviticus chapters 18 and 20.

alef/bet   The first two letters of the Hebrew alphabet; also used to denote the entire alphabet.

Aleha hashalom   May she rest in peace.

Aleinu   Ancient prayer of praise normally recited at the end of the prayer service.

aliyah (pl. aliyot)   Literally, ascent. An honor bestowed on a person who says the blessings before and after the public Torah reading.

Ameinu   Literally, our people. A clandestine group of gay and lesbian Jewish professionals in the 1980s.

Aron HaKodesh   Literally, the holy ark (or closet). The original name for a clandestine group of gay and lesbian Jewish professionals in the 1980s.

aufruf (Yiddish)   Prenuptial aliyah.

bar/bat mitzvah (pl. b'nai mitzvah)   Son or daughter of the commandments. Celebration upon reaching the age of majority in Jewish tradition (for girls at twelve or thirteen and for boys at thirteen).

beit din   Rabbinical court.

beit midrash   House of study.

Bereshit   The biblical book of Genesis, called in Hebrew by its first word, *bereshit,* meaning "in the beginning."

b'h   Abbreviation of *b'ezrat hashem,* with God's help.

bimah   Raised section in the synagogue where the leader stands and the Torah is read.

biphobia(English)   Fear of bisexuality.

b'li milah   Without circumcision.

brit   Covenant.

brit ahavah   A Jewish commitment ceremony performed in place of the legal marriage ceremony.

brit milah   Ritual circumcision of eight-day-old boys, which, according to biblical commandment, symbolizes entrance into the covenant of the Jewish people. In the last two decades, feminists have developed **brit bat** naming ceremonies to welcome children of both sexes into the community equally, or special ceremonies for girls.

challah   Twisted loaf of rich egg bread eaten by Jews on the Sabbath and holidays.

chalutzim   Pioneers in the land of Israel.

chametz   Food forbidden on Passover.

chavurah (pl. chavurot)   Small group of Jews who worship, study, and celebrate together.

Chaye Sarah   The portion of the Torah from the book of Genesis that begins with Sarah's death and concludes with the marriage of Isaac and Rebekah.

chayim   Life.

cheder   Literally, room. Traditional Jewish school for young children.

chevruta (Aramaic)   Study partner.

chiddush Innovation.

chuppah The canopy under which the couple stands at a Jewish wedding.

davven (Yiddish) To pray in a traditional Jewish mode, including singsong intonation, body movements, and soulful intention.

dreidel (Yiddish) The small spinning top with which a game of chance is played during the festival of Chanukah.

d'var Torah (pl. **divrei Torah**) Literally, words of Torah. An explanation of a text from the Torah.

erev Evening.

Gemara Commentary portion of the Talmud.

ger Literally, stranger.

ger v'toshav Literally, stranger and resident. Biblical term applied to those who attach themselves to the Jewish community.

GLBT (sometimes in different order) Abbreviation for Gay, Lesbian, Bisexual, and Transgender.

grogger (Yiddish) Noisemaker used on the holiday of Purim.

haftarah Prophetic portion that complements the Torah reading.

haggadah(ot) Liturgy for the Passover seder.

halachah Literally, path. Jewish law.

hamentaschen (Yiddish) Triangular cakes filled with poppy seeds or fruit, and eaten during the festival of Purim.

Hamevin yavin Literally, the one who understands will understand.

Hasid A person who follows the pietistic tradition of Eastern European Jewry founded by the Baal Shem Tov; also used to denote the faithful follower of a leader or spiritual path.

havdalah Literally, distinction. The ceremony that marks the end of the Sabbath.

heterosexism   The assumption that heterosexuality is universal.

Hinenu   Literally, we are here. A group of gay and lesbian rabbinical students at Hebrew Union College, New York, in the 1990s.

homophobia   Fear of gay men and lesbians.

Ish tzadik b'dorotav   Literally, one who is wise in his generation, said in reference to Noah.

Kabbalat Shabbat   The ceremony for welcoming the Sabbath.

Kaddish   Literally, sanctification. Aramaic prayer recited during religious services, and as a memorial prayer for the dead.

kashrut   The system of laws that regulates the dietary and kitchen habits of observant Jews.

Ken yehi ratzon   May it be so.

ketubah   Literally, document. Written marriage contract.

Kiddush   Literally, sanctification. The term usually refers to the blessing said over wine on Sabbath and holidays.

kiddush ahava   Literally, sanctification of love. Used as a synonym for "wedding" by gay and lesbian couples.

kiddushin   Literally, a sanctified relationship. Jewish wedding ceremony.

kippah (pl. **kippot.** Yiddish, **yarmulke**)   Head covering, traditionally worn by Jewish males, adopted by some Jewish women in recent times.

klezmer   Traditional Eastern European instrumental music, often played at weddings and other celebrations.

kol ishah   Literally, woman's voice. Rabbinic interdiction against women's public speech.

Kol Nidre   Literally, all vows. Text that precedes the Yom Kippur evening service, from which the service gets its name. The words refer to a legal annulment of vows. The text is chanted to a haunting melody.

Kulanu   Literally, all of us.

leyning (Yiddish)   Reading Torah.

mabul   Flood.

mazal tov   Literally, good luck. Congratulations.

mechitzah   The wall, curtain, or lattice that marks distinct areas for sitting and standing during communal prayer; used to separate men and women during a traditional prayer service.

menorah   Candelabrum.

mesader (f. mesaderet) kiddushin   Person who presides over a wedding ritual.

mezuzah   Ritual object containing the words of the Sh'ma (Deuteronomy 6:4), placed on the doorposts of Jewish homes.

Mi chamocha   Literally, who is like You? Biblical verse from the book of Exodus chanted at the crossing of the Red Sea and incorporated into the liturgy.

Midrash   Stories and interpretations explaining the meaning of texts.

minyan   A quorum of ten necessary for public prayer. In the past, only men were included; today all but the most traditional Jews include women as well.

mishkan   Place where the divine presence is understood to dwell.

Mishnah   Second-century compilation of Jewish law.

Mitzrayim   Literally, narrow places. Hebrew name for Egypt.

mitzvah (pl. **mitzvot**)   Literally, commandment. Also denotes good deed.

Modah ani   Literally, I praise. Female version of the first line of a morning prayer.

niddah   Laws regulating sexual relations in marriage; a menstruating woman.

olam habah   The world to come; the afterlife.

oneg Shabbat   A celebration of joy; eating and drinking following Sabbath services.

parasha   Torah portion.

Pesach   Passover, the springtime festival that marks the Jewish people's liberation from Egypt.

pintele yid (Yiddish)   The Jewish soul.

Pirke Avot   Sayings (or Ethics, or Teachings) of the Fathers (Sages, Ancestors); part of the Mishnah.

rebbe (Yiddish for rabbi)   Highly venerated teacher.

rebbetzin (Yiddish)   The wife of the rabbi.

responsa (Latin)   Classical Jewish form of questions and answers.

rosh chodesh   Literally, the head (beginning) of the month. Celebration of the New Moon.

Rosh Hashanah   The Jewish New Year.

Sabra   Native-born Israeli.

schepping naches (Yiddish)   Deriving satisfaction from someone else's good fortune.

seder   Ritual and meal in celebration of Passover.

Shabbat (Yiddish, **Shabbos**)   The Jewish Sabbath, observed from sundown Friday to sunset on Saturday.

Shabbat Shirah   The Sabbath on which the Song of the Sea (Exodus 15) is read in the synagogue.

Shabbaton   Retreat held on the Sabbath.

Shanah tovah   Greeting for a good new year.

shaliach tzibur (pl. **shlichei tzibur**)   Service leader.

sheva brachot   Seven blessings recited at a wedding.

Shvat   Month on the Hebrew calendar that falls in late winter.

shidduch   The process of arranging a marriage or relationship.

shiva minyan   Prayer quorum held daily in the home of a mourner during the first week after a death.

shlemut   Wholeness.

shlep (Yiddish)   To drag.

shlichut   Literally, mission. Representing Israel to the outside world.

shul (Yiddish)   Literally, school. Synagogue.

shofar   A ram's horn, used as a sacred musical instrument to herald the beginning of the Jewish year.

simchah (pl. **smachot**)   Joyous occasion.

Simchat Torah   Literally, rejoicing over the Torah. The holiday that commemorates the beginning of the annual cycle of the public reading of the Torah.

smichah   Rabbinic ordination, symbolized by a laying on of hands.

sukkah (pl. **sukkot**)   Literally, booth. Temporary dwelling place during the holiday of Sukkot.

Sukkot   The holiday that commemorates the fall harvest and the wandering of the Jews in the desert, described in Exodus.

tallit (Yiddish, **tallis**)   Prayer shawl.

Talmud   The multivolume compendium of Jewish law and lore consisting of the Mishnah and Gemara (commentary on the Mishnah) compiled during the fifth century C.E.

tefillin   Phylacteries, leather amulets placed on the head and arm during weekday morning prayers in fulfillment of the biblical command, "You shall bind them for a sign on your hand, and they shall be for frontlets between your eyes" (Deuteronomy 6:4).

tevah   Ark, as, e.g., the one build by Noah.

tikkun olam Literally, the repair of the world. The obligation to pursue peace, justice, and compassion.

tzedakah Literally, righteousness. Acts of giving, considered obligatory under Jewish law.

uzi Automatic submachine gun invented in Israel.

yad Literally, hand. Torah pointer.

yarmulke See **kippah.**

yerushah Inheritance.

yeshiva A house of study or Jewish day school.

Yom Kippur The final day of the High Holy Days, observed through fasting, prayer, self-examination, and redirection.

z'l (abbreviation of **zichrono/a l'vracha**) May his/her memory be a blessing. Written after the name of deceased people to honor their memory.

z'mirot Songs, specifically those often sung after the Sabbath meal.

About the Contributors

Anonymous was ordained by the Jewish Theological Seminary.

Rebecca T. Alpert is the codirector of the women's studies program and assistant professor of religion and women's studies at Temple University. She is a rabbi and the former dean of students at the Reconstructionist Rabbinical College. She is the coauthor of *Exploring Judaism: A Reconstructionist Approach* (1986, 2000), author of *Like Bread on the Seder Plate: Jewish Lesbians and the Transformation of Tradition* (1997), and editor of *Voices of the Religious Left: A Contemporary Sourcebook* (2000).

Karen Bender was ordained by the Hebrew Union College-Jewish Institute of Religion in June 1994 and has served since ordination as the assistant and then associate rabbi of Temple Beth-El in Great Neck, New York. She has published numerous sermons and poems. Rabbi Bender has been married to Rachel Bernstein since July 1, 1995, and they are the proud parents of a daughter and a son.

Leila Gal Berner received her Ph.D. in medieval Jewish history from the University of California in Los Angeles in 1986. In 1989 she graduated from the Reconstructionist Rabbinical College. She currently teaches at George Washington University and American University in Washington, D.C. She has published extensively in the areas of medieval Spanish history, Jewish ritual, and feminism. Her commentaries on Jewish liturgy appear in *Kol HaNeshama*, the prayer book series published by the Reconstructionist movement. She lives in Virginia with her life partner, Renee Gal Primack, and their daughter, Kayla Moriya Gal.

Lisa A. Edwards is rabbi of Beth Chayim Chadashim (BCC) in Los Angeles, the world's first and oldest gay and lesbian synagogue. She was ordained in 1994 by the Hebrew Union College-Jewish Institute of Religion in New York, and holds a Ph.D. in literature from the University of Iowa (1984), where she wrote a dissertation on post-Holocaust Jewish American fiction. She lives in Los Angeles with her partner, Tracy Moore, editor of the book *Lesbiot*, an oral history of Israeli lesbians.

Denise L. Eger is the founding rabbi of Congregation Kol Ami, West Hollywood's Reform synagogue. She was ordained in 1988 by the Hebrew Union College-Jewish Institute of Religion in New York. She was the founding chair of the Gay, Lesbian and Bisexual Interfaith Clergy Association. She is chair of the Central Conference of American Rabbis(CCAR) Task Force on Lesbians and Gays in the Rabbinate. She lives in Los Angeles with her partner, Karen Siteman, and their son, Benjamin.

Sue Levi Elwell, Ph.D., serves as the director of the Pennsylvania Council of the Union of American Hebrew Congregations. Ordained in 1986 by the Hebrew Union College-Jewish Institute of Religion in Cincinnati, Elwell has served congregations in California and New Jersey. The founding director of the Los Angeles Jewish Feminist Center and the first rabbinic director of Ma'yan, Elwell is editor of the forthcoming CCAR haggadah. She lives in Philadelphia with her partner, Nurit Levi Shein.

Julie Greenberg, a graduate of the Reconstructionist Rabbinical College, founded and now directs the Jewish Renewal Life Center, a program that offers training in spiritual community building. She speaks on college campuses about the issues discussed here. She is the mother of Rosi, Raffi, Zoe, Jonah, and Mozelle.

Linda Holtzman graduated from the Reconstructionist Rabbinical College in 1979. She is currently the director of practical rabbinics at RRC. Linda lives in Philadelphia with her partner, Betsy, and their sons, Jordan and Zachary. She is a founder of the Reconstructionist Hevra Kadisha of Philadelphia and served as the educational director of Reconstructionist congregation Mishkan Shalom.

Shirley Idelson, who was ordained by the Hebrew Union College-Jewish Institute of Religion in New York, served as director of religious activities at Vassar College until 1998, when she moved to Minneapolis with her partner. She continues to work in college chaplaincy at Macalester College in St. Paul, Minnesota, and Carleton College in Northfield, Minnesota.

Sharon Kleinbaum is the senior rabbi of Congregation Beth Simchat Torah, New York City's gay and lesbian synagogue. She graduated from the Reconstructionist Rabbinical College in 1990. She lives in Brooklyn with her partner, Rabbi Margaret Moers Wenig, and their two daughters, Liba and Molly.

Benay Lappe was ordained by the Jewish Theological Seminary of America in 1997 and is a member of the Rabbinical Assembly. She is currently scholar in residence at the Milken Community High School in Los Angeles, California, and an associate at CLAL—The National Jewish Center for Learning and Leadership. She was founding director of Congregation Beth Simchat Torah's Gay & Lesbian Lehrhaus Judaica in New York City and recently founded The Lesbian, Gay, Bisexual and Transgendered Jewish Youth Project for queer Jewish youth ages thirteen through eighteen. Her partner, Noemi Masliah, an immigration attorney, is one of the founders of the Lesbian and Gay Immigration Rights Task Force.

Ellen Lippmann, ordained in 1991 by the Hebrew Union College-Jewish Institute of Religion in New York, is rabbi of Kolot Chayeinu in Brooklyn, New York, where she lives with her partner, their teenage daughter, and an assortment of animals.

Sydney Mintz was ordained by the Hebrew Union College-Jewish Institute of Religion in 1997. She is currently the assistant rabbi at Congregation Emanu-El in San Francisco, California, where she lives with her partner, Deborah Newbrun, and their sons, Elijah Newbrun-Mintz and Gabriel Ray Newbrun-Mintz.

Dawn Robinson Rose received her Ph.D. in 1996 from the Jewish Theological Seminary, where she taught Jewish feminist theology for two years. She is completing her rabbinic studies at the Academy for Jewish Religion. She is the rabbinic leader of the Durham Community Synagogue in Durham, New Hampshire, where she lives with her lover, Marla Brettschneider, and their daughter, Paris Mayan.

Elizabeth Tikvah Sarah received ordination from the Leo Baeck College in 1989, where she now teaches Hebrew and spirituality and chairs the rabbinic in-service training program. She is rabbi of Brighton and Hove Progressive Synagogue and corabbi, with Rabbi Mark Solomon, of London's Jewish Gay and Lesbian Group. She has edited three books and published three dozen articles and several poems on feminist/lesbian/Jewish themes in various anthologies and journals, and is currently writing *Teasing Texts and Telling Tales: A Jewish Feminist Exploration of Torah* (forthcoming).

Julie R. Spitzer, who was ordained by the Hebrew Union College-Jewish Institute of Religion in Cincinnati, served congregations in New Jersey and Maryland before becoming director of the Mid-Atlantic and then the New York region of the Union of American Hebrew Congregations. She was the author of the pioneering *When Love Is Not Enough: Spousal Abuse in Rabbinic and Contemporary Judaism* (1995). Her life was cut short by ovarian cancer. She is survived by her partner, Abbe Tiger.

Nancy Wiener, D.Min., teaches pastoral counseling at the Hebrew Union College-Jewish Institute in New York, where she also serves as fieldwork coordinator. Ordained by the Hebrew Union College, she serves part-time as the rabbi of the Pound Ridge Jewish Community in Pound Ridge, New York. She lives in New York with her spouse, Judith Tax.

Index

ACT-UP, 167

Ad Hoc Committee on Homosexuality and the Rabbinate, 58–59, 62–63

AIDS, 11, 46, 149, 150, 156, 166–167, 232, 233

Alpert, Rebecca T., 1–36, 29, 30, 41, 145, 173–180

Ameinu (Our People), 24, 47, 183–185

American Jewish Congress, 70

Anti-Defamation League (ADL), 164

Aronsohn, Lena, 13

Baltimore Hebrew Congregation, 59, 60

Barnard College, 142

Beck, Evelyn Torton, 10

Beit HaChiduch, Amsterdam, 88

Beit Klal Yisrael, London, 90n2

Bender, Karen, 24, 28, 116–130

Bennett, Allen B., 19, 162

Berlin Academy for the Scientific Study of Judaism, 13

Berner, Leila Gal, 28, 30, 93–105

Bernstein, Rachel, 117–118, 122, 125, 129

Beth Ahavah, Philadelphia, 44

Bet Haverim, Atlanta, 145–146

Beth Chayim Chadashim, Los Angeles, 29, 153, 155–157, 158–159, 161–163

Beth El, Great Neck, 122, 123–130

Beth Simchat Torah, New York, 29, 114, 146–147, 149–151, 213, 231

bisexuality, 20, 23, 35n37

Blanchard, Tsvi, 112

Blue, Lionel, 78, 80

Blumenthal, Marc, 156

B'nai Jeshurun, New York, 218

Borts, Barbara, 75–76, 78–79

Buber, Martin, 173–174

Buddhism, 200, 201

Camp Tawonga, 135, 136–137

Central Conference of American Rabbis (CCAR), 22, 24, 25, 58–59, 61, 62, 138, 156, 160n6

Central Synagogue, New York, 120, 122

chaplaincy, 51–52

chavurah, 52, 53–54

Clinton, Bill (U. S. president), 120–121

Coalition for Personal Freedom, 166

Cohen, Sharon, 145

coming out: during job search, 63–64, 122, 123–124; in mainstream congregation, 44, 95–99, 102–105, 106–107, 124–125; nothing to lose in, 157–158; as on-going process, 93; of rabbinical students, 118–119, 131–132; of seminary faculty, 52–54, 56

commitment ceremonies. See weddings, same-sex

Committee on Jewish Law and Standards, 7–8, 205, 210, 223–224, 230

congregational rabbis: in Britain, 76,
80–83, 89; closeted, 22–23, 42–44,
59–60, 95, 96, 232–233; and
coming-out process, 44, 95–99,
102–105, 106–107; and feminist
agenda, 81–82; inclusionary agenda
of, 81–82, 99–101, 104, 124; in integrated communities, 108–115, 168;
job placement of, 23, 63–65, 96,
119–124, 135; lipstick Lesbians, 121;
in political/personality conflicts,
82–83; pregnancy and parenthood
of, 17–18, 129–130, 185; press coverage of, 39, 85, 124, 136; spokesper-
sons on lesbian/gay issues, 82, 101,
128–129, 178; support of senior
rabbi for, 124, 126, 127, 136; wedding (commitment) ceremonies of,
43–44, 102, 125–127; see also gay
and lesbian congregations
Conservative Judaism: access to
Responsa, 205; closeted rabbis in,
42–43, 44, 232–233; Committee on
Jewish Law and Standards, 7–8, 205,
210, 223–224, 230; exclusion of
gays/lesbians from rabbinate, 25, 30,
204–205, 214–215, 230–231; hearings on gay/lesbian issue, 223–224;
history and development of, 7–8;
prohibition on witch hunts, 209–
210; Rabbinical Assembly, 7, 25,
205, 214; see also Jewish Theological
Seminary
counseling, pastoral, 54–55

Davidson, Jerome K., 123, 124, 125,
126, 127
Davka: A Journal of Jewish Concerns,
31n7
Deborah, Golda and Me (Pogrebin), 98
Defense of Marriage Act (DOMA),
167
denominational administration, 28–29,
60–61, 83–87
Dobkin, Barbara, 72
Dorff, Elliot, 210
Dyke Shabbos, 182

Edwards, Lisa A., 29, 118, 152–160
Eger, Denise L., 23, 29, 156, 161–169
Eilberg, Amy, 14
Einstein, Arik, 190
Elwell, Sue Levi, 1–36, 28, 66–74
Emanu-El, San Francisco, 135–136
employment. See job opportunities; job
search
Enlightenment, 3, 6

faculty, seminary, 44, 46, 48, 52–53,
54–55, 88, 144, 176–177, 224–225
Faith and Practice: Reform Judaism
Today (Romain), 84
Federation of Reconstructionist Congregations, 45
feminism, Jewish, 9–10, 32n10, 70,
75–76, 174
Frank, Ray (Rachel), 13
Frisch Yeshiva High School, New Jersey, 141–142

Gay and Lesbian Alliance Against
Defamation (GLAAD), 164
gay and lesbian congregations, 19,
28–29, 44, 213; and AIDS crisis,
149, 150, 156, 166–167; employment in, 23, 152, 161–162; feminist
agenda in, 10–11; life cycle events
in, 146–147, 149; open-door tradition of, 150–151; outreach to gay
and lesbian Jews, 162–164, 165; outreach to heterosexual world, 164;
parenting support in, 169; political
activism in, 165–166, 167–168; in
radical tradition, 29, 154–155; as
religious alternative, 148–149; social
activism in, 149–150, 155–157, 163,
164; transformational potential of,
145–147; umbrella groups, 25, 165
gay and lesbian Jewish community:
counseling model for, 55; and Jewish
identity, 143–144, 163, 164–165,
199–202; parenting movement in,
109, 168–169; and Reconstructionism, 8, 24, 47–48, 180; and Reform
movement, 51, 60–63, 84–87; unaf-

filiated, 179–180; visibility and acceptance of, 11–12; *see also* homophobia

Gay and Lesbian Lehrhaus Judaica, 214

Gay and Lesbian Rabbinical Network (GLRN), 24

gay rabbis: closeted, 16, 19, 184; in gay and lesbian congregations, 18–19, 156, 162; organizations of, 24–25; *see also* Lesbian rabbis

Geiger, Abraham, 4

Geller, Laura, 22, 70

German (Jewish) Reform movement, 4

Gilman, Neil, 224

Gordis, Danny, 204

Greenberg, Julie, 23, 24, 29–30, 181–189

Greenberg, Steven, 153

Greengross, Wendy, 84

Gubbay, Jacob, 146

Halacha, 191–192, 205, 215

Half Empty Bookcase—Progressive Jewish Women's Study Network, 88

Hebrew Union College-Jewish Institute of Religion (HUC-JIR), 4, 23, 45, 61, 66, 107; admission of women, 13, 21–22; American Jewish Archives at, 66; closeted students in, 24, 57, 114, 116–118, 144, 177; gay and lesbian organization in, 24; openly gay faculty in, 52–53, 54–55, 156; openly gay students in, 118–119, 131–132, 144, 152, 192–193

Hirsch, Samson Raphael, 6

Historical School, 7

Hoffman, Lawrence, 111

Holtzman, Linda, 22, 24, 27, 39–49, 144, 145

homophobia, 27, 28, 46, 48, 69, 100; community activism against, 156, 163, 164, 165–166, 167–168; in Conservative Judaism, 204, 205, 223, 230–231; during job search, 120, 122–123, 156, 162, 182, 187; and lesbian sexuality, 20; in traditional texts, 20, 40, 227–228

Hyman, Paula, 142

Idelson, Shirley, 30, 190–193

Incognito Club, 24, 222–223

interfaith families, 186–187

International Conference of Gay and Lesbian Jews, 43

Jewish Bulletin of Northern California, 136

Jewish Catalogue, The, 31–32n7, 155

Jewish Chronicle, 85

Jewish Healing Movement, 15

Jewish Reconstructionist Federation, 8, 47

Jewish Renewal Life Center, 30, 187–188

Jewish Theological Seminary, 7, 8, 199; admission of women, 8, 13; closeted students in, 203–204, 205–209, 217–221, 224–225, 226–232; gay/lesbian organization in, 24, 221–222; openly gay faculty in, 224–225; outing of lesbian students, 197–198, 209–213, 218, 219–220; refusal to ordain gays/lesbians, 25, 144, 197, 204–205; text education in, 202–203

Jewish Week, 124

job opportunities: chaplaincy, 51–52; in chavurah, 52, 53–54; in denominational administration, 27–28, 60–61, 83–87; with marginal groups, 178–180, 186–187, 193; seminary faculty, 44, 46, 48, 52–53, 54–55, 88, 176–177, 224–225; in social justice work, 107, 165–168, 169; *see also* congregational rabbis; gay and lesbian congregations

job search: of closeted applicants, 42, 58–59, 96, 119, 123; coming out during, 63–64, 122, 123–124; discrimination in, 23, 156, 162, 182, 187; of openly gay applicants, 23, 48, 64–65, 119–123, 135

Jonas, Regina, 13

Kahn, Yoel, 19, 162

Kaplan, Judith, 8

Kaplan, Mordecai, 8, 32n9

King, Martin Luther Jr., 78, 80
Kleinbaum, Sharon, 24, 29, 46, 141–151, 212, 213, 214
Kol Ami, West Hollywood, 29, 156, 168
Kolot Chayeinu/Voices of Our Lives, Brooklyn, 108–115
Kulanu: A Program for Congregations Implementing Gay and Lesbian Inclusion, 62

Lansky, Aaron, 143, 144
Lappe, Benay, 25, 30, 197–216
Leeser, Isaac, 7
Leo Baeck College, 14, 75–76, 88
lesbian identity: *vs* Jewish identity, 27, 178, 207–208, 228–230; self-definition process in, 26, 39, 57–58, 67–72, 76–77, 116–117, 176, 199
lesbian rabbis: closeted, 21, 23, 30, 42–44, 59–60, 182, 232–233; double burden and legacy of, 12; education of (*see* rabbinical students, lesbian/gay; seminaries); employment of (*see* job opportunities; job search); family choices of, 16, 20–21, 23; and Jewish *vs* lesbian identity, 27, 178, 207–208, 228–230; loneliness of pioneers, 22–23, 76; numbers of, 35n39, 75; organizations of, 24–25; vocation of, 42, 66–67, 77–80, 103–104, 132, 144, 151, 175, 190–191, 202–204; *see also* coming out; homophobia; pregnancy; weddings, same-sex; women rabbis
lesbian sexuality, 20, 21
Leviticus (Book of), 18, 20
life cycle ceremonies, 15
Limmer, Stephen, 125–126
Lippman, Ellen, 24, 28, 106–115
lipstick lesbians, 121
Los Angeles Jewish Feminist Center, 70

March on Washington, 118, 119
Marcus, Jacob Rader, 67
Marder, Janet Ross, 153, 156

Matalon, Rolando, 218
Matt, Hershel, 45
Ma'yan, 72
MAZON: A Jewish Response to Hunger, 107
Metropolitan Community Church, Los Angeles, 157, 162
Meyer, Marshall, 218
Mintz, Sydney, 28, 131–140
Mishnah, *Pirkei Avot*, 14–15, 73, 115, 201
Moore, Tracy, 152
Movement for a New Society (MNS), 187
Moykher-Sforim, Mendele, 143

National Federation of Temple Brotherhoods (NFTB), 62
National Federation of Temple Youth (NFTY), 62
National Gay and Lesbian Task Force, 149
National Jewish Center for Learning and Leadership (CLAL), 213
National Yiddish Book Center, 143, 144
Neumark, Martha, 13
"New Jews," 8–9, 31n7
Nice Jewish Girls: A Lesbian Anthology (Beck), 10
Nineteen Letters on Judaism (Hirsch), 6

Offner, Stacy, 22–23
ordination: refusal to ordain gays and lesbians, 25, 144, 197, 204–205; of women, 13–16
Orthodox Judaism, 6–7, 141–142, 153, 184, 191–192

Pappenheim, Bertha, 32n9
Parenting movement, 108–109, 168–169
Parents and Friends of Lesbians and Gays (PFLAG), 129
Passover Seder, 16, 70
Perry, Troy, 162
Piercy, Marge, 97

Pirkei Avot, 14–15, 73, 115, 201
Pittsburgh Platform, 4–5
P'nai Or Kallah, 183
Pogrebin, Letty Cottin, 98
pregnancy, 46, 137; congregational
    support for lesbian rabbi, 129; and
    gay parenting movement, 108–109,
    168–169; of lesbian rabbinical stu-
    dent, 23, 181–182, 185, 188; preju-
    dice against rabbi's pregnancy, 17–18
Priesand, Sally, 13

Rabbinical Assembly, 7, 25, 205, 214
rabbinical students, lesbian/gay: at
    Ameinu conferences, 183–185; in
    Britain, 75–76; closeted, 24, 57, 114,
    116–119, 144, 145, 176, 182–183,
    203–204, 205–209, 217–221, 224–
    232; commitment ceremony of, 132–
    35; counseling of, 46; "Inclusive
    Community" course for, 48; openly
    gay, 18–119, 131–132, 144, 152,
    192–193; organizations of, 24,
    221–222; in Orthodox yeshiva,
    191–192; ostracized, 218, 220, 223,
    224–225; pregnant, 23, 181–182, 185,
    188; *see also* job search; seminaries
rebbetzin, role of, 16
Reconstructionist Commission on
    Homosexuality, 47
Reconstructionist Judaism: history and
    development of, 8; inclusion of gays
    and lesbians, 8, 24, 47–48, 180; les-
    bian rabbis in, 48, 95–99, 178; ordi-
    nation of women, 13–14
Reconstructionist Rabbinical Associa-
    tion, 8, 45, 47, 48
Reconstructionist Rabbinical College
    (RRC), 8, 13–14, 23, 39; admission
    of women, 21–22, 175; counseling of
    gay and lesbian students, 46; homo-
    phobia workshop at, 46; "Inclusive
    Community" course at, 48; openly
    gay faculty in, 44, 144, 176–177,
    224; reaction to pregnant student,
    181, 185; rejection of openly gay
    applicants, 24, 40–41, 176; shift to

open admissions, 44–46, 144–145,
    176–177, 183
Reform Judaism: Ad Hoc Committee
    on Homosexuality and the Rab-
    binate, 58–59, 62–63; in Britain,
    75–87; gay and lesbian congrega-
    tions in, 11, 153, 155– 159, 161–
    163; Gay and Lesbian Rabbinical
    Network (GLRN), 24; history and
    development of, 3–5, 153–154; inclu-
    sion of gays and lesbians, 51, 60–63,
    73; lesbian rabbis in, 22–23, 120–130,
    135–136; radical change within,
    153–155; *see also* Hebrew Union Col-
    lege-Jewish Institute of Religion
Response magazine, 31n7
Rich, Adrienne, 69–70, 192
Rose, Dawn Robinson, 25, 30, 217–225
Rosh Chodesh, 16
Rubinstein, Peter, 120

Sarah, Elizabeth Tikvah, 27, 28, 75–90
Sasso, Sandy Eisenberg, 13
Schechter, Solomon, 7
Schorsch, Ismar, 219, 230, 231
Schulweis, Harold, 116
seminaries: admission of women, 13,
    21–22, 175; interrogation on sexual
    orientation, 197, 209–213, 219–220;
    lesbian faculty in, 44, 46, 48, 52–53,
    54–55, 88, 144, 176–177, 224–225;
    open admissions policy of, 44–46,
    144–145, 176–177, 183; rejection of
    openly gay applicants, 24, 40, 41,
    176; *see also* Hebrew Union College;
    Jewish Theological Seminary; rab-
    binical students, lesbian/gay; Recon-
    structionist Rabbinical College
sexuality, lesbian, 20–21
Sha'ar Zahav (Golden Gate), San
    Francisco, 11, 19, 162
Sher, Arnold, 119–120, 122–123
Shulman, Sheila, 75, 76, 84, 90n2
Silverman, Ira, 45, 144
Smith-Rosenberg, Carroll, 67
social justice work, 107, 165–168, 169
Solomon, Mark, 90n2

Song of Songs, 15
Southern California Board of Rabbis, 163
Spare Rib, 77
Spitzer, Julie R., 24, 27, 28, 57–65
Staub, Jacob, 145
Sternberg Center, 83, 84
Stonewall riot, 157
Szold, Henrietta, 13

Tabick, Jacqueline, 14
Talmud, 158, 178
Tarfon, Rabbi, 115
Task Force on Lesbian and Gay Inclusion, 61–62
Twice Blessed: On Being Lesbian or Gay and Jewish, 10

Uilenburger synagogue, 88
unaffiliated population, 179–180
Union of American Hebrew Congregations (UAHC), 4, 60–62, 64–65, 153, 159
Union of Liberal and Progressive Synagogues (ULPS), 76, 89, 90n1
United Synagogue, 8
Universal Fellowship of Metropolitan Community Churches (UFMCC). See Metropolitan Community Church
University of Judaism, 8, 217

Vassar College, 193
Vipassana meditation, 200, 202

weddings, same-sex: and British Reform movement, 84–86, 87; of congregational rabbis, 43–44, 102, 125–127; of faculty member, 53; in gay and lesbian synagogues, 147; of rabbinical student, 132–135; transformational nature of, 154–155, 186
Wiener, Nancy, 24, 27–28, 50–56
Wise, Isaac Mayer, 7
Wissenschaft des Judenthums, 3
Wolf-Prusan, Peretz, 132–133
Women rabbis: fresh perspective of, 15–16; loneliness of pioneers, 22; ordination of, 13–14; pregnancy of, 17–18, 129; as sexual beings, 16–17; and traditional texts, 14–15; *see also* lesbian rabbis
Women of Reform Judaism, 61–62
Women's Rabbinical Alliance (WRA), 21–22
Women's Rabbinic Network (WRN), 22
Women's status in Judaism: within Conservative Judaism, 7–8; and Enlightenment, 3; and feminist movement, 9–10; within Orthodoxy, 6–7; within Reconstructionism, 8; within Reform Judaism, 5
World Congress of Gay, Lesbian, Bisexual and Transgendered Jews, 25

Yeshiva University (New York), 6